Praise for the First Edition of *The Brain-Targeted Teaching Model* by Mariale M. Hardiman

"This book will encourage many educators to teach 21st century students via 21st century policies and practices that are grounded in the dramatic advances occurring in the cognitive neurosciences."

—Robert Sylwester
Author of *A Child's Brain: The Need for Nurture*
Emeritus Professor of Education
University of Oregon, Eugene, OR

"Teachers will find the content valuable and can implement the Brain-Targeting Teaching® concept very easily."

—Steve Hutton
School Improvement Specialist
Villa Hills, KY

"Mariale Hardiman offers a unique model that teachers can use to assess the extent to which they are considering brain-friendly concepts when they plan their lessons."

—David Sousa
Consultant in Educational Neuroscience
Author of *How the Brain Learns*
Palm Beach, FL

"The emphasis on integrating the arts with content areas is timely and welcome. An additional strength are the examples from 'expert teachers' which show how the model can be implemented while addressing curriculum standards."

—Jacqueline LaRose
Assistant Professor of Education
Eastern Michigan University, Ypsilanti, MI

"This book provides a teacher-friendly model that teachers can use to establish student-friendly classroom environments and effective teaching strategies and activities."

—Darla Mallein
Director of Secondary Social Sciences Education
Emporia State University, Emporia, KS

"The Brain-Targeted Teaching Model for 21st Century Schools *has much to offer all educators. The book contains a wealth of knowledge from cognitive and neuroscience and presents it in a way that is accurate and accessible. Hardiman's work creates a vision of education in which scientific discoveries about thinking and learning are taken full advantage of."*

—Jay N. Giedd
Chief of Brain Imaging Unit
Child Psychiatry Branch, NIMH
Bethesda, MD

"Few educators bring Dr. Hardiman's ability, experience, and scholarliness to the increasingly rich exchange between educators and neuroscientists. She has succinctly synthesized a large body of information into a must-read for educators, researchers, and anyone else interested in how neuroscience and cognitive science can make a difference in the classroom."

—Kenneth S. Kosik, MD
Harriman Professor of Neuroscience
University of California, Santa Barbara, CA

"Hardiman's book provides a practical way for educators to operationalize theoretical principles and teach in a way that can effectively engage students on different and meaningful levels. The research and strategies presented in this book emphasize the very important notion of supporting students' personal, social, and academic development and achievement."

—Fay E. Brown
Director of Child and Adolescent Development
Yale School Development Program
Yale University, New Haven, CT

"One of the central components of Hardiman's remarkable book is creativity—the ability to generate something new. Promoting the development of this unique attribute is critically important for the success of our students, and I applaud Dr. Hardiman for showing that neuroscience can and should inform the process of education."

—Charles J. Limb, MD
Associate Professor
Johns Hopkins University Schools of Medicine and Education
Baltimore, MD

"This book is a tour de force, providing not only a comprehensive understanding of cognitive and neuroscience research, but also a well-constructed model providing teachers with the practical tools they need to integrate it into their classrooms. Dr. Hardiman has become a leading authority in the emerging field of neuroeducation."

—Paula Tallal
Board of Governors Professor of Neuroscience
Rutgers University, Cream Ridge, NJ

"Dr. Hardiman provides clear explanations of what is currently known about the functions of the human brain, along with practical examples of ways to apply these understandings in the classroom. With this book she offers a significant contribution to the field of education."

—Dee Dickinson
Founder
New Horizons for Learning
Seattle, WA

"Dr. Hardiman's Brain-Targeted Teaching® Model is one of the most powerful and research-based methods of achieving greater learning retention—its focus on the arts and creative problem-solving moves teaching from traditional 'drill and kill' methods to one that engages students for the demands of 21st century teaching and learning."

—Linda Casto
Advisory Board
Johns Hopkins University Neuro-Education Initiative
Malibu, CA

"The Brain-Targeted Teaching® Model has informed my teaching in so many ways. I love the model's infusion of the arts as the arts lend themselves to creative expression for all children. There is no question that the Brain-Targeted Teaching® Model enhanced the quality of my teaching."

—Andrea Jackson
5th Grade Teacher
Baltimore, MD

"The Brain-Targeted Teaching® Model provides a framework for teaching that makes sense not only in K–12 but also in higher education settings. I hope to continue spreading the word that higher education coursework can be significantly enhanced by using the tenets of Brain-Targeted Teaching®."

—Vicky M. Krug
Assistant Professor
Pittsburgh, PA

The Brain-Targeted Teaching Model

Second Edition

Dedicated with much love to Walker, Bennett, and Molly. May you always seek the joy of learning in all of life's endeavors and adventures.

To family, friends, colleagues, and students who have embraced making a difference in the lives of others through the generous sharing of your knowledge and wisdom.

The Brain-Targeted Teaching Model

A Framework for Joyful Learning and Leading

Second Edition

Mariale M. Hardiman

Forewords by Tracey Tokuhama-Espinosa and Martha Bridge Denckla

For information:

Corwin
A Sage Company
2455 Teller Road
Thousand Oaks, California 91320
(800) 233-9936
www.corwin.com

Sage Publications Ltd.
1 Oliver's Yard
55 City Road
London, EC1Y 1SP
United Kingdom

Sage Publications India Pvt. Ltd.
Unit No 323-333, Third Floor, F-Block
International Trade Tower Nehru Place
New Delhi – 110 019
India

Sage Publications Asia-Pacific Pte. Ltd.
18 Cross Street #10-10/11/12
China Square Central
Singapore 048423

Vice President and Editorial Director: Monica Eckman
Senior Publisher: Jessica Allan
Content Development and Operations Manager: Lucas Schleicher
Senior Content Development Editor: Mia Rodriguez
Senior Editorial Assistant: Natalie Delpino
Production Editor: Tori Mirsadjadi
Copy Editor: Beth Ginter
Typesetter: Hurix Digital
Cover Designer: Gail Buschman
Marketing Manager: Olivia Bartlett

Printed and bound by CPI Group (UK) Ltd, Croydon, CR0 4YY.

LCCN 2024057416

This book is printed on acid-free paper.

25 26 27 28 29 10 9 8 7 6 5 4 3 2 1

Contents

List of Expert Practitioners by Chapter

CHAPTER 8: BRAIN-TARGET FIVE

CHAPTER 9: BRAIN-TARGET SIX

CHAPTER 10: IMPLEMENTING THE BRAIN-TARGETED TEACHING® MODEL IN SCHOOLS, WORKSPACES, AND BEYOND

CHAPTER 12: IMPLEMENTING THE BRAIN-TARGETED TEACHING® MODEL AT HOME AND OUT-OF-SCHOOL LEARNING

Foreword to the Second Edition

Mariale M. Hardiman has been a leader in the learning sciences for longer than most of her graduate students at Johns Hopkins have been alive. *The Brain-Targeted Teaching Model* (2003) and its 2012 follow-up was one of the primary books in the field directed specifically at teachers and teacher educators. Now, nearly a quarter of a century later and with global evidence from different countries around the world showing the applicability of her six core *brain-targeted* goals, she continues to pave the way for teachers interested in leveraging information from neuroscience into real-live classroom settings. The strength of her work is twofold: She was among the first to challenge the neuromyths of *brain-based* popular press books and to leverage the science of learning, and she was the first to remind us how humans can be so uniquely different, yet all share core needs when it comes to learning. These core elements make up her six brain-targeted goals.

Hardiman's book ensures teachers recognize the basic needs of all students in all classrooms to learn and thrive through

1. a positive emotional climate (target one);
2. a neuroaesthetically pleasing learning environment (target two);
3. a holistic and holonic design approach that places learning goals in context (target three);
4. teaching through individual mastery of skills (target four);
5. a real-world application to stimulate creative thinking (target five); and
6. a non-traditional, multifaceted approach to evaluation through alternative forms of evidence presentation, such as the arts (target six).

While there have been dozens of books that have followed her work, all build off of these fundamental concepts. Each of the six goals could be a book on its own (and many authors have approached teaching in this piecemeal way), while Hardiman shows how weaving these elements together builds a tapestry that better frames the whole of the teaching-learning experience.

Over the past two decades, advances in neuroimaging in real classrooms (e.g., Davidesco et al., 2021), the establishment of how emotions impact cognition (e.g., Gotleib et al., 2022), and measurements of neuroplastic changes based on comparative teaching methodologies (e.g., Tymofiyeva & Gaschler, 2021) have added even more credibility to the role that neuroscience can play in shaping educational practices. This newer evidence only serves to strengthen her original model. Few educators have had the vision to both acknowledge these foundational concepts and then take the time to explain the research behind them in a way that inspires.

In 2006 to 2008, Mariale participated as one of the members of my Delphi expert panel to identify standards in Mind, Brain, and Education science, which others called neuroeducation or educational neuroscience. I will never forget her enthusiastic engagement with the process as she willingly accepted invitation after invitation to help shape the field. Kurt Fischer, also on the Delphi panel, mentored Marialc's work and encouraged her efforts to create the Mind, Brain, and Teaching program at Johns Hopkins, which served as a beacon to many teachers, shining light on science-based, evidence-informed ideas to guide their practices as he and Howard Gardner created the Mind, Brain, and Education program at Harvard. Soon, other programs began around the world, following their lead. Their tireless work to encourage teachers to become learning scientists catalyzed a whole generation of educators into action, myself among them. It is now common to see many of the fundamental ideas Mariale promotes in her book in numerous educational programs around the world and her influence on the work of countless other educators.

Mariale's revision to this second editor is focused; she has been careful not to throw the baby out with the bathwater. Rather than a complete rewrite, she offers important updates and newer citations from relevant research. While others have gone from the *lab to the classroom and back* in their work with teachers, Mariale begins with the wisdom from expert teachers themselves, which is refreshing. The supplemental sections on culturally relevant pedagogies and the acknowledgment of more embodied cognition research to explain the vital partnership of the mind and body are also welcome additions. Finally, the new chapters that expand the view of educational contexts by looking at different kinds of educators and settings, as well as a review of the research on Brain-Targeted Teaching® in multiple global contexts end the book with two important messages, which are both intuitive, but which also require explicit descriptions. First, we are all more alike than we are different. Second, humans around the world share ideal conditions in which they grow, learn, and thrive best, and these conditions can and should be designed by teachers, starting with you.

Tracey Tokuhama-Espinosa, PhD

Instructor, "Neuroscience of Learning: An Introduction to Mind, Brain, Health and Education" at the Harvard University Summer and Extension Schools

traceytokuhamaespinosa@fas.harvard.edu

Associated Editor, Nature Partner Journal's *Science of Learning*

Author of *Making Classrooms Better: 50 Practical Applications of Mind, Brain, and Education Science; Bringing the Neuroscience of Learning to Online Teaching; Neuromyths: Debunking False Ideas About the Brain; Five Pillars of the Mind: Redesigning Education to Suit the Brain; What Do Kids Want to Know About Their Own Brains; Writing, Thinking, and the Brain.*

References

Davidesco, I., Matuk, C., Bevilacqua, D., Poeppel, D., & Dikker, S. (2021). Neuroscience research in the classroom: Portable brain technologies in education research. *Educational Researcher, 50*(9), 649–656.

Gotlieb, R. J., Yang, X. F., & Immordino-Yang, M. H. (2022). Concrete and abstract dimensions of diverse adolescents' social-emotional meaning-making, and associations with broader functioning. *Journal of Adolescent Research*, 07435584221091498.

Tymofiyeva, O., & Gaschler, R. (2021). Training-induced neural plasticity in youth: A systematic review of structural and functional MRI studies. *Frontiers in Human Neuroscience, 14*, 497245.

Foreword to the First Edition

The Brain-Targeted Teaching Model for 21st-Century Schools is a welcome update to the 2003 book that introduced educators to Dr. Hardiman's Brain-Targeted Teaching® Model. Both that book and the new edition share the ambitious goal of providing teachers with valuable knowledge from the neuro- and cognitive sciences in a form that can be readily understood and applied in practice. The strength of Dr. Hardiman's approach is that in addition to carefully describing research findings, she frames those findings in terms of an accompanying pedagogical model that educators can use to interpret, organize, and apply the information they are receiving. From the viewpoint of a researcher and clinician, this is exactly what teachers need—a way to connect the information we provide with the kind of practical expertise that can only be gained in real-life school settings.

Too often, efforts to translate scientific research for use by educators run into serious difficulties. One way to go wrong is to water down the science and describe important ideas only colloquially or metaphorically, with little or no documentation of sources. Broad-brush *research-based* recommendations for practice may be offered, but these usually represent little more than common sense, and the support they garner from scientific research tends to be trivial. Allusions to brain science serve to make existing ideas seem *cutting edge*—as though they hold some great new promise for *fixing* education in one fell swoop.

Despite widespread enthusiasm for the idea of joining together the work of scientists and educators, other frameworks like the Brain-Targeted Teaching® Model have not emerged. Instead, there has unfortunately been only a proliferation of pseudoscientific *brain-based* educational products and workshops, many promoted in the media. Though research scientists are wise to steer well clear of these enterprises, this leaves no one to counter the *neuromyths* or misconceptions teachers are left with. In contrast, Dr. Hardiman is unique in her vigilance to avoid overreaching beyond what can be reasonably concluded from scientific research. This is one of the main reasons why scientific researchers are willing to work with her. Though her background is that of an educator—foremost as a long-time, nationally honored urban school principal—she has forged professional relationships with research scientists at her own institution, Johns Hopkins University, as well as others around the country.

She is determined to make sure that her claims are grounded in rigorous scientific research and are well-referenced. This does not mean, however, that research findings relevant to education must be presented as they would be in a scientific journal, without thorough explanations of vocabulary, basic concepts, or logical implications for practice. When educators have to try on their own to understand research conclusions and *translate* them into educational frames of reference, they become vulnerable to the possibility that much is lost in translation; they may misunderstand or overgeneralize. Teachers (like anyone) may go astray when the work of helping them understand and apply scientific ideas is left undone. Teachers do not work in a vacuum, and their success often depends on collaboration with others whose belief in rigorous, evidence-based practices provides the format for practice. A global commitment to the training of all who provide educational services to students at all levels must include a commitment to this scientific approach to understanding learning, the cognitive processes associated with learning from the earliest grades through higher education, and the use of research to promote innovative, creative, and effective teaching.

Whereas many educational researchers exhibit a strong ideological bent and often try to recruit scientific research to support a predetermined agenda, Dr. Hardiman starts with rigorous research and works in a highly pragmatic way to build a pedagogical framework on the foundations of scientific knowledge. She is able to lean on her experience as a long-time practitioner to consider the needs of teachers and schools. Because Dr. Hardiman understands so well how teachers think, she is able to seek out the scientific information that teachers want to know and deliver that information in a way that makes it accessible and useful.

With all of the advances that have come in the neuro- and cognitive sciences since Dr. Hardiman's 2003 book, it is great to have an updated version of the Brain-Targeted Teaching® Model. Many educators are already familiar and comfortable with her framework; they will finish this book and return to the classroom with great new ideas that are based in up-to-date and sound research. For those who may only now be learning about Dr. Hardiman's work, this book will reveal a pedagogical model that resonates with educators' goals and strategies as well as a plethora of useful information from the brain sciences. The collective hope is that this book serves as a road map toward creating ever-better outcomes for your students and better collaborative professional practices in your school.

Martha Bridge Denckla, MD
Batza Family Endowed Chair
Director, Developmental Cognitive Neurology
Kennedy Krieger Institute
Professor, Neurology, Pediatrics, Psychiatry
Johns Hopkins University
School of Medicine

Preface

The Brain-Targeted Teaching Model

I am pleased to present *The Brain-Targeted Teaching Model: A Framework for Joyful Learning and Leading* and offer this book as a new edition of *The Brain-Targeted Teaching Model for 21st-Century Schools*. Since the publication of the first edition in 2012 and my first book in 2003, the field of neuroeducation has continued to evolve, becoming a recognized interdisciplinary approach to education. Research from the learning sciences has produced numerous findings that are increasingly viewed as important to expanding an understanding of how we best acquire and apply knowledge (see Ozernov-Palchik et al., 2024). Like professionals in other emerging *neuro* fields—neurolaw, neuroeconomics, neuroaesthethics, neuroethics—many practitioners seek to not only become familiar with the advancing knowledge of human cognition and learning, but also to understand how this knowledge can inform their work.

Still, research from the scientific community that is *specifically intended* for practitioners must continue and accelerate. Findings from neuro- and cognitive science research in areas such as attention, memory, emotions, creativity, executive function, embodied cognition, sleep, exercise, and more must continue to expand our understanding of cognition and learning. This growing knowledge, however, creates the need for translation of relevant research findings to determine appropriate connections to practical applications within multiple fields (Hardiman et al., 2012).

Who Should Read This Book

This book is intended to serve as a bridge between research and practice by providing any practitioner with a cohesive, usable model of effective instruction informed by education research as well as findings from the learning sciences. The research and instructional strategies presented are designed to be relevant to a wide range of practitioners.

Since the publication of the 2012 edition, I have been amazed at the array of professionals—nationally and internationally—who have used the Brain-Targeted Teaching® (BTT) Model in their work. Some have enrolled in our academic courses at Johns Hopkins University. Others attended professional development sessions, conference presentations, or simply read the book and adopted the model for use in their own context. Many who have used the BTT Model have been educators, from early childhood practitioners to higher education faculty. Others include organizational leaders, corporate trainers, strategic planners, policymakers, athletic coaches, home school practitioners, and parents. Based on their work, feedback, and research, it is a great honor to present this current book on the Brain-Targeted Teaching® Model as a tool to inform teaching, leading, and learning.

For practitioners in any field, it is critical that relevant research on cognition and learning be approached systematically and realistically, rendering a better understanding of the developing child and adult learner, greater precision in instructional techniques, and enhanced educational outcomes.

In my own work as a school principal in an urban school district and now at the university level, I have found that too often practitioners are handed an ever-changing array of initiatives and programs that rapidly come and go. Well-meaning leaders may not understand how this serves only to dilute productivity rather than support it. Practitioners may *wait out* one initiative in hopes that a better one will come along or feel confused as they try to meld a new program with the previous one.

Accordingly, without a cohesive model, practitioners may easily be confused by the plethora of strategies that claim (some appropriately, some not) to be based on research from the learning sciences. Usable knowledge may be confounded with myths that divert time and waste valuable resources.

The Central Purpose of This Book

A Pedagogical Framework—The Brain-Targeted Teaching® Model

The basis of this book is to bring relevant research from the learning sciences to practitioners through a pedagogical framework, the Brain-Targeted Teaching® (BTT) Model (Hardiman, 2003; 2012). The model provides a cohesive structure for interpreting research findings from the learning sciences and applying them to their own practice. The BTT Model is neither a curriculum nor a marketed product. Rather, it is a way to plan effective learning and leading informed by research from the learning sciences and research-based effective instruction. It was designed, in part, from the thinking skills frameworks of Dimensions of Learning (Marzano, 1992), Multiple Intelligences (Gardner, 1983, 1993), and Bloom's Taxonomy (Bloom & Krathwohl, 1956). It aligns with the Universal Design for Learning (Cast, 2011; Rose & Meyer, 2002) with an emphasis on reaching all learners through techniques that honor culturally relevant pedagogy and neurodiversity. At the core of the BTT Model is a focus on activities that tap into creative thinking, problem-solving, and application of content to real-world contexts. Practitioners also have recounted how meaningful integration of the arts into learning activities leads to heightened student engagement and more effective retention of content.

The model presents six important domains, or *brain targets*, of the teaching and learning process. These include the following:

- Brain-Target One—Establishing the emotional climate for learning
- Brain-Target Two—Creating the physical learning environment
- Brain-Target Three—Designing the learning experience for *big-picture* understanding
- Brain-Target Four—Teaching for the mastery of content, skills, and concepts
- Brain-Target Five—Teaching for the extension and creative application of knowledge
- Brain-Target Six—Evaluation *for* learning, not just *of* learning

Special Features of the Second Edition

Similar to the 2012 version, this book reviews research from the learning sciences; discusses how the findings can inform practice; and shares activities from practitioners who have used the model in classrooms, higher education courses, corporate training sessions, strategic planning, and more. It begins with a consideration of current practices and how the emerging field of neuroeducation can promote innovative and creative problem-solving. It then examines themes from the learning sciences that practitioners should know, including discerning the differences between meaningful uses of research and common misapplications of findings, known as *neuromyths*. Next, in order to help with understanding of research in subsequent chapters, the book provides fundamental information of how the brain works, including its structure and function. Chapter 3 provides an overview of the BTT Model, and the chapters that follow focus on each of the six brain targets, including research supporting the target as well as concrete examples of applications from educators and practitioners from related fields. Finally, readers will see how the model can be used as a unifying framework in a school or any organization.

Those familiar with the first edition will note that the components of the BTT Model have not changed. In fact, research that supports each of the brain targets described above has continued to grow. Thus, this edition includes newer studies along with some of the seminal research studies described in the last edition. In addition, I have invited researchers and colleagues to share their knowledge and experiences with the BTT Model, resulting in multiple new "Expert Practitioner" excerpts that appear in each of the chapters describing the six brain targets and offer rich new approaches to learning and leading.

I present four new chapters for this edition, written or cowritten by colleagues who have used the BTT Model in their work. The new chapters include Chapter 11, which focuses on Culturally Relevant Pedagogy within the BTT Model and how this content informs online and hybrid learning. Chapter 12 addresses how parents and home school entities such as microschools can align strategies with the BTT Model. Cutting-edge technology in the form of Virtual Reality is discussed in Chapter 13 along with more common forms of technology as it is used in educational applications. I am excited to share Chapter 14, which demonstrates ways in which the BTT Model has been examined in research studies nationally and internationally, providing evidence of its effectiveness in programs servicing early childhood to adult learners. Chapter 15, "Last Words," recount the inspiring story of the late Gordon Porterfield and how his graduate students responded to an activity that required them to learn in a way outside of their comfort zone yet triggered a meaningful learning experience. The Appendices include a checklist of instructional strategies to help guide practitioners and leaders in implementing each of the components of the BTT Model. In addition, the two sample learning units that threaded through each of the chapters of the first edition (Hatchett and Genetics & Heredity) are now offered in Appendices II and III.

It is important to note that in many cases, you will see the model shown within teaching and learning environments. To any reader who is not in the field of education, I would like to point out that broadly, educators exist in every walk of life. Beyond the traditional role of classroom teachers, educators include leaders of any organization, corporate trainers, athletic coaches, parents, consultants, and many more and varied professionals. In fact, we are all educators when we impart information to students, colleagues, workers, and our children. As you move through the various chapters of this book, think about how the content applies within your own context.

Finally, it is important that I explain why I find the concept of *brain-targeted teaching* (a description I coined in the last book) to be more useful than the term *brain-based learning*. A number of people have justly criticized the use of the term *brain-based* as an adjective describing learning. The silliness of the term is exemplified by the question, "Doesn't all learning occur in the brain? After all, we don't think with our feet!" I concur that labeling learning as *brain-based* seems uninformative, as learning indeed occurs in the brain and embodied memory systems. In contrast, *all teaching does not result in learning*, so while all learning is *brain-based,* all teaching is not. Accordingly, I wanted to focus on how pedagogy can be informed by knowledge of how the brain learns—how people perceive, process, and remember information. Therefore, the term *brain-targeted teaching* seemed particularly apt.

Research from the learning sciences has demonstrated that the essence of learning is about biological changes. In view of that, focusing on the *science of learning* should be as central to discussions about education as the focus on accountability for the *product of learning*. It is time that policy and practices reflect a focus on the way humans think and learn. The emerging field of neuroeducation and the Brain-Targeted Teaching® Model can be the linchpin in this work.

Acknowledgments

It is with great pleasure that I acknowledge those whose contributions have been critical in conceptualizing and writing this book. I begin by recognizing the dedicated work of the team of core professionals who have been constant collaborators and support of the Brain-Targeted Teaching® (BTT) Model from its beginnings in the early 2000s to now. As collaborators, they have been thought partners, researchers, teachers of academic courses and professional development programs, coauthors, editors, and more. While there are many who fit into this group, I want to recognize especially the work of Clare O'Malley Grizzard, Ranjini JohnBull, Joe Meredith, and Rachael Barillari.

The voices of the many Expert Practitioners turn research and theory into rich images of real-world application of the BTT Model. Their excerpts add context to each of the brain targets. I am so grateful for the many ways in which they shared their wisdom and amazing practices to make a difference for others in schools, workplaces, and homes. They are teachers and leaders in public and independent schools, universities, and corporations. In the first pages of this edition, I list their names and the titles of their excerpts in the order they appear throughout the chapters in the book. In particular, much gratitude goes to Clare O'Malley Grizzard, who brings the arts into the BTT Model for the chapters that describe each brain target (Chapters 4 through 9).

I would also like to thank those who authored or coauthored chapters that have been added to this edition. In Chapter 11, Ranjini JohnBull shares her wisdom on Culturally Relevant Pedagogy within the BTT Model in online and hybrid learning environments. Clare O'Malley Grizzard and Jacqueline Renfrow contributed expert advice in Chapter 12 on Implementing the BTT Model at home and out-of-school learning environments. In Chapter 13, David Toia describes Virtual Reality and Katherine Fu technology in education. Chapter 14 reviews research studies showing evidence of the effects of the BTT Model on a variety of interventions nationally and internationally. I am grateful to Katherine Fu for her dedicated work in researching studies to be included in this review.

I am incredibly humbled by the Foreword for this edition written by a giant in the field of Educational Neuroscience, Tracey Tokuhama-Espinosa. Her contributions to the field are enormous at Harvard University, her work in academic organizations, and her many publications. Her generous words are greatly appreciated and valued.

I would also like to thank those who contributed in multiple and varied ways through ideas, edits, images, and supportive suggestions: Melody Huang, Bob Lessick, Thom Grizzard, Clara Fangfang Ma, Carolyn Freeland, Tara Chadwick, Krysta Herring, Don Perry, and Sam Clayton. And, finally, many thanks to all of the educators and professionals in other fields who have used the Brain-Targeted Teaching® Model over the years to enhance their practice and share their work with colleagues and friends.

I also want to recognize those who contributed to the first edition of this book. At the time they were postdoctoral fellows at the Johns Hopkins University School of Education—Emma Gregory, Luke Rinne, and Julia Yarmolinskaya. I also want to recognize Martha Bridge Denckla, who authored the Foreword for the first edition and all of the many researchers and authors who provided reviews of the book from the first edition of this book. I would like to acknowledge the graphic designer, Bennett Grizzard, for the creative graphics that depict each brain target in the icons that appear in the book. The learning units in the Appendices of the book appeared in the first edition. Special thanks again to Clare O'Malley Grizzard and Suzanne McNamara for wonderful examples of how the BTT Model can be used in elementary and high school.

Finally, many thanks to Corwin's Jessica Allan and her team for expert guidance and support of this second edition.

About the Author

Dr. Mariale M. Hardiman is Professor Emeritus at Johns Hopkins University in Baltimore, MD. Her work has contributed to advancing the field of neuroeducation through various roles including professor, researcher, school principal, consultant, and author of books, book chapters, journal articles, and multi-media presentations. She founded the Neuro-Education Initiative and the Mind, Brain, and Teaching programs at the Johns Hopkins University School of Education. Through academic courses and professional development, her work connects research from the learning sciences with teaching and learning strategies for professionals in education and related fields. She has conducted pioneering research on the effects of arts integration on long-term retention of academic content. She also examined how knowledge of the learning sciences influences teaching practices and efficacy beliefs. Her National Science Foundation-funded research investigated teachers' perceptions of creative thinking strategies and creativity assessments. Additionally, Hardiman's administrative roles at the Johns Hopkins School of Education include Department Chair, Vice Dean of Academic Affairs, and two appointments as Interim Dean.

In her time as a school principal in Baltimore City, Hardiman developed a teaching framework, the Brain-Targeted Teaching® Model that promotes arts integration and creative problem-solving. Hardiman presents her work nationally and internationally on topics related to the intersection of research in the learning sciences with effective teaching, leading, and learning. Her research on arts integration has been featured in various popular news outlets including the *New York Times, Forbes, Psychology Today, Pacific Standard*, and *Southern Living*.

Hardiman can be reached at mmhardiman@jhu.edu

Visit her website www.braintargetedteaching.org

Introduction

The Emerging Field of Neuroeducation

> *Because of its broad implications for individual and social well-being, there is now a consensus in the scientific community that the biology of mind will be to the twenty-first century what the biology of the gene was to the twentieth century.*
>
> —Eric Kandel, *In Search of Memory*, p. xiii

How do we prepare our learners, from young children to adults, for a rapidly changing world? How do we ensure the effective transfer and creative application of knowledge for learners at all levels and in multiple contexts from education to the world of work and general life endeavors? As technology has enabled a global, interconnected world, how do we prepare for greater cultural awareness? How do we support the well-being and mental health of our students and workers? How can we address the inequities in opportunities and accessibility to quality education? All of these issues and more have clearly come to light, especially in the wake of the pandemic, which has changed how we think about schooling, employment, and lifestyles.

There are no simplistic answers to addressing these questions. Yet with the resolve and collaboration of educators, leaders, policymakers, parents, and all related constituents, no challenge is beyond our knowledge and wisdom. But we must be open to conducting our work in different ways. In education, for example, despite the calls for greater emphasis on critical and creative learning, traditional approaches to curriculum and instruction still dominate what happens in our nation's schools. While higher pay and working conditions may address the teacher shortage, my experience with practicing professionals points to their desire for more agency in what and how they teach. And in increasing numbers, educators are pursuing professional learning experiences to increase their knowledge of how the human mind thinks and learns, focusing on the needs of the learner rather than how they score on standardized tests (Privitera, 2021).

Indeed, efforts to reform American schools should begin by changing the very notion of how to measure educational success, driven by the movement of 21st century learning, and ultimately informed by new knowledge from the learning sciences. At present, with no national consensus on what makes an effective school, policies have largely reduced the notion of measuring successful schooling to merely tracking achievement scores in reading and mathematics.

Clearly, educators must not shrink from accountability for student performance. The current practices that measure educational effectiveness, however, are driving school policies and practices and have resulted in a well-documented narrowing of the curriculum, reducing time spent on the social studies and the sciences and—at the same time—diminishing opportunities for many children to participate in the visual and performing arts, physical education, and even recess. This is especially true in under-resourced schools, where budgets are tight and many educators believe that children require more time to work in the tested subject areas. Narrow accountability measures fail to give the public, from parents to policymakers, the broad measures of school effectiveness they want and deserve.

While the practice of high-stakes accountability helps identify expectations of student learning, it also cuts down on the time they have to provide students with deeper and more engaging learning experiences (Guggino & Brint, 2010). Practices that support narrow, *spoon-fed* thinking are incompatible with our nation's need for workers capable of collaboration, innovation, and creative problem-solving—the hallmark of 21st century skills. Educating the citizens of tomorrow will require the redesign of school policies and practices so that students do not merely acquire information, but also are provided with opportunities to apply what they have learned in novel, creative ways.

As we redefine American education, the emerging field of neuroeducation can play an important role by focusing educators on *how students learn* rather than on merely *what they learn*. As neuro- and cognitive science researchers continue to accrue knowledge about the science of learning, it is important that relevant findings reach educators in a manner that allows them to incorporate this knowledge into policies and practices. As is the norm in medicine, neuroeducation can bring to educators the *bench to bedside* approach through which research informs practice and the needs of practitioners drive research questions.

Interest and research into the field of neuroeducation has continued to grow internationally. Examples include the Organization for Economic Co-Operation and Development (OECD) panel on how the learning sciences can change the nature of teaching (Guerriero, 2017), and two Delphi panels of scientists and educators address how the learning sciences should shape education practices and policies (Tokuhama-Espinosa, 2017). Other reviews examined the impact of neuroeducation training on teachers' beliefs and pedagogical practices. For example, Privitera (2021) reviewed existing research on how neuroscience training influenced instruction. He found that teachers who received training in topics related to neuroeducation were more likely to adopt pedagogical practices that reflected students' cognitive development and diverse learning needs. Moreover, teachers' general and personal self-efficacy beliefs—the power of education to reach all children—significantly improved after they participated in professional development in the learning sciences (JohnBull & Hardiman, 2023). It is clear that a growing number of educators see the potential of the science of learning to inform the field of education. During the last fifteen years, teacher attendance at national, regional, and local conferences related to learning and the brain has grown significantly (Privitera, 2021), and teachers report that information from the learning sciences is highly relevant to their work (Howard-Jones et al., 2007).

As professional development programs, books, and journal articles have proliferated, however, there has emerged a strong need for some way to separate the wheat from the chaff when it comes to commercial products and textbooks that increasingly tout the use of *brain-based* strategies to improve student achievement (Sylvan & Christodoulou, 2010). Practitioners must have ongoing information that helps them become informed consumers of research claims and a cohesive way to apply relevant research to effective practice.

The BTT Model is presented as a tool for applying the learning sciences to educational practice that is consistent with the skills associated with 21st century learning—preparing all students to become the creative and innovative thinkers and learners of tomorrow.

Information From the Neuro- and Cognitive Sciences That Educators Should Know

1

Separating Neuromyth From Neuroscience

The field of neuroeducation continues to produce a solid literature base and a growing number of research findings and can and indeed should inform the teaching and learning process. Unfortunately—and for a variety of reasons—these worthwhile findings are sometimes oversimplified or misinterpreted when attempts are made to apply them to pedagogy. In this chapter, I begin by identifying some of these erroneous constructs of the science, often referred to as neuromyths. Next, this chapter highlights some general themes from the learning sciences that can give educators a broader perspective of child development and learning. Many of these general themes (and associated neuromyths) will be revisited in subsequent chapters as we explore the Brain-Targeted Teaching® Model.

There exists a solid literature base and a growing number of research findings from the neuro- and cognitive sciences that can and indeed should inform the teaching and learning process.

Neuromyth in Education

Despite more than two decades of research and commentaries, beliefs in neuromyths on the part of the general public and educators in particular continue to proliferate (e.g., Dekker et al., 2012;

Grospietsch & Lins, 2021; Howard-Jones, P. A., 2014; Rousseau, L., 2021; Tokuhama-Espinosa, 2018). In considering neuromyths, we must be aware of not only why they are incorrect but also how they came to be widely believed, especially among educators. Although the media and manufacturers and marketers of commercial educational products improperly sensationalize findings, teachers are the ones who are blamed for incorrectly applying those findings (Goswami, 2006). After interviewing educators on the use of neuroscience in education, Howard-Jones et al. (2007) reported that teachers felt a sense of embarrassment and even betrayal when they discovered that programs they thought were grounded in neuroscience research actually lacked scientific support. Teachers have been encouraged, for example, to teach to the left or right side of the brain, or to inventory their students' learning styles (see section below for explanation)—activities that, while perhaps alluring, lack scientific support. Teachers' time and school resources are wasted when they are duped by false advertising or forced by policymakers to use products or methods that are not supported by research. To illustrate, I will highlight some popular neuromyths so that we can see why it is important for teachers to become more savvy consumers of research.

Teachers felt a sense of embarrassment and even betrayal when they discovered that programs they thought were grounded in neuroscience research actually lacked scientific support.

Some of Us Are Left-Brained; Some of Us Are Right-Brained

Fueled by popular media and commercial products, the notion that we can label ourselves and our students as left- or right-brained thinkers has essentially become common knowledge in many educational circles. The idea arose from research on hemispheric specialization in studies of *split-brain* patients, as researchers were able to isolate processing primarily happening in one hemisphere or the other. Scientists demonstrated that the left brain is associated with language processing, logical or *linear* thinking, and memory for facts, while the right side deals with spatial information, forms, and patterns in a more *holistic* fashion (Goswami, 2006). While each hemisphere *does have specializations*—(for example, Broca's area in the left hemisphere controls much of speech production), the two hemispheres are more similar in function than they are different. This explains why those with lesions on one side of the brain still have remarkable capacity for functioning despite damage to critical brain structures (see Immordino-Yang &

Damasio, 2007). In reality, unless one has actually had his or her corpus callosum (i.e., the bundle of fibers that connect the two hemispheres) severed, both sides of the brain are critically involved in most tasks. The idea that one hemisphere can *dominate* the other—that people who are better at some kinds of tasks than others must have better functioning in one hemisphere—has no basis in fact. There is simply no scientific evidence that would justify identifying learners as either *left-brained* or *right-brained* and gearing instruction toward one side of the brain or the other.

Unless one has actually had his or her corpus callosum (i.e., the bundle of fibers that connect the two hemispheres) severed, both sides of the brain are critically involved in most tasks.

Listening to Mozart Will Make Your Baby Smarter

The idea that listening to Mozart will increase IQ scores and help babies become smarter was endorsed by articles in such reputable sources as the *New York Times* and the *Boston Globe* as well as by books and commercial products that touted increases in mental development when infants listened to Mozart piano concertos (Campbell, 1997). This misconception was derived from a study by Rauscher et al. (1993) who investigated the effects of listening to Mozart's concertos on spatial reasoning. The researchers found that listening to Mozart produced only short-term (i.e., fifteen-minute) enhancement of spatial reasoning on a subtest of the Stanford-Binet IQ test, compared with subjects who listened to relaxation music or experienced silence. In other words, Rauscher and colleagues (1993) did indeed find an effect of listening to Mozart on one's score on an IQ test, but that effect was fleeting and was only seen for a specific subtest associated with a particular cognitive capacity and not intelligence in general. Although the researchers claim that their work was misrepresented, the impact of the study went beyond mere commercialization. In 1998, the governor of Georgia approved funding in the state budget to provide every child born in the state with a recording of classical music.

Mozart lovers need not despair. Jenkins (2001) reported impressive results in reducing epileptic attacks after patients listened to Mozart for ten-minute intervals each hour. Thompson et al. (2001) suggest that temporary changes resulting from listening to Mozart or any music may be attributed to differences in mood and arousal. Moreover, any effects from listening to Mozart are again quite narrow as the authors claim that only music perceived by the listener as enjoyable produces any effect. We will explore in subsequent chapters how the arts, including music, enhances engagement and learning.

After Critical Periods of Development, Learning Shuts Down

Often used interchangeably, the terms *critical period* and *sensitive period* (a deliberate softening of the former) refer to a time during development when children best acquire knowledge or skills in some domain. The notion is that if appropriate stimulation during this period does not occur, the *window of opportunity* for learning closes and the particular skill will never be developed. Although there is certainly evidence of critical and sensitive periods for certain aspects of development, it is important not to overgeneralize this idea to domains for which there is no evidence. And further, for domains in which a critical or sensitive period can be demonstrated, it appears that in most cases the window may narrow somewhat, but only rarely does it completely close. We could certainly learn to play a musical instrument at sixty, but we might want to think twice about booking Carnegie Hall.

Language acquisition is a key area in which researchers have proposed the existence of a critical period. Much of this work is based on studies of feral children who, due to abandonment or abuse, were not exposed to language and failed to ever develop language skills fully. Jean Itard's work with Victor of Aveyron in the early 1800s and the case of Genie, who was discovered in 1970, led to the theory that language exposure must occur early in life or language fails to develop. Additional evidence of a critical period for language is based on studies of individuals with brain damage; ensuing language impairments tend to be more severe when the incident occurs in adulthood compared with in childhood. Perhaps the most compelling evidence for a critical period for language acquisition (where the lack of linguistic input is not confounded with extreme social deprivation) comes from deaf children of hearing parents. Some of these children are often deprived of good sign language input until elementary school or later. Unlike children exposed to sign language early in life, children exposed later will not learn sign language in a native-like way (Grimshaw et al., 1998).

Language acquisition is a particularly key area in which researchers have proposed the existence of a critical period.

Second language learning is another, much more controversial area in the study of critical periods. Younger children seem to be advantaged in ultimate attainment of a second language. Even though native-like pronunciation is almost never observed in late learners, adolescents and adults can master a second language, especially with respect to vocabulary and syntax (Robertson, 2002). So although some kind of specialized *critical period* for second language acquisition could exist especially in phonology, there is evidence for high ultimate achievement even among late second language learners.

Although the window of opportunity for language learning seems only to narrow, the same cannot be said of the development of vision. Based on the work of Nobel Prize winners David Hubel and Torsten Wiesel (1970), a kitten temporarily blinded in one eye at an early developmental stage would never recover sight in that eye after the blindfold was removed, thus demonstrating that there is a critical period for the development of the visual cortex.

Research in the area of sensitive periods continues to advance, particularly in the area of adolescent development. Studies reveal changes in brain structure and function at the onset of puberty and into early adulthood (Dahl, 2004; Giedd, 2010). Although this, along with the examples described previously, may provide evidence in favor of the existence of critical or sensitive periods in certain domains, the idea that this is characteristic of all or even most areas of learning is not supported by scientific research. Similarly unfounded is the idea that it is pointless to try to learn new information after a demonstrable critical or sensitive period has ended. This appears to be true only in rare or extreme cases. So for anyone so inclined, do sign up for those tuba lessons!

Recent studies reveal changes in brain structure and function at the onset of puberty and into early adulthood.

We Only Use 10% of Our Brain

With all of the attention about the workings of the human brain, it is amazing that this myth still perpetuates and appears to be one of the most prevalent myths coming from the popular press (Takuhama-Espinosa, 2018). Indeed, many believe that 90% of the brain is inactive. There are multiple explanations for how this myth came about. For example, University of Washington neuroscientist Eric Chudler (2010) offers several sources for this myth, including the work of Karl Lashley in the 1930s. Lashley found that rats were still able to perform certain tasks even after having large areas of the cerebral cortex removed.

This may be one of several studies where results were misrepresented or exaggerated in a way that contributed to the false conclusion that large areas of the brain were inactive.

In fact, we use all of our brain. Findings from neuroimaging studies demonstrate activity throughout the brain during many different tasks. Chudler (2010) points out that studies involving functional neuroimaging generally only highlight *differences* in brain activity that arise due to the performance of specific tasks. The areas of the brain that appear dark on the scan are likely still active; they simply do not change in response to the task being studied. Thus, when a graphical representation shows only a tiny island of activation, this is in no way indicative of the amount of activity taking place in the brain as a whole. It is clearly established that brain networks work together as we engage in activities that require motor control, sensory processing, and cognitive tasks like language processing, problem-solving, and decision-making.

Cognition and learning involve multiple networks of the brain and bodily movements.

Teachers Should Assess and Teach to Each Child's Learning Style

A recently debunked neuromyth in educational literature concerns the concept of *learning styles*. Learning style theory assumes that some children learn best through visual, auditory, or kinesthetic methods. According to the theory, teachers should inventory each child's preferred style and adjust instructional strategies to meet each child's assessed style of learning.

This neuromyth is certainly widespread: About 90% of people surveyed reported a belief that everyone has a preferred style of learning (Willingham, 2009). Willingham (2009) argues that this misunderstanding likely comes from popular notions of multiple intelligences and left/right brain processing theories. Unfortunately, the learning style theory as applied to classroom instruction has been aggressively perpetrated by vendors of educational products that promote learning style assessments and strategies for tailoring instruction to specific groups of students. Specifically, learning style theory has been promoted as a way for educators to differentiate instruction based on the *needs* of particular learners. Despite the pervasiveness of learning style theory in educational settings, in an extensive review of the literature, Pashler et al. (2008) found no evidence that children taught in their preferred learning style performed any better than if they were taught through a nonpreferred style. In studies conducted by Rogowsky et al. (2020), findings clearly showed that instruction matched to students' perceived learning styles did not produce better learning. Teachers and trainers should be encouraged to differentiate instruction based on a number of metrics available. Matching instruction to a particular modality is not an effective way to differentiate learning activities.

With regard to meeting individual needs, there are potentially more efficient means of differentiation, such as considering prior knowledge, background in the content, level of mastery of skills, interest level, or learning differences and goals identified in individualized educational programs.

We Can Effectively Work on Tasks Simultaneously Through a Process Known as Multitasking

Multitasking is actually not a good way to get work done. The brain's attentional system requires focusing on concepts and thoughts sequentially, one after the other. This may seem confusing because we are able to do two things at once like walking and talking at the same time. But in that example, we see that walking and talking don't necessarily require focused attention. The brain's attentional network requires us to switch focus every time we move from one mental task to another. We may think that we are doing two mental tasks at the same time, however, there is a cost in loss of working memory when we switch tasks. If you have a good working memory, you may not notice the memory cost; however, for some, switching tasks may require going back to figure out where you were in the first task before you switched to a different one. Given what we now know about multitasking, using a cell phone or texting while driving is a serious safety threat (see Różańska & Gruszka, 2020). Moreover, findings from a review of research on media multitasking—using two or more medias at the same time—revealed that dividing attention has significant negative effects on students' academic performance (May & Elder, 2018).

We Are Born With All the Brain Cells We Will Ever Have

Many of us believe that the brain is a static organ incapable of any significant changes. This is one of the most important myths to dispel for educators as it may influence teachers' attitudes and perceptions about children's capacity to learn (Hardiman & Denckla, 2010). As we will see from the discussion of plasticity and neurogenesis below, the brain is an amazing organ capable of tremendous change throughout life.

The brain is an amazing organ capable of tremendous change throughout life.

Important Themes From the Neuro- and Cognitive Sciences That Educators Should Know

Now that we have dispelled a number of the most insidious neuromyths, I turn to areas from the learning sciences that can and should inform beliefs as well as practices at all levels and in any context. Each of these topics will also be considered in discussing the related components of the Brain-Targeted Teaching® Model in subsequent chapters.

Plasticity

Plasticity is the term used to explain how the brain is modified with experience. Learning involves changes in the strength between neural synapses after a sensory input or motor activity. Neurons branch new dendrites, grow new axons, develop new synapses, and modify or eliminate established neural connections over the lifespan of the human being. Genetic makeup and environmental interactions set the course for the brain to change with experience (Shonkoff & Phillips, 2000). Just as muscles are strengthened with repeated exercise, brain networks are strengthened with repeated use. Knowledge that the brain continues to change based on experiences is important for all practitioners. Understanding that the brain continues to develop throughout one's lifetime promotes the mindset that the capacity for learning is not fixed—an important concept that we all must embrace as we work with children and adult learners.

Just as muscles are strengthened with repeated exercise, brain networks are strengthened with repeated use.

Neurogenesis

Neurogenesis refers to the growth of new brain cells. Neurogenesis is critical in the developing embryo, but researchers have found that the brain continues to grow new cells in certain brain regions after birth and throughout our lifespan. Only about twenty years ago, scientists knew that the brain changed when neurons connected and formed neural networks (plasticity), but the common belief was that the brain did not grow new cells. Now we know that the brain has the capacity in certain circumstances to grow new cells at any age.

Researchers have demonstrated the genesis of new brain cells in the cerebellum and in other important regions such as the hippocampus, an area associated with memory (Alonso et al., 2024; Denoth-Lippuner & Jessberger, 2021; Hussain et al., 2024). In addition, it appears that neurogenesis can be enhanced through exercise, nutrition, and stress reduction (Kempermann et al., 2004). Like the concept of plasticity, knowing that the brain is constantly growing and changing helps to promote a *growth mindset* with the profound understanding that experiences can produce not only behavioral changes but biological changes as well.

The discovery of neurogenesis, the production of new cells in certain brain regions, represented an enormous breakthrough in understanding the human brain.

Emotion and Stress

Study of brain structure and function reveals the intricate interplay between cognition and emotion. Perhaps the words of Jill Bolte Taylor, a neuroscientist recovering from a severe stroke, best express this interplay. Taylor explains a major breakthrough in her thinking about brain function as she chronicles her brain's healing process. She states, "Although many of us may think of ourselves as *thinking creatures that feel,* biologically we are *feeling creatures that think*" (Taylor, 2008, p. 19).

Many of us were trained in our teacher preparation programs to believe that rational and emotional processing should not mix. We believed that educators must focus on developing cognitive processes; emotion must be shut down for learning to take place. Now we know that it is impossible to separate emotions and learning. We will explore this topic in more depth in the chapter on Brain-Target One, Establishing the Emotional Climate for Learning.

The Role of Attention in Learning

Attention is clearly critical for learning. The more attention the brain pays to a stimulus, the more elaborately the information will be retained. The brain is constantly bombarded with sensory stimuli; that which is attended to will encode into the short-term and working memory system. Events that carry emotional arousal are more likely to attract attention than neutral events. These events then stay longer in our memory systems and are later recalled with greater accuracy.

New and ongoing research in the area of attention is showing that it can be enhanced through specific training and by introducing novelty and visual images into the physical learning environment.

Posner and Rothbart (2007) identify three neural networks—or systems of interconnected brain regions—involved in attending behaviors: the alerting network, which allows us to maintain an alert state; the orienting network, which helps us attend to sensory events; and the executive network, which sustains attention to an event. They point out that effortful control of attention develops from early childhood into adolescence. Their studies have shown changes in patterns of neural activity underlying attentional processes and improvement in behavioral measures of attention after subjects received specific training in tasks requiring effortful control of attention. The chapter on Brain-Target Two will address how the classroom environment can be shaped to maximize attending behaviors in children.

Effortful control of attention develops from early childhood into adolescence.

Executive Function

The term *executive function* is used to describe basic cognitive processes that underlie ongoing, goal-directed behaviors and higher order thinking skills. These basic functions, which are often associated with neural processing in the frontal lobe, include holding information in working memory, initiating as well as inhibiting an action, and shifting perspective or the focus of attention. Together these functions allow us to carry out complex actions such as planning future events, organizing processes, self-monitoring, and regulating emotional response. Far from becoming active all at once, executive function skills develop over time. Scientists believe that some competencies such as emotional regulation are not fully developed until the mid-to-late twenties or even later.

Some researchers posit that executive function skills can be enhanced through certain training programs that range from commercial brain-training programs to mindfulness initiatives (Diamond & Ling, 2016). Much research is needed to determine how to best develop specific skills associated with executive function. For example, self-regulation training is an area of great interest in the research community.

In short, executive function skills are critical for effective learning and are more predictive of academic success than IQ or socioeconomic status

(Diamond & Ling, 2016). These skills allow the learner to draw novel associations and flexibly use information in different contexts. It is important to note that newer notions of behavior and learning posit that not all behaviors are consciously controlled but arise from more of a *whole brain* process. We next look at how the brain and body are both critical for cognition and learning.

Executive function is especially critical for effective learning as it requires being able to draw novel associations and flexibly use information in different contexts.

Embodied Cognition: The Importance of Movement and Learning

Cognition is defined as the process of acquiring knowledge and understanding. *Top-down* processing is a term often used to refer to effortful control of cognitive thoughts and actions, whereas *bottom-up* refers to the processing of an array of sensory-motor information in real time and not driven by effortful cognitive thought; researchers think that both ways of processing information operate together.

The term, embodied cognition, is based on the notion that human cognition is originally rooted in sensory-motor processes and thus determined by bodily experiences. This relatively new approach to cognition challenges traditional theories that the body is *passive* as the brain processes information. The theories suggest that learning is grounded in the learners' sensory-motor system that interacts with the environment and culture (Shapiro & Stolz, 2019). In other words, thought and movement are not separate neurological systems. Cognitive neuroscience research suggests that acquiring academic skills is linked to areas of the brain responsible for body movement in space.

Long recognizing the importance of movement in cognition and learning, Maria Montessori (1967) noted that "one of the greatest mistakes of our day is to think of movement by itself, as something apart from the higher functions . . . . Mental development must be connected with movement and be dependent on it" (pp. 141–142).

Consistent with Montessori's idea, in his book, *Spark,* John Ratey (2008) explains that movement and exercise do more than just produce chemicals that make us feel good; physical activity actually affects cognitive development by accelerating the production of specific chemicals necessary for memory consolidation and spurring the development of new neurons from the hippocampus. Within the Brain-Targeted Teaching® Model, we will see the critical role of movement on attention in Brain-Target Two as well as in content acquisition and retention when we consider Brain-Target Four, which emphasizes active learning and arts integration.

Arts and Learning

Although the number of arts programs seems to be shrinking in our nations' schools, a growing body of research maintains that there are important positive effects of arts engagement in educational settings. Besides serving as a creative and enriching experience for children, the arts have been shown to have benefits on learning, student engagement, and self-efficacy. For instance, heading the Dana Foundation Arts and Cognition Consortium, Michael Gazzaniga (2008) reports a tight correlation between the study of the arts and improvement in attention and various cognitive abilities. In addition, researchers report significant differences in academic achievement and social behaviors between youth highly involved in arts programs compared with those with no arts engagement (e.g., Bowen & Kisida, 2019; Caterall, 2009; National Endowment for the Arts, 2024). What is more, researchers have shown changes in brain structure even with relatively small amounts of music training (Hyde et al., 2009). Hyde and colleagues found that students who were given just fifteen months of music training showed significant changes in specific brain regions that were also correlated with improvements in musically relevant motor and auditory skills. Numerous studies over the last twenty years have shown academic and social benefits when students engaged in various art forms including theater, dance, visual arts, instrumental music, and creative writing. Building from these connections between the arts and learning, the chapter on Brain-Target Four (Chapter 7) explores how integrating the arts into content instruction may play a role in long-term retention of information and more robust habits of mind that transfer to all tasks. In Chapter 7, we share our research on the effects of arts integration, in which we found clear advantages for memory of science content when students were given arts-integrated lessons compared to traditional instruction (Hardiman et al., 2014, 2019).

Researchers have shown changes in brain structure even with relatively small amounts of music training.

Adolescents, Sleep, and Learning

Research in the neuro- and cognitive sciences sheds light on the way the brain changes during adolescence as well as on what patterns of neural activity may accompany at least some of those changes. National

Institutes of Health researcher Jay Giedd (2009, 2010), for example, points out that the onset in puberty brings dramatic brain changes. Compared with prepubescent children, children entering puberty exhibit greater connectivity among various brain regions during task completion, reduction in grey matter volume, and changing balance between connections in the limbic and frontal executive function systems. Research has demonstrated significant brain plasticity during the teen years evidenced by both biological and behavioral measures. Ramsden and colleagues (2011) found changes in verbal and nonverbal IQ scores (both higher and lower) during the teen years compared to earlier testing. These scores correlated with changes in associated local brain structures involved with verbal and nonverbal processing.

In addition to changes in neural and cognitive processing, sleep patterns also typically show significant changes. The circadian rhythms of adolescents point to a tendency for later sleep onset in the evening and later arousal in the morning (Dahl, 2004). This finding suggests that a school day that begins later in the morning may be more consistent with the sleep patterns of adolescents. In general, studies have shown how sleep optimizes the consolidation of newly acquired information in our memory systems in all individuals including children, adolescents and adults (Diekelman & Born, 2010; Saraji et al., 2024; Zahran et al., 2024).

Circadian rhythms of adolescents point to a tendency for later sleep onset in the evening and later arousal in the morning.

Brain changes may also account for the tendency of adolescents to shift from seeking approval from adults to seeking approval from same-age peers as well as for adolescents having a greater propensity toward thrill-seeking behaviors (Giedd, 2009). Promising new research in this area could be used to assist educators and caregivers in understanding and preventing the increase of morbidity and mortality that comes with this sensitive time in human development. We will examine adolescent emotional development in discussions of Brain-Target One.

Creativity

As a hallmark of *21st century skills*, creativity in teaching and learning has become a topic of conversation and heightened interest in both academic literature and popular media. The World Economic Forum (2023) continues to cite creativity as a critical skill for successful employment. Thus, the demands of the world marketplace challenge educational institutions to prepare students to be creative thinkers who will shape our future world.

However, Bronson and Merryman (2010) point out that although IQ scores for children over the last thirty years have improved, creativity indices have declined. They cite analyses that examined the declining scores of more than three hundred thousand children and adults on the Torrance test, a popular measure of creative thinking. The late Sir Ken Robinson observed that concentrating on high stakes testing in relation to an ever-increasing multitude of content standards is squeezing creativity out of our schools and classrooms (Tabor, 2024).

Concentrating on high stakes testing in relation to an ever-increasing multitude of content standards is squeezing creativity out of our schools and classrooms.

While educators grapple with how to build more creative activities into overcrowded curricula, scientists have continued to demonstrate differences in how the brain processes information when people are engaged in creative, spontaneous tasks, as opposed to ordinary activities that depend on rote knowledge (see Beaty et al., 2023). In our discussion of Brain-Target Five, we will examine this research on creativity, considering neuroimaging studies as well as behavioral studies. We will explore how teachers might be able to teach content in greater depth to move children beyond the acquisition of information to creative thinking and problem-solving tasks.

The next chapter provides a basic overview of brain structure and function, information that is important as we discuss research that supports the components of the Brain-Targeted Teaching® Model.

Brain Structure and Function

2

In a similar chapter in my first book, I suggested that knowing basic information about brain anatomy was not necessary to implement teaching methods based on knowledge of the workings of the human mind and brain (Hardiman, 2003). However, after observing and studying how findings from the brain sciences can inform teaching, I believe that practitioners need at least some knowledge of brain structure and function in order to incorporate these findings into their practice. As emerging research in neuro- and cognitive sciences continues to detail how we learn, fundamental knowledge of how the brain works should be an important component of any field in which teaching and learning takes place. Though practitioners might not need sophisticated scientific knowledge of neuroscience, a fundamental understanding of brain structure and function will allow them to become better consumers of scientific research. Armed with knowledge of how learning takes place, practitioners would be better able to discern usable information from sensational headlines that serve only to propagate neuromyths. Moreover, students at all ages also benefit from knowing fundamental information about the brain. The work of Tracey Tokuhama-Espinosa (2024) demonstrates the curiosity that children from around the world have about how their brain works. So let's take a brief journey through the human brain, starting with the basics of its parts and processes and then examining in more detail how the brain is organized.

Fundamental understanding of brain structure and function will allow educators to become better consumers of scientific research.

Brain Facts

Looking at a human brain, one would describe it as the size of a grapefruit and the shape of a walnut. It weighs just under three pounds, most of which is water (about 78%), fat (about 10%), and protein (about 8%). It makes up about 2.5% of total body weight and consumes about 20% of the body's energy, a rate ten times that of other body organs.

The brain is part of the human nervous system, a system that receives, processes, and stores information in order to coordinate actions. The nervous system is divided into two major parts: the central nervous system (CNS) and the peripheral nervous system (PNS). The CNS includes the brain and spinal cord, and the PNS consists of sensory and motor neurons that extend to all parts of the body. The CNS acts as the conductor, storing and analyzing the sensory signals it receives from the PNS and directing motor and chemical responses. The PNS sends sensory signals to the CNS and transports motor signals from the CNS to muscles, glands, and organs.

The brain is part of the human nervous system, a system that receives, processes, and stores information in order to coordinate actions.

Brain Cells: Neurons and Glial Cells

The brain consists of several hundred billion cells of two main types: neurons and glial cells.

Neurons

Nerve cells or neurons receive and transmit information to other cells through electrochemical signals (see Figure 2.1). Looking like a bulb with sprouting roots and a long tail, neurons typically consist of a cell body or soma (the bulb), dendrites (the sprouting roots), and an axon (the long tail). Each part of the neuron has a specific function. Like all other cells, the cell body of the neuron serves a metabolic function and contains molecules in cytoplasm within a cell membrane. The axon and dendrites are features unique to neurons, however. Dendrites branch out from the cell body and receive information from other neurons while the axon carries messages from the nerve cell to dendrites of other cells. Furthermore, the cell body of each neuron, in addition to its metabolic functions, processes or *sums up* the signals it receives from other neurons and responds by passing along signals of its own.

FIGURE 2.1 Neuron Features

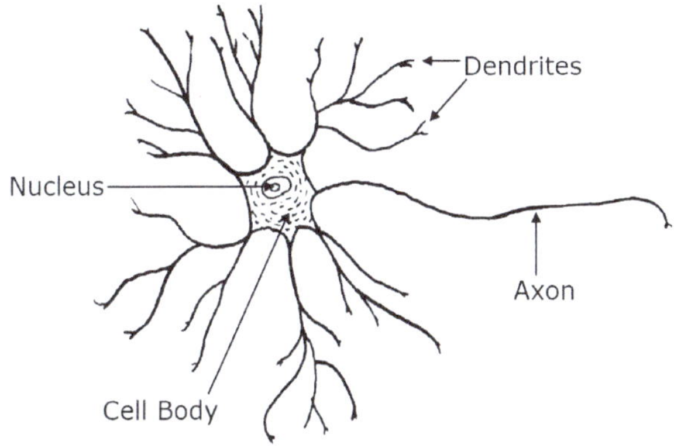

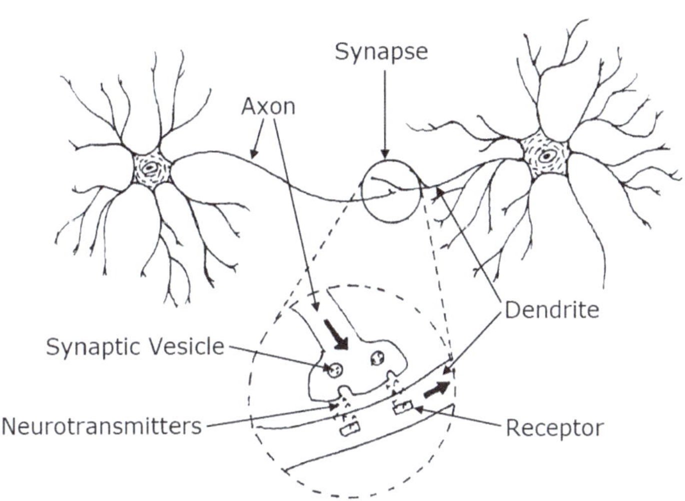

This process of cell communication is the essence of brain functioning. Signals are transmitted when neurons *fire*, sending information outward from the cell body along the axon in the form of an electrical impulse. Communication between cells occurs when signals cross a tiny gap between the axon of one neuron and the dendrite of another called a synapse. Some synapses channel electrical impulses directly while others are traversed through biochemical processes as electrical impulses

Each neuron connects with thousands of other neurons, and as a result, the process of cellular communication can involve highly intricate neural pathways.

produce a release of chemicals called neurotransmitters from sacs at the end of the axon. These neurotransmitters bind to specialized receptors on the receiving (dendrite) side of the synapse, sending signals from one neuron to the next. Each neuron connects with thousands of other neurons, and as a result, the process of cellular communication can involve highly intricate neural pathways.

Glial Cells

Accounting for more than half of the brain's volume and far outnumbering neurons are glial or neuroglial cells. One function of these cells, whose name derives from the Greek word for glue, can be to provide structural support to neurons (Gazzaniga et al., 2009). Another critical function of glial cells is the formation of myelin, a fatty sheath that surrounds the axons. Myelin is essential for protecting and insulating the axon and also allows electrical impulses to travel at greater speeds, making communication between brain cells more efficient. Because myelin is white in color, these cells are referred to as the white matter of the brain.

Cerebral Organization

Before we review three major sections of the brain—the hindbrain, the limbic system, and the cerebrum—we should note that the brain consists of two halves or hemispheres and the majority of brain structures discussed below are paired or occur in corresponding areas of the left and right hemispheres.

The Hindbrain

The hindbrain, consisting of the pons, medulla oblongata, and cerebellum (see Figure 2.2), is considered the oldest part of the evolving human brain.

Pons and Medulla Oblongata. The pons and medulla oblongata control autonomic functions such as respiration, heart rhythms, and states of consciousness such as wakefulness and sleep. They control sensory processes, including auditory and visual sensation and motor control of the face, mouth, throat, respiratory system, and heart. These structures are located along the midline of the brain and thus are not paired.

Cerebellum. Though small in size, the cerebellum, sometimes referred to as the little cerebrum, plays a large role in brain and body functioning. Although it consists of only 10% of the brain, it contains approximately eleven billion cells that control important motor and sensory processes (Pinel, 2000). It is central to the body's balance, posture,

FIGURE 2.2 The Hind Brain

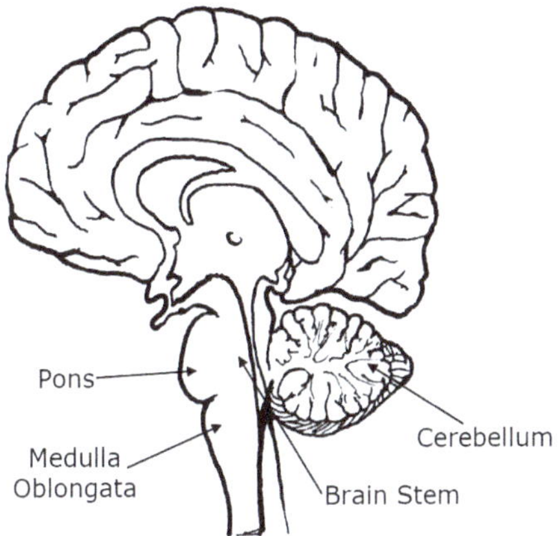

When you hit that perfect forehand in tennis without giving it a thought, your cerebellum is actively engaged.

walking, and planning motor commands for the coordination of harmonious movements. When you hit that perfect forehand in tennis without giving it a thought, your cerebellum is actively engaged. The ability to perform tasks automatically—like riding a bicycle, driving a car, or writing—relies heavily on the cerebellum; this automatic muscle memory frees up the higher cortical areas to process new information (Ratey, 2008). Researchers now know that the cerebellum performs functions well beyond muscle memory. For example, patients with damage to the cerebellum have demonstrated difficulties with verbal tasks and regulating emotion. Brain imaging studies suggest that children with Attention Deficit Hyperactivity Disorder (ADHD) who demonstrate lack of impulse control have a cerebellum that is reduced in size (Castellanos et al., 2002).

The Limbic System

Moving up from the hindbrain, we find the limbic system, a collection of structures that play an important role in emotional processing, learning, and memory. The structures we will examine here include the thalamus, hypothalamus, hippocampus, and amygdala (see Figure 2.3).

Thalamus. At the core of the brain rests a walnut-sized structure that serves as the traffic cop, directing information received from the senses (excluding the olfactory) to other parts of the brain for further processing.

Hypothalamus. This structure serves as a relay station as it monitors information coming from the autonomic nervous system. It regulates the body's functions to maintain homeostasis. For example, when the body's temperature rises, the hypothalamus will increase perspiration to lower body temperature. The hypothalamus also regulates the endocrine system and some emotional processes.

Hippocampus. The shape of a seahorse, the hippocampus may be thought of as the workhorse of the memory system. It holds memories of the immediate past and serves to consolidate memories into the long-term memory system.

Amygdala. This almond-shaped structure is mostly associated with emotional states and processes. Although multiple neural systems are involved in processing emotional information, the amygdala is considered to have a key role (Gazzaniga et al., 2009). The amygdala is especially involved in our response to fearful situations. It is interesting to note that sensory information extracted from the external environment arrives in the amygdala for emotional processing before it reaches the cortex, the part of the brain where rational thought takes place (Sapolsky, 2004). More specifically, according to LeDoux (1996), the amygdala receives stimuli forty milliseconds before the cortex. This finding indicates that fearful responses precede any conscious, thoughtful responses to stimuli.

FIGURE 2.3 The Limbic System

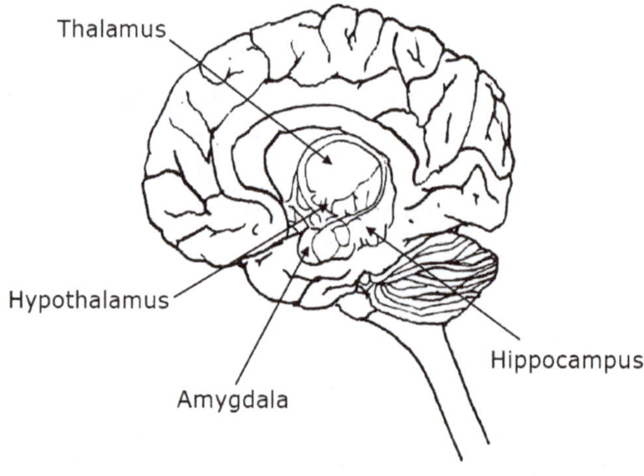

The Cerebrum

The cerebrum is the largest area of the brain, accounting for more than 80% of the brain's weight. It is divided into halves referred to as cerebral hemispheres. The left and right hemispheres are connected by a thick bundle of nerve fibers called the corpus callosum. The corpus callosum contains about two hundred million tightly packed axons that bridge communications between the brain's hemispheres. Within each hemisphere, the cortex is divided into four lobes, each associated with particular brain functions (see Figure 2.4).

The corpus callosum contains two hundred million or so tightly packed axons that bridge communications between the brain's hemispheres.

Occipital Lobe. Located at the back of the brain, the occipital lobe perceives and processes visual stimuli and their properties, including color, luminance, visual orientation, spatial orientation, and motion (Gazzaniga et al., 2009).

Temporal Lobe. The temporal lobe is located just above and around the ears. This lobe is where auditory stimuli are initially processed. The left temporal lobe includes Wernicke's area, one of several areas that specialize in processing spoken language.

Parietal Lobe. The parietal lobe is located on the top and side of each hemisphere and is responsible for processing sensory information such as pain, body position, temperature sense, limb position, and touch.

FIGURE 2.4 The Four Lobes of the Cerebrum

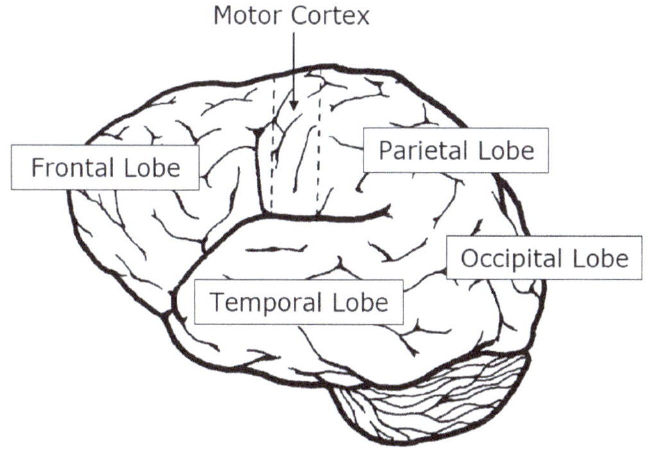

Frontal Lobe. Considered the center of thought, the frontal lobe includes the prefrontal cortex and the motor cortex. The prefrontal cortex is associated with executive functions such as planning, carrying out conscious actions, and inhibiting responses. The motor cortex lies between the prefrontal areas and parietal lobe and contains some of the largest neurons in the cerebral cortex, with axons that extend several feet down the spinal cord (Gazzaniga et al., 2009).

Hemispheric Differences

As pointed out in the previous chapter, differences in information processing between the left and right hemispheres of the brain were established and popularized as a result of studies of *split-brain* patients who underwent surgery to disconnect the two hemispheres of the brain in an effort to minimize seizure activity due to severe epilepsy. Specifically, split-brain surgery consists of severing the corpus callosum, the bundle of nerve fibers that serve as an *information superhighway* between the two hemispheres. Early notions of brain asymmetry characterized the left hemisphere as responsible for verbal and *linear* information processing, and the right hemisphere as responsible for spatial and *holistic* processing.

In contrast, more recently developed views of hemispheric specialization suggest that both hemispheres are involved in most tasks, though contributions from each may not be equal (Gazzaniga et al., 2009). Modern neuroimaging techniques such as functional magnetic resonance imaging (fMRI) and positron emission tomography (PET) confirm, for example, that the left side of the brain indeed plays a prominent role in language processing. However, neuroimaging studies also indicate that regions in the right hemisphere are important for some aspects of language as well, in particular for comprehension of abstract thought (Bookheimer, 2002) and prosody, the ability to detect affect or intonation in speech.

Both hemispheres are involved in most tasks, though contributions from each may not be equal.

From Research to Practice

This research in left/right brain specializations demonstrates an important point: As research evolves, popular notions of how the brain works also need to evolve to reflect the latest scientific thinking. As we saw in the last chapter, there is no such thing as being a *left-* or *right-brained* thinker. And although it is harmless for anyone to profess to be left- or right-brained, it is unwise to base instruction on this or any other unscientific pop-culture notion. With a basic understanding of brain structure and function, educators can avoid using mere popular notions of how the brain works and instead translate usable findings on cognition and learning into instructional practices.

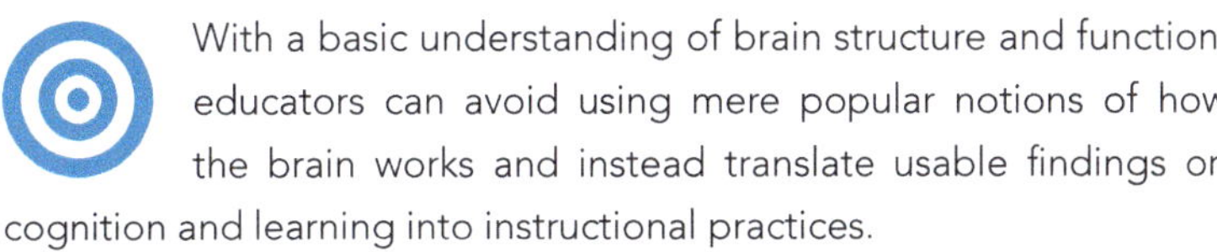

Armed now with some basic information of brain anatomy, in the next chapter, we begin our study of the Brain-Targeted Teaching® Model, an instructional framework designed to assist teachers in basing instruction on what we know from research from the learning sciences about how the brain and mind work.

The Brain-Targeted Teaching® Model

3

The Brain-Targeted Teaching Model

The Brain-Targeted Teaching® (BTT) Model is an instructional framework designed to guide teaching and leading, informed by research from the learning sciences. Rather than merely a list of strategies, the BTT Model offers a cohesive framework that educators and other professionals have applied over the years in PK–12 classrooms, higher education, corporate training, athletic coaching, strategic planning, professional development, parenting, and more.

The model consists of six stages of the teaching and learning process that I refer to as *brain targets*—that is, teaching targeted to what we know about how we think and learn. As discussed in previous chapters, scientific discoveries in cognition and learning can and should inform the work of educators, leaders, and professionals in any context. However, without a guiding framework, making sense of usable knowledge from this research and integrating it into practices can become challenging. This model synthesizes relevant research into a cohesive pedagogical system for using effective practices in any instructional program from early childhood to adult learning in any content. The model also is relevant for use in noneducational contexts, such as strategic planning or leadership training in any field. As such, it is not a curriculum nor a stand-alone product, and most sound teaching and learning programs and practices align with one or more of the brain targets, such as the Universal Design for Learning (Rao et al., 2023; Rose & Meyer, 2002) or Framework for Teaching (Danielson, 1996).

Without a guiding framework, making sense of usable knowledge from this research and integrating it into instructional practices can become challenging.

Although each of the targets is presented as a separate component, all six are interrelated. Thus, the model should not be viewed as linear, but as an organic system that guides and informs an approach to learning, leading, or strategic planning in any context. Fundamental to that approach are practices that lead not only to mastery of content but also to apply knowledge in creative problem-solving, often referred to as *21st century skills*. Also central to the model is the purposeful focus of positive emotional and physical learning and work environments; an instructional design that demonstrates *big-picture* concepts; continuous evaluation of learning and skill mastery; and the integration of the arts and technology to foster retention, conceptual development, and higher order thinking. The section below provides a brief description of each of the brain targets.

The model should not be viewed as linear, but as an organic system that guides and informs an approach to learning, leading, or strategic planning in any context.

Overview of the Brain-Targeted Teaching® Model

Brain-Target One: Establishing the Emotional Climate for Learning

Our study of the BTT Model begins with Brain-Target One, an exploration of the interconnection of emotions and learning. As research from the learning sciences continues to shed light on the neural systems underlying emotion, it is important to understand the influence of emotional arousal, both positive and negative, on attention, memory, and higher order thinking. For example, research is demonstrating the negative effects of stress on learning from prenatal stages to early childhood, adolescent, and adult learning. Conversely, positive emotion has been shown to improve learning and work outcomes. This research informs strategies designed to promote a positive, joyful, and purposeful climate for learning, leading, and working. We also consider ways to embed into learning tasks specific activities to provide an emotional connection to content in order to make learning more meaningful and relevant. The same is true for most of what we undertake in our world of work or broadly in our lives. When we are enthused and excited about a project or learning a new skill, we approach it with a more positive sense of purpose and intention.

Positive emotion has been shown to improve learning outcomes.

Brain-Target Two: Creating the Physical Learning Environment

Just as the emotional environment can shape learning, elements in the physical environment—the focus of Brain-Target Two—can influence attention and engagement in learning tasks. We explore how novelty engages attention and how it can be achieved by using strategies such as changing seating arrangements or displays in the classroom or workspace. We also look at ways to encourage movement and bring a sense of order and beauty into the environment. This also holds true for our work and home spaces. Novelty, order, and aesthetics can enhance a positive sense of place. And certain elements in the physical environment can support or impede learning and task outcomes. For example, think about how temperature, noise, lighting, or odors can affect how you feel about engaging in the task at hand.

Novelty engages attention. Environmental factors can enhance or impede task outcomes.

Brain-Target Three: Designing the Learning Experience

The learning sciences delve into the cognitive processes associated with information processing—how we make meaning and find relationships amidst input from various senses. Brain-Target Three is informed by the notion that we use prior knowledge to categorize stimuli and combine this prior knowledge with new knowledge to create patterns of thinking and learning. Rather than lists of facts, cognitive science tells us that knowledge is organized around global understanding or big ideas. Therefore, we design the learning experience with the use of visual representations to show *big-picture* concepts and connections between new ideas and prior knowledge. We demonstrate how learning goals and objectives connect with daily activities and lead to the attainment of targeted content, skills, and concepts. Creating visual representations in the form of graphic organizers or concept maps can help to focus on overarching goals, understand how those goals are related, and see how they transition into component parts (e.g., activities). This approach enhances visual thinking, an important skill in learning and in our daily lives.

Knowledge is organized around global understanding or big ideas.

Brain-Target Four: Teaching for Mastery of Content, Skills, and Concepts

Learning content, skills, and concepts requires that we acquire and retain information and be able to use it meaningfully. Brain-Target Four explores the connection between learning and memory, reviewing how information and experiences are processed, encoded, stored, and retrieved in our brain and embodied memory systems. Research from cognitive science and psychology demonstrates various ways to influence long-term memory. In short, in this target, we focus on how to best make *learning stick*. We consider certain *memory effects* as we explore how retention of knowledge is supported through teaching that integrates the visual and performing arts into content instruction.

Research from cognitive science and psychology demonstrates various manipulations that influence long-term memory. Retention of knowledge is supported through teaching that integrates the visual and performing arts into content instruction.

Brain-Target Five: Teaching for the Extension and Application of Knowledge—Creativity and Innovation in Education

Teaching and learning must not only lead students to mastery of content, skills, and concepts but also promote the application of knowledge in real-world creative problem-solving. The hallmark of 21st century learning is the ability to demonstrate creative and innovative thinking. Brain-Target Five focuses on the growing body of research in creativity and how findings can inform instructional practices so that learning experiences foster divergent thinking and creative problem-solving.

The hallmark of 21st century learning is the ability to demonstrate creative and innovative thinking.

Brain-Target Six: Evaluating Learning

Evaluation of learning is a critical component of the teaching and learning process. In Brain-Target Six, we explore research that demonstrates how continuous evaluation can enhance learning and memory. We consider how to expand traditional types of assessments to include the use of portfolios, student-generated products, and performance-based assessments. In this way, evaluation is not only *of* learning, evaluation is also *for* learning.

How continuous evaluation can enhance learning and memory.

Brain-Targeted Teaching®: Research to Practice

In Chapters 4 through 9, we take an in-depth look at each component of the BTT Model. For each brain target, we first review research from the learning sciences that informs the brain target. Then, to demonstrate application of the research into practice, each chapter includes strategies that logically stem from the research. These strategies are embedded in the text and also are offered in special sections written by *expert practitioners* who have used the model in PK–12, higher education, corporate settings, and at home. Their experiences add depth and context to an understanding of how research can inform practice in multiple and diverse ways. I hope you enjoy reading about their experiences and perhaps even try out their strategies in your own work.

Brain-Target One

4

Establishing the Emotional Climate for Learning

A teacher who is attempting to teach without inspiring the pupil with a desire to learn is hammering on cold iron.

—Horace Mann

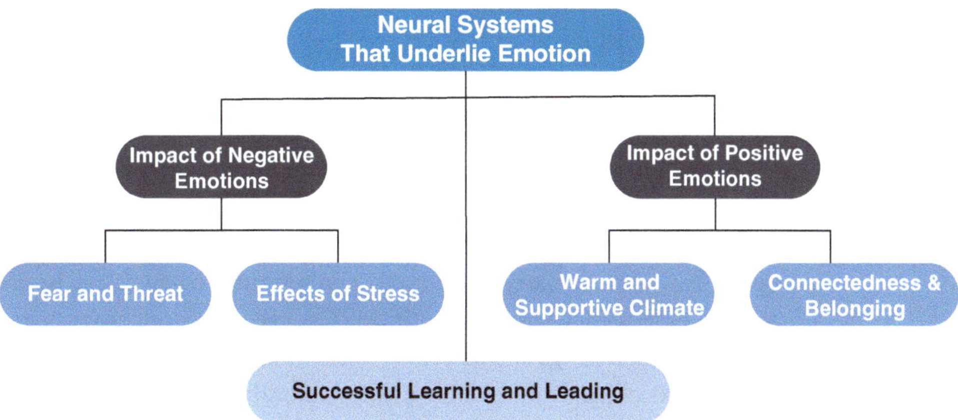

I ask you to take a few moments to think back to your own school experiences. Think of a time when you may have been publicly embarrassed by an insensitive remark by a teacher or classmate. Think about how you felt immediately after the incident. Were you able to concentrate on the learning task after that event? Did it affect how you performed in that teacher's class in the subsequent days or even months? What elements do you remember most about the experience? Similarly, in the workspace, how do you feel if your contribution in a meeting is ignored or ridiculed? You might have feelings of embarrassment, anger, or self-doubt. How does the work environment support or diminish your productivity?

These are questions that I've asked thousands of participants in workshops, conferences, and graduate education classes. And the responses are always riveting. At seventy-two, Sarah, for example, described a vivid memory of an event she experienced as a six-year-old. Sarah shared how her excitement for learning numbers was squelched by her first-grade teacher who criticized her mistakes when she was asked to count by fives. She said that she clearly remembers the teacher saying, "Sit down and be better prepared the next time you try to answer . . . not all of us understand math as well as others." Sarah expressed how, after that remark, she was frightened to respond to any question posed by the teacher, especially in a math lesson. When I asked her how that affected her performance in math that school year, her response was not surprising. She stated, "That incident affected my performance in math for the rest of my school career. I avoided the subject and always struggled with confidence in any math work in the future." Sarah was not the first to share a story that she remembered with such clarity and to view the incident as having a negative impact on her schooling. Jeremy shared a similar situation stemming from an oral report in a seventh-grade social studies class. Negative and embarrassing feedback from the teacher in front of the class prompted him to refuse to speak publicly for the rest of his middle school experience. Martha shared how her boss at work regularly ignored her ideas but embraced the same exact content when offered by a different colleague.

My rather risky workshop presentation activity may seem strange to the audience; after all, most speakers want the audience to be happy during a presentation, not provoke them into thinking uncomfortable thoughts! Like many others, Sarah, Jeremy, and Martha openly shared their experiences to help illustrate a critical idea: Each of these shared experiences clearly demonstrates the role of emotions in learning. When placed in situations like those described above, most of us become caught up in negative or stressful feelings and our attention is shifted away from the higher cognitive processes required for learning or working. It is important here to recognize that individuals might perceive the events described above differently. Some may feel threatened while others may ignore or even be motivated by a negative interaction. Tracy Tokuhama-Espinosa (2024) points out that emotions are our biological response to an event, but how we feel about the event is our psychological reaction. This reaction may or may not be under our control depending on factors such as our prior experiences and dispositions. That said, it is crucial that learners and leaders understand the effects of emotions on learning and performance and strive to create a positive environment that encourages a sense of safety, respect, and belonging.

Understanding and preventing how attention is shifted under stress is crucial, especially in a school environment, if any learning is to occur.

We begin our journey through the Brain-Targeted Teaching® (BTT) Model by studying the effects of emotions on learning, including how stress impedes learning and also how positive feelings enhance the learning experience. The effects of emotions on learning have been a topic of rigorous study in the learning sciences. For example, the National Academy of Sciences, Engineering, and Medicine (2018) released the second volume of the publication *How People Learn*. In summary, the report stressed that the learning environment sets the stage for effective learning and must include a focus on the learner's emotions, interests, motivation, and culture. Setting the emotional climate for learning may be the most important task a practitioner or leader embarks on each day. This is true for traditional schooling, informal learning, the work site, and technology rich learning environments (Graesser, 2020).

In Brain-Target One of the BTT Model, practitioners consider the emotional climate through two lenses. First, they design the general climate of the classroom or workspace to promote a joyful, productive, and safe learning or work environment. Second, they purposefully plan activities that will provide an emotional connection to the content, making the subject matter or work task more personal, relevant, and meaningful. In this chapter, we explore findings from the learning sciences that shed light on the relationship between emotions and learning as well as what those findings advocate in terms of establishing an emotional climate for learning and leading. We will review how the brain processes emotion, the troubling effects of negative emotions and stress, how positive emotions support productive engagement, and more effective learning and work outcomes. Finally, this chapter suggests strategies that support the work of practitioners and leaders in establishing positive environments for every member of the school or work community.

Setting the emotional climate for learning may be the most important task practitioners or leaders embark on each day.

Neural Systems Underlying Emotion

In order to consider how practitioners and leaders might address the emotional climate in the classroom or workplace, we should have some understanding of how the brain processes emotions—whether they are negative or positive—and how that functioning influences feelings that affect the capacity to attend to, perceive, and remember information. Although researchers now recognize that multiple areas of the brain are engaged when we process emotion, studies of the brain's emotional response must begin with the limbic system (Gazzaniga et al., 2009). The amygdala, located in the brain's medial temporal lobes, is part of the limbic system and is an important structure for processing emotion (see Li et al., 2020). The amygdala is engaged not only in implicit emotional reaction, such as an unexpected fearful event, but also in explicit emotional learning, such as learning about a danger and remembering the information.

In addition to the amygdala, explicit emotional learning engages the hippocampus, a key structure involved in memory. We may intuitively know that an emotionally charged event stays in our memory. This relationship between emotion and memory is supported by research demonstrating that the engagement of the amygdala does indeed strengthen memories (Lupien et al., 2009). In other words, the involvement of the amygdala in declarative memories explains why we remember emotionally charged events better than ordinary day-to-day occurrences.

How We Perceive Stress, Fear, and Threat

One critical aspect of emotional processing, and therefore of emotional learning, is how our brains respond to stress, fear, and threat. In particular, our brain processes threat so that we can both think about and respond to it. To take a step back, as we receive information from our senses, the sensory signal projects to the thalamus, which then sends information to various brain systems for processing including the cortex, associated with higher order thinking. At the same time, the thalamus sends the signal to the amygdala to assess if the sensory input involves danger or threat. The signal, however, travels from the thalamus to the amygdala through a *quicker* pathway than the signal that is sent to the cortex. Joseph LeDoux (1996) calls this the *low road*, a quick and dirty route that allows the brain to prepare for an immediate response to potential threat (p. 163). In contrast, the signal projected to the cortex, the *high road*, is slower but more thorough in its analysis. This high road signal, once processed by the cortex, is then routed to the amygdala for a fuller emotional response.

This dual system for sensory perception of threat has its purposes. The quick route to the amygdala, the low road, allows us to act in a potentially dangerous situation before we fully know the extent of the threat or even if a danger actually exists. In evolutionary terms, the quick but incomplete response system is necessary for survival, as it allows an organism to protect itself from environmental dangers. Yet although fast and efficient, this system is not designed to be precise in its assessment. Consistent with this imprecision, LeDoux (1996) explains that when we react to fear, our brain systems are in fact designed to respond to sensory information that has not been fully analyzed in the cortex. In this way, the emotional processing system, mostly in the amygdala, "has a greater influence on the cortex than the cortex has on the amygdala, allowing emotional arousal to dominate and control thinking" (p. 303).

When we react to fear, our brain systems are in fact designed to respond to sensory information that has not been fully analyzed in the cortex.

Our emotions and thinking are not the only functions affected when we perceive threat and fear. Once the amygdala senses threat, a cascade of *physical* responses follows. The information processed by the amygdala triggers structures in the limbic system, specifically the hypothalamus, which activates hormones and neurotransmitters to prepare the body for the fight-or-flight response and promotes bodily changes, including elevating blood pressure, increasing heart rate, and contracting muscles.

This biological system—emotional processing of threat that in turn generates a physical response—evolved as a result of stressful events that lasted for a short time. We either were able to run from the saber tooth tiger or we were its lunch. In our lives today, however, stress is often an ongoing event and the effects of constant stress hormones may not be beneficial. Chronic stress is known to impair body systems such as the cardiovascular, digestive, and immune systems. In addition, research has shown that constant stress may cause damage in the hippocampus and frontal cortex, affecting memory and information processing (Immordino-Yang et al., 2018). In the following section, we consider in more detail how these neural and physiological consequences of stress impact cognitive function and learning.

Chronic stress is known to impair body systems such as the cardiovascular, digestive, and immune systems.

Effects of Stress on Learning

An area of great concern to the research communities across multiple disciplines is the effects of stress on the developing child. In particular, a growing body of research is examining how Adverse Childhood Experiences (ACEs) affect health, cognition, and learning. ACEs refer to traumatic events that children and adolescents experience that can have troubling biological and behavioral consequences. These harmful events include abuse (physical, emotional, sexual), neglect (physical and emotional), and household disfunction (substance abuse, mental illness, domestic violence, parental separation or divorce, and incarcerated family member). Research has shown that four or more ACE events significantly increase susceptibility to poor health; diminished cognitive, attentional, emotional, and social skills; poor academic performance; increased school absences; and higher rates of behavior problems (Bethell et al., 2014). Children living in under-resourced communities are especially vulnerable to experiencing a number of these stressors (Darling-Hammond et al., 2020; Farah et al., 2008). The findings underscore the importance of early identification and targeted interventions to foster resilience. Interventions such as school-based health and wellness centers have shown promise in helping children improve academic and social outcomes (Blodgett & Lanigan, 2018). Research has shown how protective factors can buffer the effect of stressful experiences. Interventions include establishing supportive relationships, maintaining positive school environments, and accessing a network of community resources—all important factors to foster resilience and improve educational outcomes (Darling-Hammond et al., 2020; Jimenez et al., 2016; Porche et al., 2011; Shonkoff et al., 2012).

Parental nurturance seems to have an important role not only in the development of cognitive function but also in maturation of the physical brain.

These findings are similar to studies conducted within the general population. Such lab-based studies not only support the effect of stress on learning but also demonstrate the extent to which performance on a simple task is affected when a study participant is under stress. For example, Schwabe and Wolf (2010) found that, when placed in a stressful situation while learning new words, participants' performance declined by at least 30%. Although mild stress in specific contexts may enhance performance and recall, prolonged stress appears to reduce the ability to acquire, retain, and recall information (Tan et al., 2021).

Although mild stress in specific contexts may enhance performance and recall, prolonged stress appears to reduce the ability to acquire, retain, and recall information.

Stress in School and Work Environments

Given that stress has been shown to affect one's ability to learn and work effectively, it is imperative that we understand the stress levels of students in schools and individuals in the workplace. Ideally, the school or workplace is a safe, joyful, and inviting experience and not a stress-inducing environment.

In exploring this topic, it is important to first consider the effects of the pandemic on school and work environments. Multiple studies and reports have documented the learning loss due to school closures and the shift to remote learning (Brookings Institution, 2022) and highlight the emotional stress on children and families (Garbe et al., 2020). The World Economic Forum (2023) reports that school closures worldwide affected 1.5 billion students and notes that children in marginalized, under-resourced communities suffered the most debilitating effects, exacerbating existing inequalities. Studies also focus on the challenges that teachers experienced as they shifted quickly to remote learning (Goodrich et al., 2022). Many teachers report the struggles they faced when students returned to on-site learning with chronic absenteeism and students' social-emotional issues.

The work environment was also significantly changed by the pandemic, with a quick transition to remote work that affected productivity and worker satisfaction. Many organizations recognized the need to promote employee well-being through flexible work arrangements, strong communication systems, and mental health resources (Brynjolfsson et al., 2020; Carnevale & Hatak, 2020; Kniffin et al., 2021).

Unfortunately, pre-pandemic, the rates of dropouts and suspensions across school districts as well as stories of bullying filled news reports and school district statistics. Studies on school environments have long shed light on the emotional world of students in school. Pekrun et al., (2002), for example, conducted a series of studies to determine the emotions that students say they experience during the school day. Although a broad range of emotions were cited, including positive emotions associated with learning, the most frequent emotion identified was anxiety, accounting for up to 25% of all emotions reported. In addition, the researchers tested the physiological reaction to stress-related episodes by testing levels of cortisol, a hormone associated with stress. Not surprisingly, they found that students with high anxiety had high cortisol levels. In contrast, students who were able to employ stress-reducing coping strategies did not produce high cortisol levels, suggesting the importance of including purposeful activities to reduce stress in the learning environment. Behavioral problems associated with anxiety have also been linked to cortisol levels (Ruttle et al., 2011). The research demonstrates that when anxiety-driven behavioral problems begin, individuals have increased stress and cortisol levels that become abnormally elevated. If the behavioral problems and thus the stress continue over an extended period of time, stress and cortisol levels become abnormally low, as the body is trying to protect itself from negative effects associated with high levels of cortisol. Unfortunately, this reaction to continual stress may cause the individuals not to worry or care about their performance in school, which in turn leads to poor academic performance. This work suggests that interventions should be put in place as soon as behavioral problems are observed.

Recent behavioral studies have continued to show the effects of negative emotions on learning. In a systematic review of literature on the effects of emotions on learning, Tan et al. (2021) found that negative emotions lead to reduced learning efficiency including diminished attending skills and memory. Negative emotions such as fear, anger, embarrassment, sadness, grief, or shame have been associated with poor memory performance and accuracy, diminished executive function skills, and poor social interactions (e.g., Vogel & Schwabe, 2016; Zareyan et al., 2021).

Studies on school environments shed light on the emotional world of students in school. As research continues to demonstrate behavioral and biological effects of stress on learning, it would seem that high priority must be given to producing a school and work climate that promotes a positive learning environment. As a first step, practitioners and leaders might do well to take an *emotional inventory* to determine what might be stressful triggers for those in learning and work environments. Such an inventory should also involve assessing the perceptions about causes of stress as these perceptions may affect actual stress levels. Students can also self-assess through inventories that can help them understand their levels of stress (Gunnar, 2021). Tan et al. (2021) recommend the observation of facial expressions, which they believe can be an easy but powerful nonverbal communication method to capture emotional states. They believe that the development of artificial intelligence technology may provide another approach to predict emotional states.

In a study involving children and adults, even young children appeared to be aware of the kinds of stressful situations that would impede academic performance. The participants were presented with stories in which the main character experienced either a positive or negative event, and then the character had to perform a difficult cognitive task. The participants were asked to predict the character's performance on the cognitive task. Even young children understood the detrimental effects that negative events such as an argument with a peer, a noisy environment, or even messy hair might have on performance (Amsterlaw et al., 2009).

It is clearly impossible to avoid negative stressful events in our lives and the lives of those we nurture. However, by focusing on maintaining a positive environment, practitioners can create protective learning and work spaces in which all members thrive.

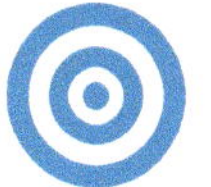

As research continues to demonstrate behavioral and biological effects of stress on learning, it would seem that high priority must be given to producing a school climate that promotes a positive learning environment.

The Impact of Positive Emotions

We have seen how emotion, especially the negative effects of stress, impacts attention, learning, and memory. As there are detrimental effects of negative emotion on learning, there are also beneficial effects of positive emotion on learning (Pekrun & Garcia, 2014). Research shows that positive emotions broaden attention whereas negative emotions have the opposite effect, diminishing attending behaviors. Positive emotions have beneficial effects on multiple aspects of learning including promoting intrinsic and sustained motivation, cognitive flexibility, confidence, self-efficacy, and resilience (Gilchrist et al., 2022; Tan et al., 2021). Alexander et al. (2021) present a thorough review of the neurophysiological correlates of positive emotions that modify brain function and support general well-being. Consistent with the work of The Human Affectome Project (http://neuroqualia.org/background.php), the authors consider environmental factors and how healthy social relationships promote positive emotions in children, adolescents, and adults. Similarly, Li et al. (2020) point out how neuroscience research illuminates the connections of emotions and the important cognitive processes of memory, attention, and motivation. They highlight research showing that positive emotions such as happiness, pride, and hope are triggers for motivation, which is closely tied to self-regulation and academic success. They also point out that emotions work within a social context and spread within a social group through mirroring networks (observing actions of others) and mentalizing networks (making inferences about what is observed). This provides strong evidence for the critical need to foster positive emotions within classrooms, schools, and the workplace. Below, we see how Dr. Ranjini JohnBull fosters a positive emotional climate by fostering a sense of community within online instruction.

From the Expert Practitioner

Culturally Relevant BTT Introductions: Demonstrating Identity and Safety in Online Learning

Based on emotional climate principles from Brain-Target One, I design my learning environment in online platforms to engage students' attention and facilitate their social and emotional connections in the online learning spaces (i.e., using Canvas, Flip, VoiceThread, Padlet, etc.). To address the tenets of Brain-Target One, I design the environment as an inclusive and warm online classroom. To promote identity safety, I model the type of introduction that I hope will make students feel safe with a recorded video, and then, I provide "Meet and Greet" forums for students to follow my lead. This leverages both Brain-Target One and the Culturally Relevant Pedagogy principle of building upon students' strengths and building their own

cultural competence about their personal intersectional identities. Before the course opens, I post my short video in an announcement, and I talk about both my personal and professional identities.

During the video, I share photos of my family to help them see I am a real person who understands the complexity of navigating personal and professional responsibilities. By sharing my intersectional multicultural identity, my students feel free to share their identities. They feel assured that I will support them and create a safe space for them in our online classroom. Then, students engage in our "Meet and Greet" video discussion forum to introduce themselves via recorded videos, share about their identities and interests, and begin making connections with their peers.

It is common for students to share how they feel welcomed and included through these video introductions. What I've learned is that when I share my background, they feel safe to share about their identities and be themselves in our online classroom. They are more willing to share their mistakes, their challenges, and their need for support or instructional adaptations. Through learning about their identities, I try to build upon their knowledge and find connections within the course and assignments to affirm their strengths and identities. While I cannot physically change my students' learning environment, what I can do is provide them with the most engaging and inclusive online experience so that they feel less stressed and more engaged every time they open their computers to interact in our learning environment. These basic strategies set the tone for my online courses, and they have been the beginnings of long-lasting connections between me and my students that allow me to support them in their academic journeys. These practices that I've developed from Brain-Target One and culturally relevant pedagogy have provided me with the added benefits of aligning my practice with my values, and it has resulted in a deep sense of fulfilment in my career.

Ranjini Mahinda JohnBull, PhD
Associate Professor

As there are detrimental effects of negative emotion on learning, there are also beneficial effects of positive emotion on learning.

In setting up an emotional climate for learning, another important factor to consider is motivation to learn, which can vary from one student to the next. In fact, recent research by Hart and Albarracín (2009) has demonstrated that individuals who are typically motivated by achievement goals perform better when a task is presented as achievement-oriented (e.g., a challenging puzzle) compared with when that task is presented as fun-oriented (e.g., a fun game). The reverse pattern—better performance when a task is presented as fun-oriented—is observed for individuals who are not typically motivated by achievement goals. These results highlight the importance of goal-state in teaching and learning: Both student groups can perform well with the appropriate kind of motivation. For underachieving children, learning activities in which the students feel they are having fun, such as in a learning game or arts activity, may be important for motivation for learning and to foster emotional connections to the content.

For underachieving children, learning activities in which the students feel they are having fun, such as in a learning game or arts activity, may be important for motivation for learning and to foster emotional connections to the content.

Emotions and the Adolescent

Ask any parent or teacher of an adolescent how behavior changes in those important years, and you are sure to get a laundry list of both the difficulty and delight that come with this important time of life. Scientists are now demonstrating what teachers and caregivers have long known: Adolescence is a time of rapid physical and emotional changes paired with social changes; together, these factors lead to significant variations in behavior and biology. Immordino-Yang et al. (2018) point out that "adolescence is the most dramatic period of brain development after infancy" (p. 7) leading to rapid growth in cognition and social-emotional development. Puberty-related hormones trigger the reward structures in the brain and affect sensitivity to social cues, which may result in risk-taking and emotional swings. Most notably, the peer group typically replaces the adult as the source of approval, and the tendency for risk-taking and thrill-seeking behaviors increases from the onset of puberty into early adulthood (Giedd, 2009; Immordino-Yang et al., 2018; Steinberg, 2008).

In addition to physical, social, and emotional changes, sleep patterns change during adolescence. In fact, at the onset of adolescence, there are important changes to the neural systems of sleep and circadian rhythms

(Dahl, 2004; Immordino-Yang et al., 2018). Moreover, as technology facilitates increased social opportunities in the evenings coupled with physiological changes leading to later onset of sleepiness, adolescents are at risk of sleep deprivation. Understanding and preventing such sleep deprivation is critical as growing evidence demonstrates that lack of sleep can create emotional as well as cognitive and physical health problems (Tan et al., 2021).

As technology facilitates increased social opportunities in the evenings coupled with physiological changes leading to later onset of sleepiness, adolescents are at risk of sleep deprivation.

Though adolescence brings a number of potentially negative effects on emotions (and therefore on learning), at the same time, educators who enjoy working with adolescents cannot help but notice the many benefits of the high-intensity feelings that are part of this developmental period. In addition, the development of the frontal lobes influences executive function skills and higher order thinking, leading to abstract and creative thinking. The challenge and reward for practitioners and caregivers is to attend to the process of sculpting that passion through exciting learning activities; self-expression in the arts; and collaboration on sports fields, in special interest clubs, and with human service projects.

Emotions in the Work Environment

As demonstrated by the vignettes at the start of this chapter, the effects of a negative or positive emotional climate do not stop at the end of formal schooling but also impact how adults learn and work in any organizational structure. Ashkanasy and Dirrusm (2017) point out that the study of emotions in the workplace is limited; however, organizational scholars are beginning to make headway in shedding light on the importance of the emotional environment on workplace satisfaction and production. They point out that performance and job satisfaction improve when leaders attend to employees' emotional resilience and self-efficacy. Strategies include identifying and rectifying negative sources in the workplace, bringing in outside experts, using personal example models, creating flexible work schedules, redesigning the task or work environment, avoiding work overload, reducing ambiguity, providing opportunities for social interaction, assigning work that is viewed as rewarding, and creating safe and aesthetically pleasing physical work environments. Similarly, Diener et al. (2020) highlight the importance of positive emotions within individuals that ultimately support the organization as a whole. Their review includes the effects of positive emotion on personal beliefs, creativity, work engagement, health, coping strategies, teamwork, collaboration, relationship, leadership, and performance outcomes.

The findings of research from organizational scholars are similar to research in educational settings. Multiple studies underscore how educators' emotions are associated with the performance of their students (Lei et al., 2018; McLean et al., 2024). For example, Cheng et al. (2022) explored how teachers' emotional states affect students' perceptions of their competence as educators. Students reported higher level of enjoyment with learning tasks when they perceived the teachers' emotions as positive. Within any work environment, the importance of self-care, work-life balance, relationships, and a feeling of belonging elevates personal and societal health and wellness.

I now invite you to read about the importance of a positive emotional climate in the workspace written by Pamela Terry, who sees the impact of emotions in her field within the nuclear power industry.

From the Expert Practitioner

Emotions in the Workplace

In the nuclear industry, as is true in many business and industry settings, an unspoken rule exists that workers participating in training leave their emotions at home and that emotions have no place at work. These ideas about employee emotions date back to the industrial era. In the modern knowledge worker era, however, we now know that worker emotions influence not only their cognitive processes but also their job satisfaction, workplace engagement, and ultimately learning outcomes and organizational performance. Therefore, it is important to attend to employee emotions both in the workplace and in training environments.

In training environments, instructors must establish social trust with their learners. Social trust, or the trust that learners have in their instructor, is critical to learner attention and acquisition of new knowledge and skills and includes two factors. First, learners must trust that they can be vulnerable and incorrect in the learning setting without threat of humiliation. Learning requires being emotionally open to not knowing and to unlearning and relearning, which can be perceived as a threat or risk in unsafe environments. Therefore, instructors need to acknowledge the vulnerability of adult learners and safeguard their emotions during learning.

Secondly, social trust involves the learners' trust in their instructor's technical competence with the subject matter. As we mature from childhood, adults develop the capacity to doubt the validity of other's representation of facts. In the learning environment, adult learners' brains compare the instructor's knowledge with their own background knowledge, experience, and expertise. If learners determine that the instructor is not credible, the learners' ability and desire to attend to the information presented is negatively impacted. In addition, negative emotions that may come about because of lack of social trust (or many other factors for that matter) can increase learners' cognitive load, or their perception of learning difficulty, while positive emotions facilitate more efficient cognitive processing.

As a result, the nuclear industry emphasizes the importance of not only the technical competence of its instructors but also acknowledges that learner emotions are not only relevant but have a tremendous impact on student learning outcomes and ultimately organizational performance. It is to an organization's benefit to support positive emotions and mitigate negative emotions in the classroom and in the workplace.

Pamela Terry, EdD
Manager, Nuclear Industry Training

Implementing Brain-Target One: Establishing the Emotional Climate for Learning

Whether working with young children, adolescents, or adults, practitioners must be aware of the powerful role in establishing and maintaining a positive and productive environment in the schools and organizational settings. As our examples at the beginning of this chapter demonstrate, even the best of educators or leaders may inadvertently engage in a practice that induces stress and inhibits learning and working. If practitioners and leaders are armed with a basic understanding of the effects of stress on learning (as presented in this chapter), they will be better able to mitigate stress-inducing practices and promote positive environments.

Educators must be aware of their powerful role in establishing and maintaining a positive and productive environment in the school and classroom.

Research from biological and behavioral studies clearly speaks to the importance of purposeful activities to establish positive emotional climates. As we design learning units or strategic plans in the Brain-Targeted Teaching® Model, Brain-Target One contains the following goals: (a) to establish and revisit practices that promote a positive environment and (b) to design activities that engage students or workers emotionally in the content or skills of the lesson or the work task. Below I address each of these goals in turn and present areas to consider in creating the kind of environment that will support learning and will be long remembered as a time and place of joyful learning and working. Although some of the strategies described below focus on teaching and learning in the classroom, each strategy can be adapted in any formal or informal education setting and in any organizational environment.

Strategies for Promoting a Positive Learning Environment

Positive Language: Praise and Veiled Commands

Praising for positive behaviors and work often comes naturally to practitioners and leaders. But is all praise equal in its effect on learning and is it always productive? How we address students' work produces what has become largely known as growth mindsets, the belief that the capacity for learning is not fixed but can be developed (Dweck & Yeager, 2019). Research tells us that behavior-specific praise is more effective in reinforcing and shaping behaviors and mindsets than generalized praise. For example, it is more effective to call attention to a specific behavior such as, "You are each assuming full responsibilities in your cooperative learning group" rather than simply saying "Good job today, class."

Behavior-specific praise is more effective in reinforcing and shaping behaviors than generalized praise.

Positive language through praise of effort (e.g., "you must have worked hard on this task") has also been shown to be more productive than praise of ability (e.g., "you must be smart on this task"). To assess the effects of these two approaches to praise, Carol Dweck conducted multiple studies in a variety of settings with students from age four through adolescence. Results indicated that students who were praised for ability on a task were less successful on subsequent tasks than those praised for their effort on the task. For example, students who were told they were successful on math problems because they were smart were less confident and motivated to complete harder problems than those who were told that their success was due to hard work. Thus, praising based on intelligence appears to reduce confidence when an individual encounters a difficult task whereas praising effort enhances perseverance, engagement, and growth mindsets (Dweck & Yeager, 2019).

Students who were praised for ability on a task were less successful on subsequent tasks than those praised for their effort on the task.

Practitioners and leaders should avoid using "veiled commands" (Delpit, 1988, p. 289) that disguise the intent of the communication. For example, the teacher may intend for the question "*Is that where your scissors belong?*" to be a command to put the scissors away in a box. The child may interpret the question literally as a question and not respond to the indirect command. Delpit points out that cultural background may influence whether children understand the intended meaning of an indirect or veiled command. We should work toward developing a classroom and work culture in which positive language is the expectation at all times and consider how cultural differences may influence how one understands and perceives a situation.

Predictability: Classroom Routines, Rituals, Celebrations, and Motivation

Establishing routines communicates what is expected in academic and work contexts. For example, using quick review drills or journal writing is an activity that many teachers use daily to get the lesson started while they are engaged in the *housekeeping activities* of recording attendance and distributing materials. Many teachers effectively use workstations to provide students with information and materials they need on a regular basis such as a notebook of homework assignments, makeup work for absentees, work for extra credit, forms needed for fieldtrips, or other administrative tasks.

Rituals that are quick and fun, such as chants, hand signals, clapping patterns, songs, movements, or relaxation exercises, help to motivate and engage students and build a sense of group identity. Rituals can also serve as powerful social messages that become the standard for peer social interactions and work expectations. In work environments, daily rituals might include activities such as a morning yoga session, a group review of the day's activities, or brainstorming events that promote social and work relationships.

Rituals that are quick and fun, such as chants, hand signals, clapping patterns, songs, movements, or relaxation exercises, help to motivate and engage students and build a sense of group identity.

Celebrations for success; special cultural events; or reaching academic, work, or social goals often go a long way in promoting a sense of belonging and building group cohesiveness. Below, our expert practitioners, Aisha Austin and David Toia, share how embedding games into instruction creates a fun experience for students and fosters a sense of group cohesiveness.

From the Expert Practitioners

Game On: Fine Tuning the Emotional Climate Using Games

Imagine it is a Friday morning, and as the teacher, you are responsible for setting the stage for a positive emotional climate in your classroom for the day. Where to begin? You suddenly remember the lessons of Brain-Target One that "setting the emotional climate for learning may be the most important task a teacher embarks on each day" (Hardiman, 2012.) You say, "Hey, let's play a game," and suddenly the room is overflowing with excitement. You catch murmurs of students discussing their preferences for which game to choose and the reasons for their choices. Once the game is introduced, the atmosphere shifts; students are eager to form teams and focus becomes entirely on the game as strategies are formed by students. All other distractions fade away, and suddenly, all your students are fully immersed in the game play experience. This experience mirrors what psychologist Johan Huizinga's termed "the magic circle" of gameplay—you have successfully created a unique space that allows students to

connect in a creative way. In this positive, energized environment, your students feel safe, ready to learn, and valued setting a constructive and collaborative tone for the remainder of the school day. Here is a reflection from an educational specialist sharing how games and gamification can be used as an impactful tool in learning.

Aisha Austin
Education Consultant, Higher Education Instructor

Game Still On

Games create experiences that are saturated with emotions. If you don't believe me, try playing Monopoly with a 7-year-old. When I teach educational game design, I emphasize to my students how the experiences provided by games are meticulously curated and constructed to evoke specific moment-to-moment affective outcomes. Want to increase the learner's engagement? Try adding a timer into a learning activity and challenge them to see how fast they can go. Want to get students excited about doing research? Give them an "unknown information" mystery to solve and have them pretend they are historical detectives. With a bit of planning, these simple tools can interject fun into nearly any learning experience.

David Toia
Manager of Immersive Learning Media

Emotional Events: Engagement Versus Disengagement

While working toward promoting a positive environment within the classroom or workspace, most practitioners and leaders experience any number of factors that are beyond their control, including home life, peer interactions, and societal and community stressors. Coping and managing these inevitable factors are necessary for creating and maintaining a positive environment.

One decision that practitioners are often faced with is how to deal with an emotionally charged event that students or workers experienced before entering the classroom or workplace. A common scenario involves an individual who is distraught because of a situation at home, an altercation with a peer or colleague, or a multitude of other causes. A practitioner can decide to allow the individual to process the emotion through dialogue, redirect the individual through engagement in a task, or simply ignore the person's emotional state. Research may provide some answers for helping the individual to regulate emotions. In a study that assessed students' performance in an academic task following a negative emotional event, three strategies were applied. After viewing segments of a sad film, students were tested in one of the following three ways: (a) students were asked questions that engaged them in processing the feeling of sadness, (b) students were told not to feel sadness from the emotional scene and were redirected to analyzing neutral information, or (c) students were given neutral information to analyze without any mention of the emotional scene. Results showed that children who were instructed to disengage performed better on educational tasks than those who were instructed to process their feelings or those who received no acknowledgment of the emotional event (Rice et al., 2007).

Children who were instructed to disengage performed better on educational tasks than those who were instructed to process their feelings or those who received no acknowledgment of the emotional event.

These findings may help to inform those quick and important decisions that practitioners and leaders are frequently faced with when dealing with an individual's emotional stress. Although certainly some situations will require immediate interventions from the support personnel, it appears that acknowledging the emotion and redirecting the individual may be the most effective approach.

Another approach to help with emotional regulation is affect labeling, referring to the process of recognizing emotions and labeling them through words or images. Torre and Lieberman (2018) review multiple studies that show how labeling a negative emotion is a successful strategy for children and adults to mitigate the effects of negative experiences. The process of naming an emotion has been shown to significantly reduce distress promoting self-reflection, reducing biological activation in the autonomic response system (e.g., heart rate and skin temperature), and decreasing activity in the amygdala (Elsayed et al., 2021). Using this strategy is a simple but effective way to regulate emotions through writing a word or paragraph, drawing an image, or using a feelings chart, in which an individual chooses a face that depicts their feelings.

Affect labeling has also shown positive results for reducing post-traumatic stress symptoms in veterans with combat-related symptoms.

Burklund et al. (2024) report significant improvement in depression and amygdala reactivity after veterans received an affect labeling intervention.

Testing the Emotional Temperature

These findings address how to deal with an emotionally charged event that an individual has encountered. In a classroom, for example, in order to manage such emotions, teachers must first discern whether or not each child has experienced such an event. In a busy classroom environment, teachers, and especially those who teach multiple groups of students for short periods each day, may find it challenging to check the *emotional temperature* of each child. Creative teachers, however, find a way to assess how students' emotions might influence their engagement in classroom activities. One such teacher, Marian, who taught in school in an under-resourced community solved this problem with a simple strategy. Each day her first graders would come into the classroom with various issues that were affecting their performance and, as a result, impeding her ability to teach the class and maintain order. To address this difficulty, she designed a simple *emotional temperature form* with a row of emotions and corresponding adjectives (e.g., good, bad, sad, happy). Students were asked to circle how they felt that day and to write a word or sentence or draw a picture that expressed their emotion. This activity became a daily routine for the children as they entered the room. They would take the form, complete it, and then return it to a basket before beginning their work. The teacher reported two significant results of this activity. First, it served to acknowledge the emotions students were feeling, consistent with research findings described above, which then allowed them to disengage and redirect to an academic task. Second, in reviewing their responses, the teacher had better insights into the world of each child and therefore could make better decisions about the need for any follow-up activity or intervention services.

Connectedness in School With a Caring Adult

Taking the emotional temperature of a group of students or in an office environment allows a teacher or leader to know which individuals may need more support within the school, workplace, and community. Research demonstrates the importance of a connection to a caring adult to promote a sense of belonging and effective learning and working. In an extensive analysis of literature from the learning sciences, Darling-Hammond et al. (2020) stress the importance for children to have secure emotional relationships with caring adults to assist them with emotional regulation and development. Healthy relationships are key drivers for a host of positive outcomes, including academic performance, school attendance, reduction of risk-taking behaviors, school engagement, and pro-social skills (Osher et al., 2021). Hajovsky et al. (2020) found that teacher self-efficacy beliefs affect teacher-student interactions. Teachers who demonstrate high self-efficacy beliefs demonstrate more effective and supportive relationships with students, ultimately affecting students' performance and well-being.

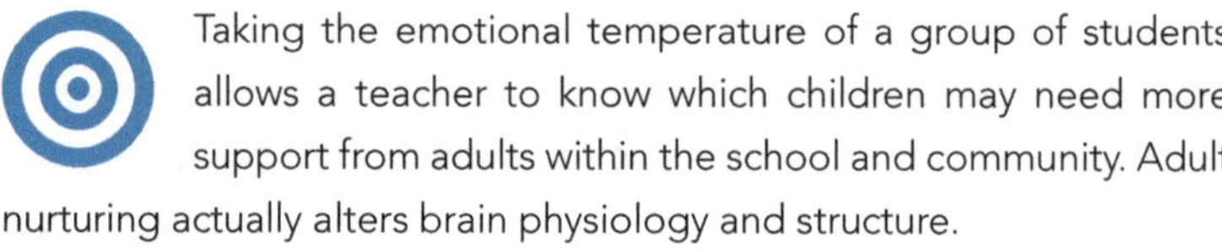

Fostering a nurturing environment where all students feel connected to a caring adult must be a priority in every classroom in every school and every workplace. Practitioners and leaders can promote the connectedness by

- Providing consistent expectations and fair, nonaggressive strategies to manage processes;
- Designing instructional activities that are rigorous, engaging, differentiated, and meaningful;
- Providing activities that are culturally relevant and support neurodiverse individuals;
- Involving all students and workers in the care of the classroom and workspace;
- Creating opportunities for peer-tutoring, cooperative group work, and colleague interaction;
- Communicating positive messages to all constituents through personal notes, newsletters, websites, media outlets, and other social communication structures;
- Creating individualized goals for learning and work products;
- Ensuring that each individual has an opportunity to participate and contribute to the learning or work of the school or organization;

- Role-playing ways to resolve conflicts, especially through content-based activities such as literature or social studies lessons;
- Establishing opportunities for cross-age interactions such as content-based tutoring, mentoring, theater, and other arts programs; and
- Modeling warmth and kindness in the classroom and workplace.

Fostering a nurturing environment where all students feel connected to a caring adult must be a priority in every classroom in every school and workplace.

Control and Choice

Offering choices relating to the content and process of learning and working has been shown to provide a sense of agency or control over outcomes and is associated with increased levels of motivation and achievement (e.g., Phung et al., 2021; Schneider et al., 2018). Whether in a school or workplace, personal agency is heightened when individuals have some control over assignments or tasks.

Within a classroom environment, given appropriate guidance and structure, teachers can motivate performance by allowing choices in content, methods, and assessment. Below are some examples in each area:

Choices in Content:

- Students have access to activity centers that reinforce skills through multiple content choices.
- Students are given a choice from a selection of reading material or genres of literature that address curriculum objectives.
- In subjects where content is flexible, groups of students choose a topic, research elements, and present findings to the class.

Teachers can motivate performance by allowing choices in content, methods, and assessment.

Choices in Methods:

- Given a specific assignment (e.g., responding to a story or reading a historical document), students choose one of several ways to demonstrate understanding such as a summary where they highlight key points of the assignment, an analysis where they compare and contrast details with other similar genres, or an application where they create a plan of action based on the content.
- Given one response strategy (e.g., summary), students pair it with an additional response mode, such as a project using an art form such as music, visual arts, role-playing, poetry, or rap.

Choices in Assessment:

- Demonstrating understanding of learning objectives through traditional methods may be required in many school districts through standardized assessments and regular benchmark curriculum-based assessments. However, teachers can supplement these assessments by allowing students to choose an art form or technology to demonstrate understanding of content, skills, or concepts.
- Assessment activities that require students to move beyond the mere acquisition of knowledge and apply content in authentic ways will allow for deeper thinking and provide choices for students to identify a problem, analyze strategies, and design action plans.

Social and Emotional Learning

The proliferation of formal social and emotional learning programs in schools demonstrates the growing acceptance that schools can no longer focus solely on students' academic performance without also addressing their emotional and social needs. As highlighted in this chapter, neuro- and cognitive sciences have shown us that cognition and emotions are not separate systems but are intricately connected in terms of brain structure and function.

Schools can no longer focus solely on students' academic performance without also addressing their emotional and social needs.

Research suggests that a child's ability to recognize and interpret emotional cues has long-term effects on social behavior and academic competence. In recent years, social and emotional learning programs (SEL) have been designed to help children recognize and manage emotions within the context of the learning and social environment. Research findings show that SEL programs improve students' academic performance and general school performance (Mahoney et al., 2021). In a meta-analysis involving more than two hundred studies of social-emotional learning programs in schools, Payton and colleagues (2008) found that students scored more than ten points higher in academic achievement and also had better school attendance, grades, and social interactions within the classroom. SEL programs include fostering awareness of emotions, regulation of emotions through stress management, developing understanding and empathy toward others, building relationships, and responsible decision-making.

Humor

We all enjoy a good laugh. But what does that have to do with learning? Research has shown that appropriate use of humor is associated with higher student engagement, enjoyment in learning, and a sense of school belonging (Erdoğdu & Çakıroğlu, 2021; St-Arman et al., 2024). Research shows that teachers also benefit from the use of humor. Teachers report that humor in the classroom helps to relieve stress, makes the learning process more enjoyable, and supports positive relationship with colleagues and students (Erduran Tekin, 2024). A word of caution—teachers must be mindful, however, to avoid sarcasm or teasing that may seem good-natured but can be hurtful and elicit peer teasing or bullying.

Reflection and Mindfulness Training

Similar to social and emotional learning programs, the growing practice of mindfulness training to help students manage stress and improve attention is gaining popularity in schools and classrooms. Mindfulness interventions provide explicit instruction in secular meditative-type relaxation exercises and quiet sitting while observing one's thoughts and feelings. Research findings with school-aged children point to improvement in subjects' attention regulation as well as reduction of anxiety and depression after receiving mindfulness training (see Dunning et al., 2019). In a pilot randomized controlled trial of school-based mindfulness and yoga training for urban youth, Mendelson and colleagues (2010) suggest that such training reduces negative physiological and cognitive reactions to stress and improves self-regulation.

Specifically, they found that children who received the mindfulness training reported significant reductions in rumination (negative, brooding, or obsessive thoughts), intrusive thoughts that divert attention, and negative emotional arousal.

In recent years, mindfulness exercises have become more popularized in schools and workplace settings. The proliferation of commercialized mindfulness tools such as smartphone apps allow individuals to practice on their own within constraints of cost, time, and space. To assess the effectiveness of this approach, Sparacio et al. (2024) designed a randomized control trial with 2,239 participants over thirty-seven sites. They compared four mindfulness exercises with the control condition of listening to a story. Participants completed fifteen-minute mindfulness sessions recorded by a certified instructor. They found that even short mindfulness sessions reduced stress compared to the control group.

Given the growing evidence of the efficacy of mindfulness training, teachers and leaders might consider adding moments during the day to allow for calm attention, awareness, and quiet reflection such as paying attention to breathing or thinking good thoughts about positive experiences or loved ones and friends. This approach to social development and emotional regulation appears to be consistent with recommendations to focus on positive interventions rather than those aimed at specific negative behavioral symptoms.

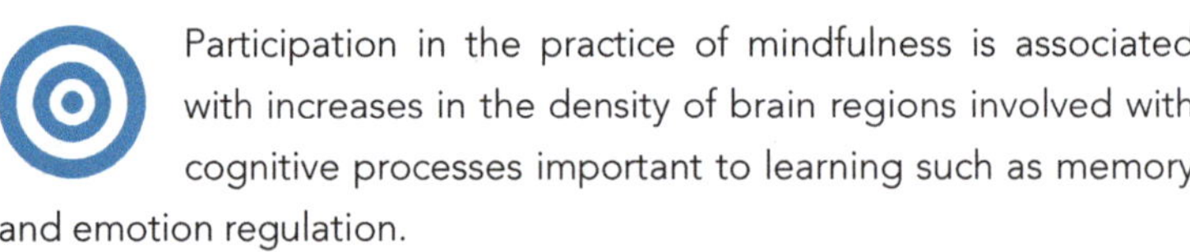

Participation in the practice of mindfulness is associated with increases in the density of brain regions involved with cognitive processes important to learning such as memory and emotion regulation.

Below you will learn some excellent examples of mindfulness exercises from our expert practitioner, Beth Snow MacMullan.

From the Expert Practitioner

Emotional Regulation Through Breath, Movement, and Mindfulness

As a career educator and expert in working with students of all ages especially those who struggle with language-based differences or ADHD, I believe the Brain-Targeted

Teaching® Model brings together many practical strategies and an approach to teaching and learning that is optimal. Brain-Target One is my favorite to put into practice each day when working with students. Often there are times, even throughout the day, when establishing an emotional climate that supports students and meets them where they are is essential. Self-regulation and employing strategies for emotional regulation for both the teacher and the student are invaluable as we know the stress response amongst students and teachers creates barriers to teaching and learning. In practice, homing in on three categories that target establishing an emotional climate (BT1) in order for students to become more available to learning is essential. These three areas are calm, energy, and focus. Within each category, the use of breath, movement, and mindfulness techniques can be used. There is no need for fancy equipment for these techniques that only take a few minutes. I encourage teachers to lead these exercises, however, students can also be leaders!

Calming Techniques Breath: It is recommended calming techniques are used as a daily practice and not suggested to students in a moment of upset. Starting each day or class session with calming breathing (Breathe in for 3, out for 6. Or breathe in for 4, hold for 2, out for 4.) is incredibly effective.

Movement: Legs Up—Inverting the body can activate the parasympathetic nervous system and create a sense of calm. One position that is easily accessible is to bring one's legs up the wall or chair.

Mindfulness: Square Visualization with Breath (4×4)—In order to promote calm, the centering technique of square breath can be extremely useful. Students visualize a square or can trace a square in the air or on a surface. With the square in mind, students breathe in for 4 (the top side of the square), hold their breath for 4 (the right side of the square), breathe out for 4 (the bottom side of the square), and then hold empty for 4 (the left side and closing the square shape).

Energizing Techniques Breath: Washing Machine—In order to energize students, the "Washing Machine" technique is extremely beneficial. Stand firm with arms in a goalpost shape, then twist side-to-side and add strong breath like the sound of a washing machine: "Whoosh, whoosh, whoosh, whoosh." Then come to stillness and reset. This can be done quickly or slowly depending on the situation. Students love this exercise!

(Continued)

(Continued)

Movement: Warrior—This strong position helps students feel brave and energized. Take one foot forward with a bent knee, extend arms, and look over the fingertips. Be sure to switch legs. Encourage students to stay for 5 full breaths. You can add affirming statements to accompany this pose like: "I am a fierce warrior" or "I am a learning warrior."

Mindfulness: 4 Syllable Energizing Affirmations—Students can stand or sit for this technique. Guide students to press their thumb and pointer fingers together, then the middle, ring, and pinky fingers on at a time with strong pressure. Four-syllable affirmations can accompany this technique and be stated out loud or silently: "I can learn now." "I can feel peace." "Free to be me." "I can do it."

Focus Techniques Breath: Chopping Wood—This technique improves focus and can be used at any time of the day. Stand firm and lift arms above the head by ears. Release arms down forcefully like chopping wood with a loud breath.

Movement: Tree—This balancing position allows students to improve focus and attention. Standing firmly on one leg with the other foot perched like a kickstand or against the standing leg as arms are at the center or above the head making the shape of a tree with branches. Eye gaze at one point to increase concentration. Be sure to switch legs. If needed, one can use a wall or chair to improve balance. Hold for 5 breaths at least. Sometimes it is fun to do a contest to see how long the pose can be held.

Mindfulness: Concentration—Sitting in a comfortable seat or standing firmly with eyes closed or with a gaze downward, observe one's breath for one minute. Focusing on the tip of the nose, watch the breath for one full minute. On the inward breath repeat "I breathe in focus" and on the outgoing breath "I breathe out distraction."

Beth Snow MacMullan, M.S. Ed.
Founder, Breathe Learn Connect Services, LLC, Executive Functioning Coach, Mindfulness and Yoga Teacher

Humor was shown to significantly reduce participants' negative emotions.

Engagement in the Arts

A growing body of research is pointing to the positive effects of the arts in students' school experiences. The visual and performing arts engage students in the fabric of the school, but they also appear to provide students with skills that support academic areas such as persistence to task, visual thinking, collaboration, and improvisation. In addition, in our study of Brain-Target Four, we explore how embedding arts activities into instruction in content areas provides a natural vehicle for enhancing long-term retention of content and deeper learning. Below we take a dive into how the arts support the Emotion Climate for Learning with the wisdom of Clare O'Malley Grizzard, arts educator and arts-integration specialist.

Embedding arts activities into instruction in content areas provides a natural vehicle for enhancing long-term retention of content and deeper learning.

From the Expert Practitioner

The Arts in Brain-Target One

Access to creative ways of knowing encourages the positive dispositions that make learning personally meaningful. As artists, musicians, and performers, learners build confidence in expressing themselves and see the world in new ways.

Build a culture of collaboration right from the start by opening the class with a divergent-thinking prompt or new material to experiment with.

For example, you could incorporate one of the following exercises:

- *Offer atypical art materials to create a collaborative day calendar: Tape pencils to long sticks; use natural materials that make marks; collage letters and images from magazines.*
- *Greet each learner with a call and response greeting. This is a musical technique that differs from an echo. Like a conversation, each person adds a unique response to the Facilitator's call.*

(Continued)

(Continued)

- *Begin with theater games including improvisation, role-play, or interview to review the day's agenda.*

Use the arts to bring content into a relatable context for learners by using contemporary art. Connect to the real world of living artists, who are making timely statements about issues that are relevant to the learner's world, as well as to the curriculum. The PBS series, Art21.org, is a fantastic educational resource of contemporary art and artists.

Calm anxiety with a creative moment:

- *Create a character that can be drawn or danced, acted out, or written. Let the character express the anxiety. This creation can be shared or kept private.*
- *Create an embellished worry box that can contain written/drawn worries of the day.*
- *The arts encourage persistence—display a visual timeline for pacing throughout the creative work session.*

The arts are not competitive, they are collaborative; they can transform the learning environment as well as an individual's relationship skills. Using tableau, composing a group song, choreographing an ensemble dance sequence, or creating a video—all require effective communication, finding common ground, setting goals, and embracing compromise—all of them lifelong skills.

The arts make us more empathetic. A strategic activity that is common in art education is critique, a discussion activity used to analyze works of art. Through guided questioning, learners can open dialogues, actively listen to others, give positive feedback, and even negotiate conflict resolution.

Clare O'Malley Grizzard
Art Educator; Arts Integration Specialist

Emotional Connection to Learning Goals and Objectives

In our study of the elements of Brain-Target One, we have focused on fostering a positive emotional climate in the classroom. The second element of Brain-Target One is designing activities that purposefully connect students emotionally with the content, skills, and concepts taught within the learning unit.

Embedding activities into lessons that connect students on an emotional level to the content can take on many forms. Our descriptions of activities from our expert teachers in this chapter are just a few examples of ways teachers can purposefully target positive emotional connections in the classroom and within content. I end this chapter with the wise words of Rachael Barillari, who introduces exciting new work in heart-brain coherence.

From the Expert Practitioner

Teaching From the Heart

As teachers, we choose to embody one of the most heart-centered professions. We teach because guiding a child toward holistic development is among the most fulfilling experiences. Teaching with love for our communities and compassion for all children is an anchoring force, even on the most challenging of school days.

I've always believed that great teaching starts from the heart. For me, this has evolved beyond a figurative statement to a scientific understanding, deeply influencing my approach as an educator and researcher. While teaching in an urban middle school, I observed the profound impact of the classroom's emotional climate on learning—both academic and social-emotional. It became clear that children need to feel they belong, that they can exhale and feel safe in a classroom before any deep skill-building, creativity, or innovation can begin. Learning about Brain-Target One from the Brain-Targeted Teaching® Model was my gateway to understanding the scientific underpinnings of this phenomenon, especially in relation to the cranial brain.

As a HeartMath Certified Trainer, I discovered that the heart is not just metaphorically central to teaching; it is also scientifically crucial. The heart's nervous system contains around 40,000 neurons. The HeartMath Institute's research shows that more neural signals travel from the heart to the brain than vice versa, indicating that our emotional state significantly influences cognitive processing. Heart-brain coherence, a state of optimal functioning achieved when the heart, brain, and nervous system work together in harmony, is vital for both teachers and students. This coherence promotes openness to learning, emotional stability, and

(Continued)

(Continued)

overall well-being. Biologically this is also connected to the production of DHEA (the vitality hormone), which promotes growth and resilience.

As educators, prioritizing our emotional states—what I refer to as "putting our oxygen masks on first"—is essential because a teacher's inner coherence significantly impacts the overall emotional climate of the classroom. As Dr. Rollin McCraty (2015) explains in Science of the Heart, the heart's magnetic field—the strongest rhythmic field produced by the body—extends into the space around us and carries information about our emotional state. This "energetic" communication, or cardio-electromagnetic communication, enables us to sense and resonate with others' emotions, fostering an empathetic and compassionate environment.

To help cultivate this environment, I use simple yet effective routines in my personal life and in the classroom. For instance, I start each day by writing my intentions for the day ahead, and what I am most grateful for from the day before, in a notebook. I take some deep breaths while I drink my morning coffee and on my travels to my classroom. This pairing of focusing on the breath while positively directing thoughts contributes to the optimal communication between the heart and brain.

Once I am with my students, I always begin with the "Small Joys" routine, where every student shares something "small and good" happening in their lives today, helping to set a warm and inclusive tone. We also practice centering with a few deep breaths, which activates the parasympathetic nervous system, reduces cortisol levels, and increases DHEA. This prepares students for higher order thinking and creativity.

Throughout the lesson, I model resilience and compassion by embracing mistakes and scaffolding productive struggles. Research shows the importance of integrating emotional and cognitive engagement in the classroom. A 2023 study by Janet N. Zadina, The Synergy Zone: Connecting the Mind, Brain, and Heart for the Ideal Classroom Learning Environment, demonstrates that creating an optimal learning space relies on connecting cognitive tasks with emotional states. When teachers intentionally align these elements, they enhance both learning readiness and retention. This synergy is crucial for developing classrooms where academic growth and emotional well-being flourish. I reinforce positive behaviors with celebrations and affirmations both one-on-one and with the entire class, which I call "Naming the Good."

This is the heart of teaching: creating a positive emotional climate for learning that is rooted in brain science, heart science, and simple, joyful routines.

Rachael Barillari
Educator and Curriculum Writer

Brain-Target One - Strategies for Establishing the Emotional Climate

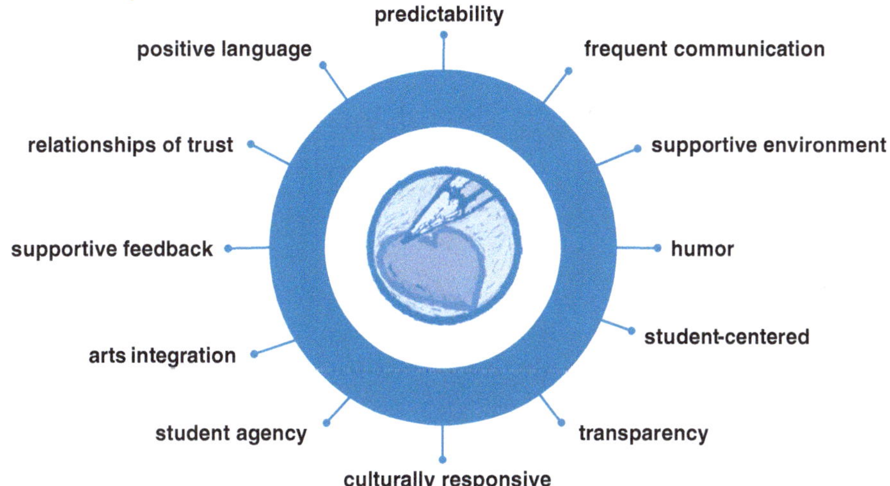

Brain-Target Two

Creating the Physical Learning Environment

5

The child, left at liberty to exercise his activities, ought to find in his surroundings something organized in direct relation to his internal organization which is developing itself by natural laws.

—Maria Montessori

Brain-Target Two - Creating a Physical Learning Environment Chapter Map

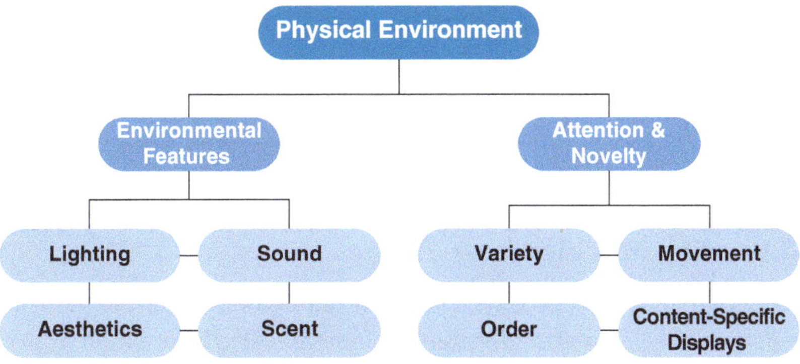

Shira could not believe her eyes when her mother's car pulled into the loading zone in front of her new school. Recently relocated from another city, Shira dreaded the move. But as she looked at the school in which she would now enroll, her attitude quickly changed. The front of the school was filled with beautiful gardens; a fanciful sculpted fence; a playground full of inviting equipment; and, flanking the front door, barrels of brightly colored potted flowers. Walking into the school's lobby, she saw a kaleidoscope of colors from murals, artwork, sculptures, and award certificates as well as posters advertising a school play and signs welcoming visitors. She heard soft music coming from a kindergarten classroom and singing coming from the auditorium. The physical environment of the school delivered an unspoken but strong message to Shira; she couldn't wait for this school to become her own.

The physical environment of a school or workplace is indeed an unspoken but powerful messenger. From the curb to classroom or office, halls to lavatories, offices to cafeteria, the physical environment not only influences how individuals feel but also affects their learning and work productivity (Byers et al., 2018). The physical environment also reflects an organization's core values, promoting a sense of place in which all individuals feel welcomed and affirmed. In the last chapter, our study of Brain-Target One led us to review how the emotional climate shapes social behaviors, cognition, and learning. Building from those concepts, this chapter focuses on how various elements in the physical learning environment influence attention, allow engagement in task-oriented activities, and reflect a sense of community and belonging.

The physical environment of a school or workplace is indeed an unspoken but powerful messenger.

Our study of Brain-Target Two, Creating the Physical Learning Environment, begins with a look at attention, the portal to learning, and how the environment can be engineered to help engage and sustain attention and motivation. We first explore how novelty is a tool to engage attention. We will also examine how the environment enhances learning and productivity, whether in a school, work environment, or at home, through the physical features of lighting, sound, and scent, as well as movement, order, and beauty.

Attention and Novelty

Attention is cognitive selection to a sensation, thought, or event. From a myriad of sensory stimuli, attention systems selectively choose which stimuli are filtered out and which become part of the conscious response system (Posner & Patoine, 2009). As discussed in Chapter 1, Posner and Rothbart (2007) identify three neural networks or systems of interconnected brain regions underlying aspects of attention. The *alerting network* engages individuals in the task at hand and is important for capturing attention; the *orienting network* keeps attention attuned to external events rather than internal thoughts; and the *executive attention network* inhibits extraneous thoughts, shifts the attention system to focus on stimuli, and regulates emotions.

Attention is cognitive selection to a sensation, thought, or event.

Selective attention to conscious thought is an important filtering mechanism as the brain discards information that it perceives as neither relevant nor useful. It is unlikely that you are aware, for example, of your clothes touching your skin, the hum of electrical lights and appliances, or the chair you are sitting on until it is called to your attention. The brain's attention system ignores these physical and sensory bits of information in order to tune into what it perceives as more meaningful and enticing.

The brain's attention system ignores these physical and sensory bits of information in order to tune into what it perceives as more meaningful and enticing.

One feature that the attending system is not likely to ignore is novel objects or events. If you want to grab the attention of your students or colleagues, try introducing something novel in the environment. Brains are wired to pay attention to something that is different from what is familiar in the surroundings; novelty triggers the alerting and orienting systems and improves memory (see Butavand et al., 2020). Educators see this attending system at work when they note how even small changes in the environment generate students' comments or questions. But how long is that stimulus novel? Regrettably, although novelty grabs attention, it does not help to sustain it, as maintaining attention involves more complex executive function processing (see Immordino-Yang et al., 2018). The new poster on the wall, for example, may foster interest at first, but if it remains there for a lengthy period of time, it becomes like wallpaper, blending into the background environment and even cluttering the space rather than enhancing it. Unchanging visual environments, whether in the classroom or workspace, create *habituation,* a term used to describe how the same stimulus presented for a long period of time produces a reduction of interest or even boredom (Schomaker & Meeter, 2015).

Novelty in the environment triggers the alerting and orienting systems. Unchanging visual environments create *habituation.*

Researchers have long demonstrated the positive influence of novelty not only on attending to information but also on retention of information. Smith et al. (1978), for example, found that alternating the room where a person studies improves retention. They conducted a study in which one group of students studied vocabulary words in one room and a second group studied the words in two different rooms. Those who studied in two rooms performed better on measures of memory for the words than those who studied in the same environment. This study and others demonstrate that when the outside surroundings are varied, information is enriched and retention of content is improved. In a similar study, after a learning session, children who were exposed to a novel experience in a different location presented better memory for the learned information than others who did not have the novel exposure (Ballarini et al., 2013). What is more, Sidney Zentall (1983; see also Zentall & Zentall, 1983) argues that children exposed to bland, unchanging environments become stimulus adapted and appear to seek out their own novel stimulation, often leading to nonoptimal behavior. In studies comparing unchanging environments with ones that provided novelty, children were generally off-task and out of seats more often in bland environments. In particular, children with attention deficit hyperactivity disorder (ADHD) were less efficient learners in classrooms where environments and teaching techniques were monotonous and predictable. They tended to seek out their own stimulation through off-task behaviors. Building from previous studies, Baumann et al. (2020) investigated how novelty affected retention of information for ADHD students. They found that introducing a novel virtual experience after learning a word list resulted in significantly better recall of the learned words compared to those who remained in a familiar environment.

When the outside surroundings are varied, information is enriched and retention of content is improved.

Regular changes in the environment seem to be an effective tool for capturing attention and providing visual stimulation. This can be accomplished in a multitude of ways, such as changing seating arrangements, rotating visual displays, and adding objects that connect to themes of content instruction. With all of the tasks on a teacher's or a leader's daily list of chores, we understand that purposeful changes to the physical environment may well drop to the bottom of the list. However, if we consider the importance of novelty to capturing attention, it is worth taking the time to make even simple changes that help engage students in schools and individuals in the workplace.

If we consider the importance of novelty to capturing students' attention, it is worth taking the time to make even simple changes that help engage students.

It must be noted, however, that while novelty is a powerful and important instructional tool, teachers and leaders should find a balance between the need for a climate that demonstrates predictable routines and providing novel experiences and environmental changes.

Here one of our expert teachers describes how she believes that changes in seating arrangements make learning more interesting and engaging for her students.

From the Expert Practitioner

Novelty in the Classroom

When I first started using the Brain-Targeted Teaching® (BTT) Model, I was intrigued by the idea that novelty in the environment was important, that I could possibly increase students' attention to learning activities by changing seating or displays. As I wrote my first BTT unit, I thought about the various ways I would change seating for my sixth-grade students based on the activity I had planned for the day. During one 2-week unit, the seating changed from traditional rows, to a large circle, to clusters, to theater-style. I brought in a different object related to our unit every few days. There was no question that changing the classroom piqued my students' interest. As soon as they entered the room, they would make the connection between how the room was arranged and the work they would be doing

(Continued)

(Continued)

that day. One day as students were lining up to enter the room, I heard several students debating how the room would look when they entered. I observed students becoming more interested in what I was teaching because of these changes. Now, for every unit that I teach, I become even more creative about changes to the environment to grab students' attention and make them more interested in the lesson.

Alexandra Fleming
Social Studies Specialist
School Social Studies Teacher and Supervisor

The Effects of Environmental Features on Attention and Learning

In this section, we focus on how environmental factors affect learning in the classroom. We then consider how those same features also apply to office work environments.

Lighting in the Classroom

Lighting the fire of learning can sometimes be as simple as lighting a classroom with natural daylight and providing outside views. Visiting schools or offices one is likely to see some rooms with no windows, or clouded plastic-like windows that provide only filtered light and no views of the outside, or window shades pulled down to eliminate all natural light and outside views. Perhaps practitioners believe that lowered light levels might produce a calming environment. Indeed, there may be times during the day when it is most appropriate to have lowered, soft light in the classroom or workspace. That said, it is not uncommon to see students sitting in dark rooms with drooping eyes and heads on desks. Constant poorly lit rooms influence pineal gland activity of synthesizing melatonin, which plays a role in arousal and the production of hormones that regulate moods (Lekan-Kehinde & Asojo, 2021; Morrow & Kanakri, 2018).

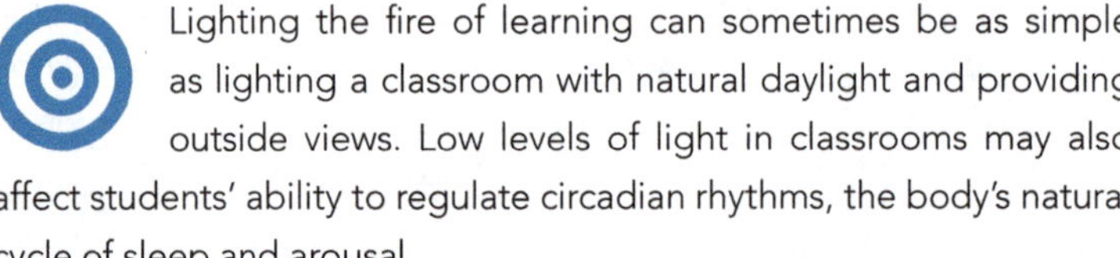

Lighting the fire of learning can sometimes be as simple as lighting a classroom with natural daylight and providing outside views. Low levels of light in classrooms may also affect students' ability to regulate circadian rhythms, the body's natural cycle of sleep and arousal.

Windows in a classroom are important for more than merely providing natural light. Tanner (2008) argues that students whose classrooms allow for outside views through window gazing are better able to redirect attention to academic tasks than if their attention strays to other activities such as doodling in a notebook or texting on a phone. He characterizes window gazing as requiring "soft attention," which is cognitively less consuming than other types of distraction that may capture students' more focused attention (p. 455).

Research now has *shed light* on the importance of lighting in learning in a classroom environment. In an extensive review of literature on the effects of lighting on learning, Lekan-Kehinde and Asojo (2021) argue that lighting is a major aspect of an optimal workspace, affecting performance, concentration, alertness, and moods. Their review reveals how optimal lighting arouses concentration, influences behaviors, and positively affects reading performance and students' ability to engage in the executive function skill of task-switching. These findings support a seminal study of more than twenty-one thousand students across three states. Heschong (1999) studied the effect of natural light on student achievement. Results showed that students who studied in classrooms with the most day lighting demonstrated 20% better scores on mathematics assessment and 26% on reading assessments. As Lekan-Kehinde and Asojo (2021) point out, the use of different lighting scenarios is typically based on selected activities, and lighting can be used as a tool to reduce or increase the activity level in a workspace. For example, warm-toned light creates a cozy, comfortable environment whereas higher intensity blue-enriched light increases concentration and cognitive performance such as processing speed and memory. Similarly, Meng et al. (2023) conducted a systematic review of thirty-two studies related to the indoor visual environments on children's health outcomes. They identified lighting and natural window views as important factors that influenced physical, psychological, and cognitive health.

Students who studied in classrooms with the most day lighting demonstrated 20% better scores on mathematics assessment and 26% on reading assessments.

As a growing number of studies show the positive effects of optimal lighting on learning, those making decisions regarding school and office construction and should take note. As one practitioner recounts below, adapting a poorly lit environment can make the space more comfortable and effective for learning and working.

From the Expert Practitioner

Let the Light Shine

The lighting in my classroom was "upgraded" as part of the school district's measures for efficiency and cost savings. The fluorescent lights, previously embedded in the ceiling tiles, were now hung several feet from the ceiling in long rows. The minute I saw the room, I was startled at the difference in ambiance and light levels. The top walls of the classroom were now barely lit. The new lights created glare for the children sitting directly under them and shadows for those between the rows of florescent lights. The room appeared dimmer now, and I could feel the loss of light affecting my own mood and I believe the moods of the children, too. I decided to counteract this effect by bringing as much light into the classroom as I could. Shades were pulled all the way to the top to allow for more natural light, and I added three standing lamps in various sections of the room. Manipulating the levels of light in the room is critical; I see every day how lighting affects my students' attention and their moods.

Amanda Kowalik
Teacher and School Leader

Acoustics and Noise in the Learning Environment

Imagine driving on a highway going on a long trip. You are relaxed and listening to your favorite song on the radio. You suddenly find yourself in the wrong lane and are forced to exit onto another highway. Cars are speeding by you on both sides, and your brain is now on high alert trying to figure out how you are going to get back on the right course. What is the first thing you do?

If you said, turn down or turn off the radio, you would join the majority response. But wait, this is the auditory system, what does that have to do with your visual tracking? Obviously, the answer is "a lot"! Background sounds, even relaxing music, can become a distraction when higher mental processes are needed.

Most practitioners would agree that they have greater control of the visual environment in the classroom than they do the acoustical. Classrooms and workspaces are often bombarded with white noise such as the buzzing of electrical lights and hums from heating and cooling systems, audiovisual equipment, and computers. Noise may also come from hallways; other classrooms and offices; and outdoor sounds from traffic, sirens, and playgrounds. Finally, at times the school's public address system could be a distraction to learning, especially if it is used inappropriately or too frequently during instructional time. Unlike the driver on the highway who might turn off the radio, these distractions are not as easily extinguished.

Most teachers would agree that they have greater control of the visual environment in the classroom than they do the acoustical.

And in reality, most schools have higher levels of background noise than they should. This is unfortunate as young children are especially vulnerable to distractions created by noise. Massonnié et al. (2019) found that excess noise affected creativity scores, especially for young children with difficulty in working memory and selective attention. In a review of fourteen studies on the effects of noise on high school students' performance, Mealings and Buchholz (2024) found a negative impact of high noise levels on students' listening skills, learning outcomes, and general well-being. Learning loss in high noise environments was the most debilitating for non-native speakers and students with special learning needs. In a review of literature on the effect of noise in the form of classroom chatter, Lamotte et al. (2021) found significantly lower performance on reading comprehension tests when students were in noisy classrooms due to chatter in the learning environment.

Background sounds, however, are not always harmful. Experimental studies show that music can have relaxing effects on children and adults (Lehmann & Seufert, 2017). Consistent with this research, sounds in the environment can be soothing for students and even mask ambient noise in the classroom. When children are at work in routine tasks, sounds can add a texture of peace and relaxation to the classroom environment. Some ideas for sound elements include the following:

- Playing background music that will relax students; classical music is often used in this way, but other musical genres can serve the same purpose;
- Hanging wind chimes in a window or just above air vents so that they tinkle when air systems come on;
- Playing recordings of sounds of nature such as waves, waterfalls, bird chirps, seagulls, or dolphins;
- Adding waterfall fountains that provide the sound and view of falling water; and
- Adding materials that produce gentle sounds such as rain sticks or small bells to sensitize children to different sounds.

Music has been shown to have relaxing effects on adults in experimental studies.

Finally, although we all love the delightful sounds that emanate from classrooms where children are engaged in active learning tasks, teachers at times may want to consider reserving some moments during the school day for quiet reflection. A good example of this practice is in a Montessori classroom. Maria Montessori promoted the regular practice of silence because she believed that it helped children regulate attention, develop inhibitory control, and become more sensitized to sounds in the environment (Lillard, 2005, p. 316).

Teachers at times may want to consider reserving some moments during the school day for quiet reflection.

Sounds in classrooms can and should vary widely. One might hear the purposeful chatter that comes from a group assignment, project-based tasks, or relaxing background sounds during routine tasks. However, periods of quiet that promote purposeful control and reflective practices are important while students are engaging in learning a new skill that requires concentration.

From the Expert Practitioner

Montessori and the Silence Game

Montessori classrooms are a buzz of activity. Children are engaged in meaningful learning—some learning by themselves and others in groups. Some children are receiving direct instruction from the adults, and others are learning by watching their older peers. With all this activity, one can imagine all the synapses in the brain being formed!

Maria Montessori recognized the benefits of engaging children in activities of their own choosing. She also appreciated the need for creating pauses in the child's day for consolidation. One of the ways she helped children learn the importance of quiet time was through the exercise called "The Silence Game." The Silence Game gives children deliberate practice in controlling their impulses and their movement. It can be practiced as a group activity or individually by choosing materials from the shelf that guide the child to silence. In either form of the game, children are learning self-control.

While observing a Montessori classroom in Beijing, I saw a child sit in the middle of a busy classroom on a mat, his eyes cast downward on the hourglass placed in front of him, practicing silence. Montessori understood that whether the game is performed as a group exercise (children collectively have to choose to be silent or the game stops) or is chosen individually, developing self-control and willpower through silence was worth the time spent practicing these skills.

Michelle Hartye
Montessori Leader, Consultant, and Teacher Educator

Scent in the Classroom

Of all sensory perceptions, scent has a unique role in human development. As explained in Chapter 2, the thalamus sorts sensory information then relays the signal to brain structures for processing. The exception is olfactory input, which bypasses the thalamus and takes a direct path to the brain's limbic system for processing by structures associated with emotion and memory (Gazzaniga et al., 2009, p. 171). This may explain why certain scents produce vivid memories such as the smell of grandmother's apple pie or the scent of a cologne connected with a person from the past.

Of all sensory perceptions, scent has a unique role in human development.

Indoor air quality in the school or workplace is a topic that deserves attention given the amount of time one spends indoors and the importance of thermal and odors to the comfort levels of individuals in indoor spaces (Korsavi et al., 2020). In particular, research on the effects of scents on human behavior suggests that scents play a role in emotion and memory. A study by Choi et al. (2022) found that pleasant aromas have the potential to enhance mood and performance. Their study showed a strong positive correlation between learning in a room scented with lemon and higher scores in vocabulary and memory retention compared to other scented or unscented conditions. In a similar study, Ma (2022) found that scented environments produced positive emotions and reduced negative emotions as measured on the Adolescent Academic Emotion Questionnaire. Using essential oils of rosemary, lavender, mint, lemon, and sweet orange, she concludes that the use of aromatherapy (especially sweet orange) is beneficial to improving students' academic emotions and promoting relaxation. Other researchers found the use of aromatherapy reduced test anxiety (e.g., Luan et al., 2023).

Subjects showed improvement in performing an attention-related task in an environment with scents such as lily of the valley and peppermint compared with an unscented environment.

These studies and others suggest that scents influence emotion and performance and may provide an additional environmental asset to enhance students' attention and memory. Below we hear how one of our expert practitioners uses scent to gain students' interest, attention, and performance. We will hear from eighth grader, Angela, as she describes her language arts teacher's classroom.

Studies suggest that scents influence emotion and performance and may provide an additional environmental asset to enhance students' attention and memory.

From the Expert Student

Vanilla Makes Me Happy

My favorite class that I go to each day is definitely language arts. I like the subject and the teacher, but I also just like the feeling of being in the room. This may sound funny, but that room is not like any ordinary classroom. The walls are painted a copper color, burgundy curtains drape the windows, and the room smells like vanilla. It makes me feel good to be there, sort of like home when my mom makes vanilla pudding. I like doing my work in the room because I feel relaxed and happy. Everyone in the class feels

the same way, and no one really goofs off during that class. It is just fun to go there. I wish more teachers would do what my teacher has with his classroom. It really makes us know that he cares about how we feel as much as what we learn.

Angela
Eighth-grade student

The Effects of Movement on Attention

Few would argue with those in the popular media who cite the growing problem of obesity and lack of movement in the lives of children. With advances in modern technology, physical activity has ceased to become a natural part of everyday lives. Yet as John Ratey (2008) points out, exercise is in the roots of our biology and strongly influences cognition; moving muscles produces proteins in the blood that affect learning. Ratey and others (e.g., Hillman et al., 2009) also note that exercise improves certain mental processes that regulate alertness, attention, and motivation. As we saw in Chapter 1, embodied cognition is critical to the *whole brain* approach to learning—thought and movement are not separate neurological systems. Learning involves not only executive skills but also movement of the body in space.

Exercise is in the roots of our biology and strongly influences cognition.

Getting students moving in the school environment may be increasingly difficult as schools continue to engage in the unfortunate practice of reducing physical education and recess programs to allow for more instructional time in tested areas. Still, teachers can provide students with opportunities for movement within the classroom and during content instruction. Purposeful movement can be created within the physical features of the classroom through the use of workstations, research space, special nooks, and alcoves for reading or other group or individual activities. In addition, movement during learning can occur through arts integration such as theater, dance, tableau, yoga, and other forms of creative movement. We will discuss arts integration strategies further in our study of Brain-Target Four.

Order and Beauty in the Classroom

The philosophies and practices of schools such as Montessori, with its focus on the prepared environment, and Reggio Emilia, with its arts studio-like educational setting, can provide wonderful models of purposeful use of the physical environment to promote engagement in learning. In both models, order and beauty are key components of a classroom. Maria Montessori, for example, strongly advocated that learning is optimized when children are in environments that are free from clutter and are aesthetically pleasing (Lillard, 2005). Reggio Emilia promotes the environment as a critical component for allowing children to develop and grow and for facilitating communication, interaction, creativity, and discovery. The environment is thought of as the *third teacher* and involves principles such as aesthetics, active learning, collaboration, relationships, and bringing elements of the outdoors to inside spaces (Mineo, 2023; Robson, 2017).

Learning is optimized when children are in environments that are free from clutter and are aesthetically pleasing.

My experience in schools leads me to believe that not all teachers understand the importance of order and beauty. Although I could site many examples of lovely classroom environments, I've also witnessed classrooms in which vertical spaces were cluttered with posters that never changed, and horizontal spaces were piled with stacks of books, papers, projects, and a myriad of other objects. Let's hear from one of our expert teachers about how she organizes the classroom to reflect order and beauty and how that affects her students.

In summary, features of the physical learning environment can attract students' interest in the lesson, give them a sense of comfort and belonging, and ultimately help to influence attention and engagement in learning. As one more tool to facilitate the teaching and learning process, practitioners should deliberately plan the physical environment as they establish the goals and objectives for each new learning unit—a component described in more detail in Brain-Target Three in Chapter 6.

Teachers should deliberately plan the physical environment as they establish the goals and objectives for each new learning unit.

From the Expert Practitioner

Using Visible Thinking Routines: Consistency and Novelty in the Classroom

When thinking how arts integration supports content within a learning environment, I always like to start by asking myself, "What do these two content areas have in common?" Noticing that both artists and scientists use observation as a starting point for their work gave me the perfect arts integration throughline for a kindergarten unit on Weather Systems. Like all skills, observation within the learning environment is something that needs to be taught and practiced. A great way to teach students to become better observers is using See, Think, Wonder, a thinking routine created by Harvard's Project Zero. The goal of this routine is to teach students to slow down and really observe an image or object by asking three questions: What do you see? What do you think? And What do you wonder?

Establishing thinking routines like See, Think, Wonder into the classroom is a great way to incorporate Brain-Target Two—Creating the Physical Learning Environment. Thinking routines can be used in any classroom at any grade to establish an organization within the classroom that students become comfortable and familiar with. Once established they allow teachers to balance novelty and consistency by using the same routine in different ways and in different parts of a lesson. To introduce the routine to kindergarten, I made a See, Think, Wonder visual and worksheet. We used the same visual and worksheet throughout the unit so students became familiar with these visuals as part of the routine. The visual and worksheet both used a combination of symbols and words to make it accessible to all students. The See, Think, Wonder visual and worksheet were used to introduce students to the routine first as a class. After practicing the routine a few times as a class, students felt comfortable with the routine and were given a chance to practice the routine independently. Once students begin to feel comfortable independently with the routine, we began using this routine at different points in the lesson to help students observe in different ways. For example, using the See, Think, Wonder routine at the beginning of a lesson was a great way to get students curious about the learning environment and allow them to tap into their prior knowledge. While using the routine at the end of a lesson helped

(Continued)

(Continued)

students to reflect on their learning and wonder what might be next. All while using the same visual and worksheet format that students knew and felt comfortable with.

When starting the unit, the arts integration goal was to help students become better observers. At first this seemed like a hard thing to measure, but by the end of the unit students had many See, Think, Wonder handouts making it easy to see students' growth in their comfort and understanding of both the routine and their skills as observers.

Katie Gill-Harvey
Art and Classroom Teacher

We now return to the wisdom of Clare O'Malley Grizzard, arts educator and arts-integration specialist in describing how Brain-Target Two looks in a physical environment.

From the Expert Practitioner

The Arts in Brain-Target Two

Cultivating a creative and innovative physical environment facilitates exploration and curiosity. Below are strategies for how the arts enhance the physical learning environment:

- *Reimagine the learner space to allow for flexibility, creative collaboration, and communication. How can students participate in creating that space?*
- *Create a dedicated performance space, or a maker space, that allows for shared exploration of art materials and group-based performances and presentations.*
- *A teacher/leader can make thinking and learning visible by displaying the process and development of ideas, rather than what is typically presented: only finished projects or graded work. As in mapping, process boards serve to connect the sometimes disparate parts of a learning event to an accessible global whole and celebrate the incremental learning of the entire lesson.*

- *Display artifacts and images that reflect the diversity of your students with culturally responsive materials.*
- *Consider a content-related temporary museum and library for your learning space.*
- *Use a soundscape technique—making sounds and music to replicate the atmosphere of a story or event.*
- *Use nonverbal cues for transitions and movement within the learning space. Use music, visual clues, and body movements to guide activity and promote engagement (songs, clapping, sound bowl, learner-created signage, dance gestures).*
- *Analyze the physical setting of a novel or an historic event, then design a stage set, utilizing theater elements, in a diorama or drawing of the concept.*

Clare O'Malley Grizzard
Arts Educator, Arts Integration Specialist

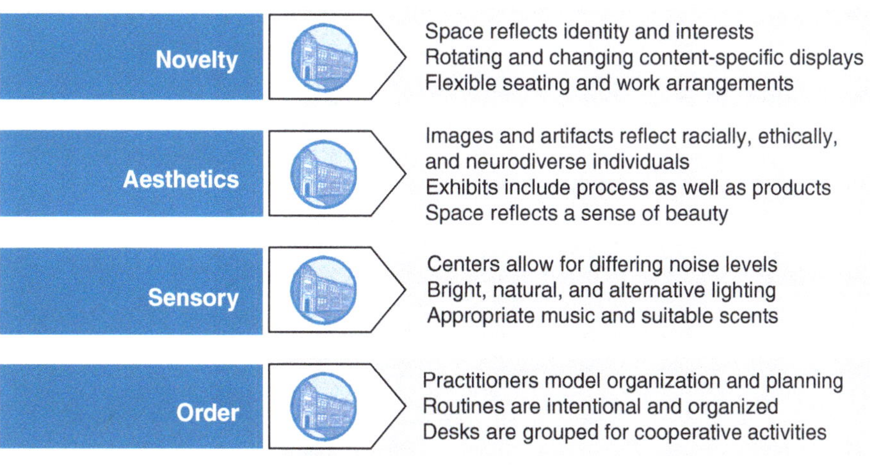

Brain-Target Three

Designing the Learning Experience

6

Here is an essential principle of education: To teach details is to bring confusion; to establish the relationship between things is to bring knowledge.

—Maria Montessori

Brain-Target Three - Designing the Learning Experience Chapter Map

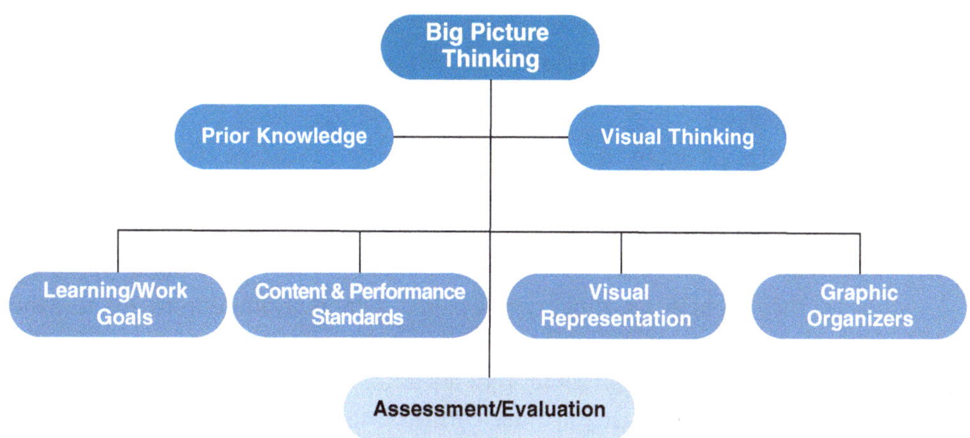

The previous two chapters highlight research and practice focused on establishing a setting that enhances a positive emotional climate for learning and leading (Brain-Target One) and creates a physical learning environment for promoting attention and engagement in learning and attaining performance goals (Brain-Target Two). Progressing through the stages of the Brain-Targeted Teaching® (BTT) Model, we now look at designing the road map for instruction or for strategic planning for any organization.

Imagine trying to put together a large jigsaw puzzle without ever having seen the completed picture usually displayed on the outside of the box. Without a doubt, having an image of the whole picture gives each individual piece of the puzzle more meaning. Likewise, when we guide learning by providing a broader view or *big picture*, we promote a visual way to understand complex ideas, interrelationships, and connections among goals, skills, and concepts. This is consistent with the brain's propensity to look for patterns and associations between information at the forefront of thought and information stored in memory (Posner & Rothbart, 2007).

In this next target, practitioners use content standards and curriculum guides to determine learning goals, activities, and assessments. These key elements are presented in a form of visual representation (e.g., concept maps or various graphic organizers) in order to display the big picture of how new learning goals connect with prior knowledge; how activities result in achieving learning goals; and how evaluations are designed to be able to demonstrate understanding of concepts, skills, and content. Similarly, in any organizational structure, visualizing elements of goals, work targets, performance standards, and evaluations in a visual format helps to convey the big picture of what the organization values and how it functions.

Visual representations of information can take on various forms. The term *concept map* is used throughout this chapter, although some may be more familiar with terms such as mind maps, graphic organizers, content webs, pictorial representations, conceptual frameworks, or other ways that promote visual, big-picture thinking.

In traditionally organized instruction, educators typically follow a sequential list of skills, chapters from a text, or topics from curriculum outlines. This kind of instruction often moves from one objective to the next without a broader context. Although this instructional approach may promote learning specific pieces of content, students might miss the larger concepts or the *big picture* essential for deep understanding and memory. Although some students make such connections on their own, too many times they are just learning isolated facts with little connection to their prior knowledge or other content. This is also important in the workspace. Understanding how one's tasks are connected to the larger goals of the organization helps to situate the work within the larger context of system goals.

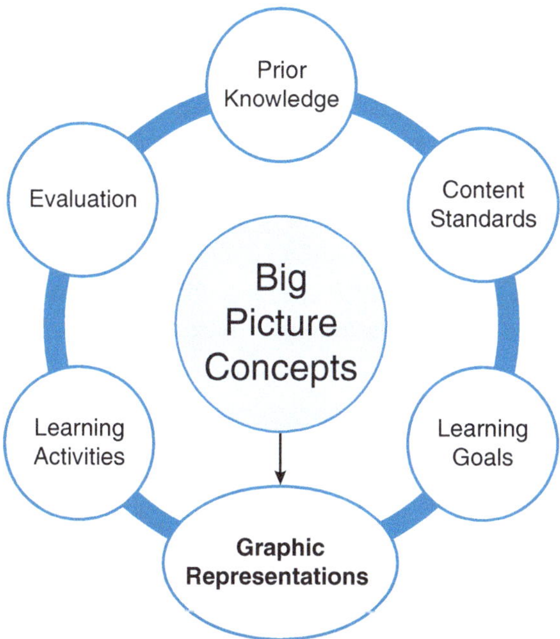

Brain-Target Three - Designing the Learning Experience

> When we guide learning by providing a broader view or *big picture*, we promote an understanding of the connections between prior knowledge and new learning and also demonstrate the relationships among learning goals.

In contrast to typical practice, we have known for some time the efficacy of explicitly teaching global concepts through visual representations such as concept maps (e.g., Luiten et al., 1980). Research continues to show that concept maps help learners and workers in multiple professions draw from prior knowledge, retain information, have deeper understanding of content and concepts, and visualize relational structure of information dissemination (Anastasiou et al., 2024; Maribal et al., 2024; Rosas, 2023). In a special review publication, Trochim and McLinden (2017) provide a historical view of the efficacy of concept mapping and outline multiple ways that concept mapping has evolved. Specifically, they focus on three main domains—the generation of ideas through brainstorming, structuring those ideas, and representing ideas in a visual form.

We have known for some time the efficacy of explicitly teaching global concepts through visual representations such as concept maps.

The ability to understand how ideas are connected is only amplified if students already have some prior knowledge to which new information can be related. In a seminal study, Recht and Leslie (1988) compared content memory in poor readers and strong readers with or without high prior knowledge in the content area. The results showed that despite their weak reading comprehension ability, poor readers with high prior knowledge remembered more than strong readers without prior knowledge. Taken together, studies suggest that, in addition to presenting a global picture of the learning, teachers must also ensure that new learning builds from what students already know.

Studies suggest that, in addition to presenting a global picture of the learning, teachers must also ensure that learning units build on what students already know.

Cognitive Development and Big-Picture Thinking

Bransford (2000) explains that knowledge is not a list of facts and formulas; rather, knowledge is organized around core concepts or big ideas that shape thinking. This view of learning is consistent with a type of cognitive structure known as *schema* (*schemata* in plural form) or "mental representation of what all instances of something have in common" (Byrnes, 2008, p. 26). According to proponents of schema theory, having global understanding of common elements in different pieces of information helps us to categorize content, remember information more effectively, comprehend concepts more deeply, and solve problems more efficiently. In addition, understanding connections among elements assists with abstract thinking and understanding relationships among disparate chunks of information (Byrnes, 2008).

Understanding connections among elements assists with abstract thinking and understanding relationships among disparate chunks of information.

Byrnes (2008) points out that, unlike some other theories of learning such as Piaget's theory of cognitive development, schema theory does not account for developmental stages of learning. It does not address, for example, how the novel or younger learner may process global understanding differently from older or expert learners. Research, however, provides a fuller picture of developmental stages regarding the development of global thinking. Poirel and colleagues (2008) investigated how visual processing evolves during childhood by comparing global visual processing (whole picture) to local processing (component parts). Results showed that children at the age of four tend to focus more on component parts of a picture—or local processing—than on the whole picture. However, findings also showed that beyond age four, children progressively demonstrated a tendency to process the picture globally. By the age of nine, subjects had an adultlike tendency for global processing—they more frequently identified a picture by its overall image and ignored the components that made up the picture. These results suggest that presenting visual information through global representations such as graphic organizers is most effective for children beginning in the early elementary grades.

Planning a Brain-Targeted Teaching® Learning Unit

In the BTT Model, Brain-Target Three encourages practitioners to design graphic organizers that include the overarching themes, content, activities, and evaluations that students will experience during the unit (Hardiman, 2003, 2012). This type of global planning allows students to see connections among topics, how activities relate to goals and objectives, and how they will demonstrate understanding of what they have learned. From the teacher's perspective, planning BTT learning units necessitates having a thorough grasp of the content while also promoting interdisciplinary planning and creative teaching activities. It is consistent with the idea of *planning backward* advocated by Tomlinson and McTighe (2006) in which teachers are encouraged to identify the essential content that should result in enduring learning, determine how students will demonstrate understanding, and plan instructional activities to meet instructional goals. In this chapter, I briefly describe various areas to be considered in developing and planning a BTT learning unit, including choosing the learning goals and objectives, designing activities, creating evaluations, and displaying key concepts through graphic organizers. This process has also been adopted by professionals working in organizational contexts outside of education, adapting the structure to align with their own context. Below are examples of how educators have used concept mapping to enhance learning.

Global planning allows students to see connections among topics, how activities relate to learning objectives, and how they will demonstrate understanding of the lesson's goals.

From the Expert Practitioner

How to Start a Learning Unit: Concept Mapping

Brain-Targeted Teaching® has become the tool that I use to drive each unit, even each lesson that I write and teach. When beginning the initial writing phase of a unit, I always begin with a concept map. I first make one for myself, with paper and pencil, which essentially conveys my thought process in print. Once the map is complete, I then make the same map again using large chart paper and colored markers to display for my students at the beginning of the unit. This allows them to see where we are heading throughout the unit and make connections between concepts and across content areas. Instead of wondering what they will do in class each day, how it all fits together and makes sense, they have a clear map to guide them. I refer to the map throughout the unit, and so do my students. At the end of the unit, I give each student their own small concept map to keep. We go through each part of the map to form a discussion of how we covered each concept. The discussion always ends with students having moments of self-discovery about what they accomplished. As a result, they show greater confidence in the content they have mastered.

Amanda Kowalik
Teacher and School Leader

Instructional Decision-Making: Content Choices for Learning Goals and Objectives

As teachers begin to plan BTT learning units, the first decision is to determine the essential concepts, content, and skills that students will need to know, not only to pass the unit test but also for long-term learning. This instructional decision-making is not always easy. Many teachers lament that they are expected to cover too much material in too little time. Unfortunately, this *inch deep mile wide* approach to curriculum has forced some teachers to move quickly through the content and avoid interactive problem-solving activities, including arts integration, that would lead to long-term retention of content as well as make learning more engaging for students. High-stakes testing in reading and mathematics, curriculum-based benchmark testing, preparation for high school assessments, and Advanced Placement tests can certainly shape curriculum decisions for teachers and school administrators. Still, it is often left to teachers to make instructional choices for learning goals and objectives, which may require sifting through content standards, curriculum guides, and textbooks to determine the knowledge and skills that students will need in order to be successful in the educational environment and become life-time learners. This same scenario often exists when corporate trainers are tasked with teaching new or seasoned employees complex skills within a short timeframe. Choosing content wisely and planning instruction that allows for retention and application of information is critical in any profession.

First decision is to determine the essential concepts, content, and skills that learners will need to know.

Learning Activities

After determining goals and objectives, the next stage of planning is to determine activities to engage learners and lead to long-term retention and application of content. Activities take on many forms, from teacher-directed instruction to problem-based inquiring learning. In the BTT Model, practitioners are encouraged to use a variety of teaching practices—more traditional forms of teaching might work for some objectives, while in other cases, learners should be led to engage in more interactive tasks such as arts-integrated learning (see Brain-Target Four) or creative problem-solving (see Brain-Target Five). The most important consideration in planning learning activities is to be sure that they are purposeful and relate to learning goals. As Tomlinson and McTighe (2006) point out, teachers should avoid activities that are like "cotton candy—pleasant enough in the moment but lacking long-term substance" (p. 28).

Teaching activities take on many forms, from teacher-directed instruction to problem-based inquiring learning.

At this stage in the planning process, practitioners should consider what evaluations are required such as district-based benchmark assessments or end-of-chapter tests. In addition to those traditional forms of tests, teachers should consider how alternative forms of assessments such as performance-based assessments will be included in the unit, including rubrics for how various activities and assignments will be graded.

From the Expert Practitioner

Mapping the Journey of Learning

Before I finished my teacher education, I used to fantasize about a "road school," where another teacher and I would have twelve students and a big RV and we would essentially take the students on a forty-week-long road trip—the ultimate experiential education. Of course, that would be completely impractical, but I have come to see my 180 days with my students as a journey. And just as I wouldn't have taken them across the country without maps, I don't teach without curriculum maps.

The curriculum maps I create for each unit detail all of the main skills and concepts I will include. Key vocabulary is also included. I use the maps to plan how I will integrate multi-arts and multi-sensory strategies for learning objectives. I also use curriculum maps (or webs) to determine the most efficient way to scaffold prior knowledge. Planning in interdisciplinary teams enriches this exponentially and allows for multidisciplinary activation of schemata. I use the web as a part of my syllabus for each class as well and have found that parents really appreciate having this scope of what their children will learn.

When beginning a unit, I present the map to the class, and we review any prior knowledge they might have. This also helps me to be more analytical in the planning of individual lessons. As a special educator, task analysis has become a huge part of my planning. Within the skills and strategies I am planning, what skills do I assume my students have previously mastered? For instance, when I teach Renaissance-era geography, I know that cartography will be a big part of the learning experience. For the group I have, how much time will I have to spend on key concepts, such as cardinal and intermediate directions, absolute and relative location, and finding accurate scale?

These are some things I think about when creating these curriculum webs: How can I make the curriculum web visually interesting without cluttering it? Where can I post it prominently in the room so that it can also be used as a checklist for mastery of skills and content? How can I include my students as part of the learning design process?

Finally, having a clear visual representation of everything that will be included in a unit of study is an important way for me to be objective about the efficacy of my teaching. I can analyze and prioritize content based on mandated content standards.

Susan Rome
Actress, Higher Education Instructor

Likewise, in any organization, evaluating the attainment of performance goals must be a carefully thought-out process that leads to growth of each member of the community. Our study of evaluation in Brain-Target Six will consider the role of evaluation in learning as well as examine different forms of evaluation.

Having a clear visual representation of everything that will be included in a unit of study is an important way for me to be objective about the efficacy of my teaching. I can analyze and prioritize content based on mandated content standards.

Use of Graphic Organizers in the Brain-Targeted Teaching® Model

The use of graphic organizers in instruction is not new. As discussed earlier, researchers established the important role of organizers for learning and memory as early as the 1960s (Ausubel, 1960). Consistent with these findings, many practitioners include some form of graphic representations of various forms including Venn diagrams, cause/effect charts, linear or cyclic sequences, spiderwebs, or concept pattern organizers. What may be different is the use of a graphic organizer as a framework for a defined unit of study (e.g., a two- or three-week unit on a topic) or a sequence of skills that might extend for the school year. Sharing this advanced organizer with students also can take many forms. Sometimes teachers give students a finished product; other times they provide the beginning of an organizer that students complete as the unit progresses. Hyerle and Alper (2011) described "Thinking Maps" as a tool for presenting a "common visual language for thinking and learning across whole learning communities [and] are taught to students in order for them to improve their unique cognitive abilities and to transfer these processes deeply into academic fields" (p. 3). Below we will see another example of how practitioners use concept maps in their work.

What may be different for some teachers as they consider the BTT Model is the use of a graphic organizer as a framework for a defined unit of study.

From the Expert Practitioner

The Power of Concept Mapping

As a special education coteacher in a secondary English II class, the general educator and I immediately understood the importance of scaffolding for our students. My proposal was that our culminating task include an essay that students submit to our local Mayor and City Council representatives. My coteacher was on board, and we began backwards planning.

Because this was being taught virtually due to school closures during the pandemic, we wanted to be sure our students knew how to construct a cohesive and persuasive argumentative essay while also feeling confident to share their writing with our local leadership. Creating a concept map was crucial for this, and we elected to present this to our classes; through this, students could monitor our collective progress toward our culminating task each week. We also wanted to ensure their writing was supported through the strategic use of graphic organizers. Lastly, because our students would be sharing their work with our local leaders, we wanted to infuse skills beyond their 10th-grade English Common Core standards that can be applied to their daily life: This included evaluating electronic sources, assessing relevant information from articles, and advocating for themselves and others.

Upon finishing the unit plan, concept map, and graphic organizer, we prepared our first lesson where we shared our big goal: drafting argumentative essays on a current-event topic of their choice and sharing that with our local government. The graphic organizer was scaffolded into priority tasks for each day and week, which provided students an opportunity both to self-monitor their use of time and self-evaluate against our concept map. As their research transitioned to writing, we infused the iterative nature of this process through multiple opportunities for peer review—which we scaffolded and modeled—and 1:1 conferencing with students to ensure they were on pace with submitting their culminating written task.

Our students flooded our mayor, city council, my coteacher, and my inboxes with their concerns about our community, cited sources supporting their argument, and suggested action steps based on existing literature. Our local leadership was so moved by this act that it resulted in a Zoom meeting with our entire tenth-grade class. This provided our students with an avenue for our local government to hear more from our students while also responding to their concerns, sharing their proposed actions to work toward solutions, and offering students an opportunity to ask further questions. All of this would not have happened if our students did not have a scaffolded approach through concept mapping to initially express themselves. And because we offered space to hear their concerns, we were able to design a learning experience that was meaningful to them in their development as lifelong learners.

Melissa Sullivan
Special Education Coteacher

From the Expert Practitioner

The Arts in Brain-Target Three

How can teachers/leaders incorporate the power of visual thinking—picture superiority—in our instruction?

Creative Mapping

We have seen how planning with organizational maps can guide the cohesive process that will reach learning goals. If we consider other uses of mapping, we see how it can represent a vast amount of information in a creative and efficient way.

(Continued)

(Continued)

Here are some examples:

- *Story mapping is a versatile graphic tool that can be used for students to learn the elements of a narrative, or in the workplace as a visual planner of, say, a journey of customer experience. Storyboarding is a version of this strategy.*
- *Concept mapping is a diagram of written ideas that are linked with terms or phrases that provide the relationship or connection between ideas.*
- *Personal geographies have learners explore themes of identity, home, and migration by mapping the geographic places that connect to their lives. Map the classroom, school grounds, or neighborhood by walking, then use drawing, video, or photography to create a personal map. (Remember the map of the Thousand Acres Woods in* Winnie the Pooh *or The Middle Earth Map in* Lord of the Rings.*)*

Drawing Is Seeing

Drawing is active learning, unlike the passive listening to a lecture. It requires recall and elaboration into another cognitive mode. In many studies, researchers have found drawing is a powerful way to boost memory, increasing recall by nearly double (e.g., Fernandes et al., 2018). (See more on Drawing strategies in The Arts in Brain-Target Four.)

Opportunities to Incorporate Drawing

Visual notetaking uses icons, diagrams, simple drawings, and symbols along with text annotations to represent ideas and information. Visual note taking is often called sketchnoting.

Graphic organizers provide nonlinguistic communication, making information and content clear and accessible. Learner's analysis of graphic organizers, charts, maps, and data displays improve their ability to communicate ideas, visualize concepts, and bring creativity to their work. Use impactful, generative imagery in instruction.

Clare O'Malley Grizzard
Arts Educator, Arts Integration Specialist

With so much learning going on at so many levels, a good concept map helps to keeps us all—students, teachers, parents, and workers in any profession—purposefully moving along toward common learning goals.

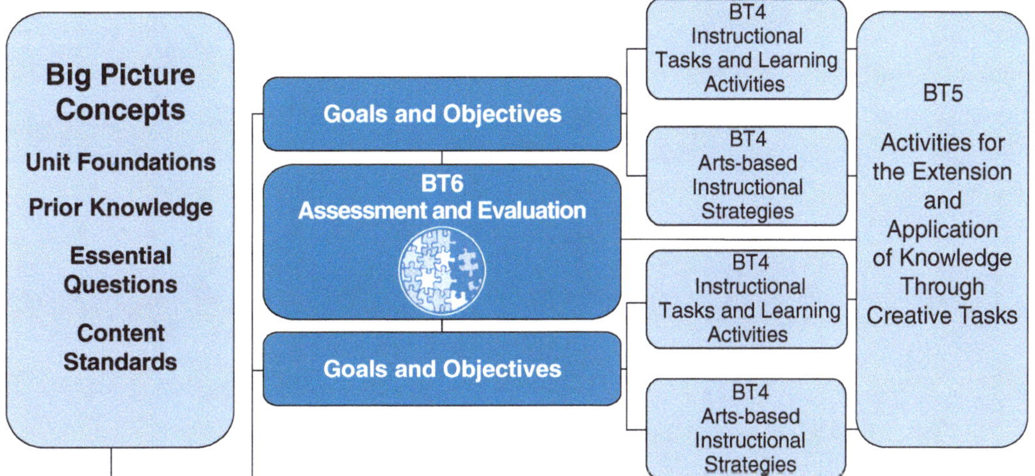

7 Brain-Target Four

Teaching for Mastery of Content, Skills, and Concepts

If teaching were the same as telling, we'd all be so smart we could hardly stand it.

—Mark Twain

Brain-Target Four - Mastery of Content, Skills and Concepts Chapter Map

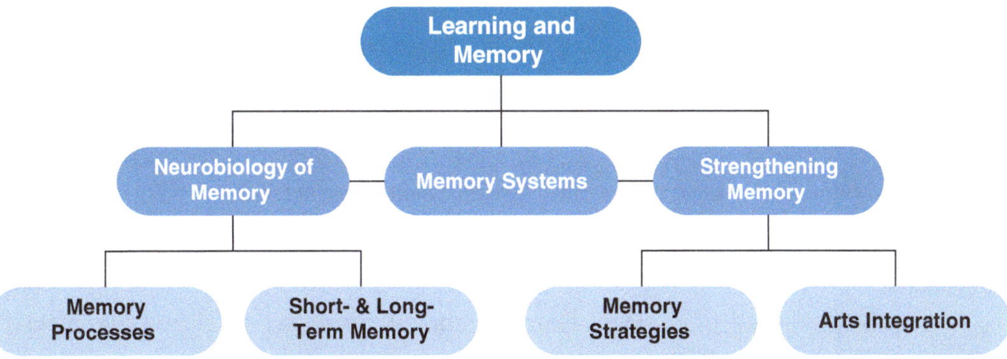

Formal schooling is built on the assumption that students learn content, skills, and concepts that will help them throughout life. Although debates continue in the educational arena over the importance of acquiring knowledge versus *learning how to think*, the Brain-Targeted Teaching® (BTT) Model is built upon the assumption that the latter is in many ways dependent on the former. In other words, in order to be effective thinkers, children must possess the background knowledge needed to be literate in today's society and perform everyday tasks at a high level. Moreover, they also must strive to become lifelong learners—creative problem-solvers who can engage in inquiry and discovery. For the next two components of the model, we review ways that teachers can promote mastery of targeted learning goals (Brain-Target Four) and help students learn to apply knowledge in creative ways in real-world problem-solving tasks (Brain-Target Five).

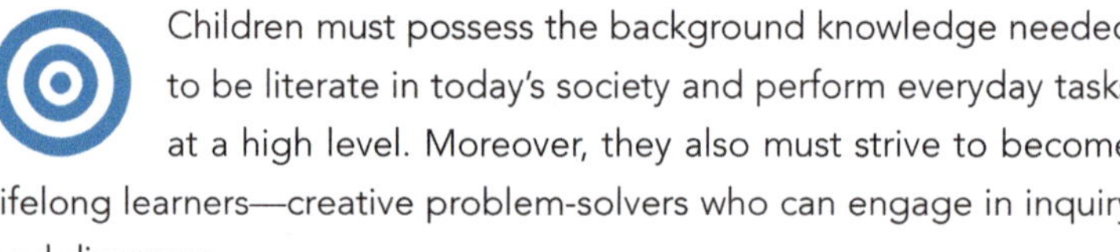

Children must possess the background knowledge needed to be literate in today's society and perform everyday tasks at a high level. Moreover, they also must strive to become lifelong learners—creative problem-solvers who can engage in inquiry and discovery.

In the discussion of Brain-Target Three in the last chapter, we focused on the *what* of teaching—the key goals upon which BTT learning units are built. We suggest displaying those goals and the activities that help students reach them in visual representations to promote big-picture thinking—both for the benefit of the teacher, who plans instruction, and for the benefit of the student, who learns from instruction. As we continue on our journey through the BTT Model, we now begin to focus on the *how* of teaching—that is, on strategies teachers can use to bring students to mastery in a given domain. In this chapter, we first consider how learning depends fundamentally on memory processes. We will review human memory systems and discuss how memories are encoded and retrieved. We then examine research from the learning sciences on factors that improve long-term memory for material that is important to retain. Finally, we will discuss how these factors can be leveraged through the use of certain instructional strategies, in particular the integration of visual and performing arts into classroom activities.

Learning and Memory

Like twin stars, learning and memory are intricately connected. Learning is the acquisition of new information, and memory allows this information to be stored and then recalled as needed at a later time. Lasting memories for some information are created after just a single exposure, while other times, memories form only after many repetitions. In 1890, William James's seminal work, *Principles of Psychology,* described memory as the recollection of *states of mind* that occurred in the past. Influenced by this early work, *information processing theory* emerged in the middle of the 20th century as a way to understand how information is received and processed through the senses, maintained in temporary memory systems, and potentially stored in long-term memory to be retrieved later for use in thought or action. The prototypical model of information processing is depicted in the figure below.

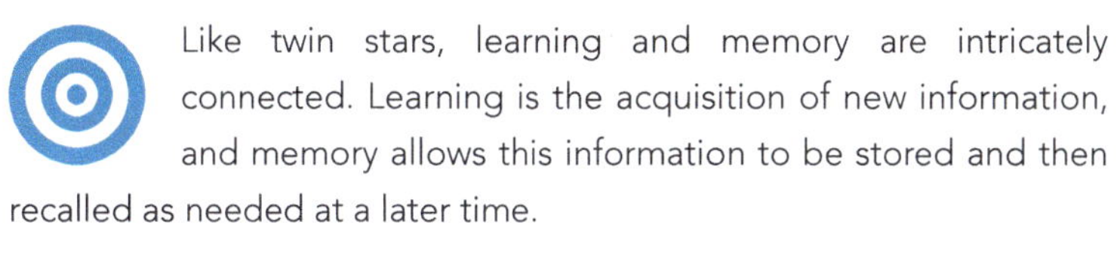

Like twin stars, learning and memory are intricately connected. Learning is the acquisition of new information, and memory allows this information to be stored and then recalled as needed at a later time.

Types of Memory Processes

Rather than being a *vessel* for information, memory is better thought of as a collection of systems and processes that serve a variety of functions. Certain *types* of memory often overlap with one another, and classifications employed by scientists are driven in many ways by distinctions among the various kinds of information people can remember.

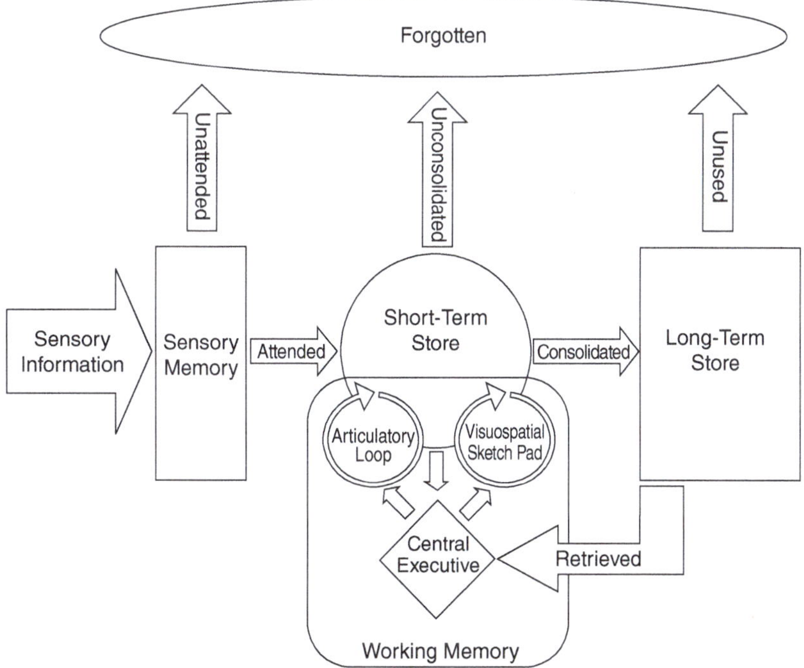

The Information Processing Model

Scientists have developed theoretical models for memory systems that deal with everything from unnoticed sensory input to information that is etched on our minds for life. Although there are differences between theorists regarding the details of these models, they generally address three different kinds of phenomena: (a) quickly fleeting memory for sensory information, (b) short-term and working memory (forms of temporary storage), and (c) long-term memory (the relatively permanent storage of information).

Sensory Memory

Sensory memory, which lasts from milliseconds to seconds, refers to the very brief storage of large amounts of visual, auditory, olfactory, or haptic input from the environment. The vast majority of this information never reaches other memory systems; our brains filter out about 99% of sensory information because it is irrelevant (Byrne, 2017). However, as was first shown for visual information by Sperling (1960), we are able to retrieve sensory data for a short time after it is received, even if we are not consciously paying attention to it. For example, even when not actively listening, we might be able to repeat back the last word we heard from a television commercial, because auditory information briefly persists in our sensory memory as a kind of *echo* that we can reproduce. However, this type of memory is fleeting, and sensory information is not processed further by other memory systems unless some kind of meaning is attached to the stimulus (Gazzaniga et al., 2009).

Our brains filter out about 99% of sensory information because it is irrelevant.

Short-Term and Working Memory

Short-term memory and *working memory* are often used interchangeably in the memory literature to describe the temporary storage of information. Though these forms of memory likely share some of the same neural or cognitive mechanisms, short-term and working memory models are conceptually distinct and account for somewhat different phenomena (Byrne, 2017; Nadel & Hardt, 2011). Fundamentally, short-term memory refers to the temporary storage of information that was just received for up to about twenty seconds (though this span can be increased if information is actively rehearsed mentally). Working memory, conversely, refers to a more complex cognitive system in which information is held in one's conscious awareness in order to perform computations or manipulate that information in some way. The first in-depth theory of working memory (and the best known) is that offered by Baddeley and Hitch (1974), who created a model to describe the basic processes through which information is received, maintained, and retrieved. Information held in working memory often comes from the environment—for example, prices that are kept in mind to do mental arithmetic and figure out how much is saved with a discount. However, working memory is also used to retrieve and manipulate information already stored in long-term memory. For instance, working memory is what allows one to bring to mind previously scheduled appointments in order to figure out when to schedule a new one.

Short-term and working memory models are conceptually distinct and account for somewhat different phenomena.

According to Baddeley (2020), working memory has three components: (a) a central executive that receives information from the senses or long-term memory, activating either (b) the *phonological loop* (for verbal information) or (c) the *visuospatial sketchpad* (for visual/spatial information). These latter two components of working memory serve to maintain information within conscious awareness so that the information can be acted upon. Repeated rehearsal of novel information within the phonological loop or visuospatial sketchpad can contribute to the formation of long-term memories, as can the deeper processing associated with performing mental operations on information. Usually, however, once information from the external environment has been acted upon, it is no longer needed and is lost from memory.

Once information from the external environment has been acted upon, it is no longer needed and is lost from memory.

It is important here to address the popular belief that short-term and/or working memory has a capacity of approximately seven items. This belief was spawned by Miller's (1956) article about *the magical number seven*, in which he noted that people's capacity for processing information appears in a variety of different cases to be limited to seven (plus or minus two) *items*, where items include things like digits or words. Following Miller's work, many people subsequently drew the conclusion that short-term or working memory capacity *in general* is limited to seven items or *chunks*. This conclusion is an overinterpretation of Miller's article, and, since its publication, numerous counterexamples and mitigating factors (e.g., expertise in a given domain, practice, etc.) have been recognized (Shiffrin & Nosofsky, 1994). Fundamentally, Miller meant only to highlight people's limited capacity for information processing. Yet the idea that working memory capacity is strictly limited to seven items still persists as a myth—despite more recent evidence (such as that offered by Cowan, 2001) that if it is reasonable to ascribe to working memory a general limit of this sort at all, this limit is probably closer to about four chunks. Complicating matters, this conclusion is based on the assumption that information can be readily divided into obvious chunks. In many practical situations, there is no one obvious way to chunk information and therefore little to no justification for carving instructional content into a preordained number of chunks. Instead, practitioners should simply rely on their intuitions and seek out relatively natural ways to chunk information. For any given task, what's important is to think about the amount of information learners might need to maintain within their conscious awareness at one time, look for helpful ways to chunk that information, and avoid overwhelming students with too many isolated pieces of information.

Based on the foundational work of Sweller (1988) and often referenced in teaching and instructional design is the theory of cognitive load—focusing on providing information that is optimal for the learners' working memory and to be aware of avoiding overloading learners with information that makes it difficult to focus on essential learning tasks. Chen and Kalyuga (2020) provide evidence that cognitive load can deplete working memory resources and suggest ways to mitigate this effect such as periods of rest and the use of chunking and spacing learning episodes over time.

Long-Term Memory

Long-term memory refers to the retention of information (without active rehearsal) for a significant amount of time, whether years or a lifetime. Though information that is not retrieved every now and then tends to be forgotten over time, the total volume of information that can be retained in long-term memory is for all practical purposes unlimited. An important overarching distinction within long-term memory is the difference between *explicit* and *implicit* memory. Further distinctions between different forms of memory can be considered within each of these broad headings.

Explicit memory. All explicit memory can also be described as *declarative* memory. This form of memory deals with knowledge that one is consciously aware of, such as events that occur in our lives or information we have knowingly acquired. When we recall events from our past, like performing in a play or winning a tennis match, this is referred to as *episodic memory*. Episodic memory does not function by storing and retrieving all the information associated with an event. As Squire and Kandel (1999) explain, unlike a video camera, we are not able to simply *mentally record* events exactly as they occur. Each time we remember an event, we use key pieces of remembered information to reconstruct the experience; this sometimes results in changes to details or more significant inaccuracies or embellishments. Episodic memory is generally contrasted with *semantic* memory, which refers to our ability to remember facts or concepts—propositions about the world, meanings of symbols and words, grammar rules, uses for objects, mathematical ideas, and so on. Both types of declarative memory, episodic and semantic, are critical for allowing us to access and use our knowledge so that we can conduct our everyday lives (Baddeley, 2020).

> When we recall events from our past, like performing in a play or winning a tennis match, this is referred to as *episodic memory.* Both types of declarative memory, episodic and semantic, are critical for allowing us to access and use our knowledge so that we can conduct our everyday lives.

Implicit memory. Fundamentally, implicit memory refers to experiences that we remember without conscious awareness that learning is taking place. Though there are several types of implicit memory, the most important one to distinguish is *procedural memory*. Procedural memory is often contrasted with declarative memory and supports our ability to *know how* to do something without thinking about it. Procedural memory explains why we can learn to perform certain tasks without being able to say precisely how we're doing them. For example, when we learn how to ride a bike, there are a few relatively vague things that others might tell us to do (e.g., "push on the pedals," "steer," etc.), but for the most part, we learn how to ride a bike through practice and trial and error. As we try and try again to ride the bicycle, a wide variety of motor processes are taking place, and movements and actions that lead to success are stored in our memory systems without our conscious awareness. Procedural memory is very important in school settings, but the ways in which children rely on procedural memory are not always easy to recognize. For instance, when learning to read, students acquire decoding skills through repeated exposure and practice—that is, through a largely hidden process of implicit, procedural learning (Byrne, 2017).

Procedural memory explains why we can learn to perform certain tasks without being able to say precisely how we're doing them.

Memory Systems in Daily Life

In summary, although our sensory, short-term, working, and long-term memory systems are distinct from one another, they are interrelated in important ways. Further, memory is influenced by many factors, including our experiences, our senses, the importance we assign to information, and what we do with information once we receive it.

To consider how the memory systems work together, imagine the following scenario: An announcement is made asking you to attend a special meeting. The meeting will be held in room 128, and, as you are walking down the hall, you pass by the lighted gym before reaching your destination. At the meeting, the leader announces that the organization will receive a grant for sixty new computers from the Azzara Foundation. What might you remember from this experience, and for how long? What types of memory will be utilized?

First, following the announcement, you must initially rehearse the room number to yourself in order to maintain it in working memory; however, once the meeting is over and this information is no longer needed, it will likely soon be forgotten. As you head toward the meeting, the directions to the designated room must be retrieved and held in working memory long enough for you to get to the right location. As you pass by the gym, the light from inside would reach your visual system, but unless this has some importance or meaning that would lead you to pay particular attention, this sensory information would likely not be retained even in short-term memory, let alone long-term memory. The Azzara Foundation may be known to you, or it may have no meaning or significance at all—in which case the name may be retained only briefly in short-term memory. When you hear that your organization will receive sixty computers, you will likely hold that information in working memory in order to figure out that since there are six teachers or employees, they will be receiving ten computers for their use. The total number of computers might be forgotten but could perhaps be reconstructed based on what you know. The memories from the meeting itself that would be most likely to stay in long-term memory would be those having to do with the computers you now see in your classrooms or workspaces.

Neurobiology of Learning and Memory

As discussed in Chapter 2, the typical neuron shares information by *firing* an electrical impulse down its axon, where this impulse causes the release of various neurotransmitter chemicals at tiny junctions between neurons called synapses. On the other side of each synapse, a dendrite attached to another neuron takes up these neurotransmitters. If the aggregate excitatory input from other neurons reaches a certain threshold, the neuron receiving these signals fires, transferring the signal on to its neighbors. Through this process, signals travel from one neuron to the next along complex neural pathways that weave their way through the brain, producing all of our thoughts and behaviors. In the 1940s, Donald Hebb (1949) proposed that neural connections are strengthened when groups of neurons are actively generating signals (i.e., firing) at the same time. This idea is the origin of the oft-heard phrase "neurons that fire together, wire together." The more often groups of neurons fire simultaneously, the more strongly and efficiently signals are transmitted among them, a process known as *long-term potentiation*. Repeated activation of neural circuits binds them together in patterns of connectivity that underlie the creation of memory traces or *engrams*. The more frequently these neural connections are used, the stronger they become, making memories longer lasting and easier to retrieve.

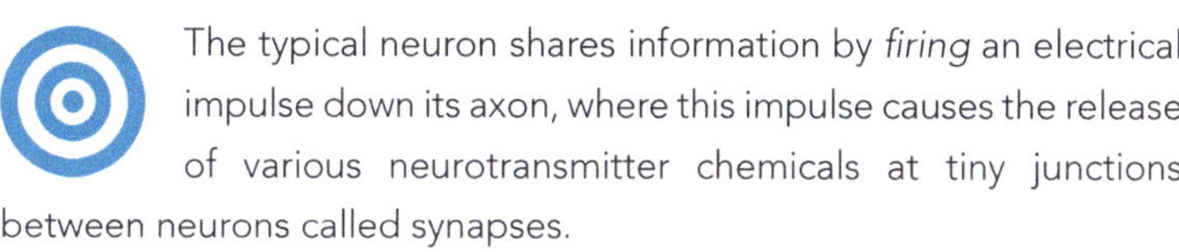
The typical neuron shares information by *firing* an electrical impulse down its axon, where this impulse causes the release of various neurotransmitter chemicals at tiny junctions between neurons called synapses.

Through studies of patients who have experienced brain damage, scientists have learned more about the biological basis of complex memory systems. Scientists have discovered that damage to the hippocampus, for example, disrupts the ability to form new long-term memories. Nobel Prize winner Eric Kandel (2006) explains that memory is a mental function distinct from perception, motor activity, or cognitive ability, and that temporary and long-term memory systems perform separate functions and involve different brain regions. Though damage to the hippocampus can affect the formation of long-term memories, this does not mean that long-term memory is located in the hippocampus, however. As is the case with many brain functions, the story is considerably more complex. Although the hippocampus has been shown to be crucial for memory formation, the patterns of activity related to long-term storage and retrieval of information spread across a variety of areas in the cerebral cortex.

Memory is a mental function distinct from perception, motor activity, or cognitive ability, and temporary and long-term memory systems perform separate functions and involve different brain regions.

The question of how and why some pieces of information are remembered long-term and others are forgotten continues to be the subject of research in various disciplines. However, some important understandings have now been firmly established by neuroscience. For example, we now know that the brain needs time to solidify memories in long-term storage, a process called *consolidation*. Another significant finding is that for temporary memory, synapses use existing proteins inside the cell, whereas the conversion from temporary to long-term memory involves the synthesis of new regulatory proteins (Kandel, 2006).

We now know that the brain needs time to solidify memories in long-term storage, a process called *consolidation*.

In summary, lifelong learning requires that new information be specifically consolidated within long-term memory to produce permanent storage. As practitioners, it is important to understand that acquiring knowledge that can be subsequently retrieved and applied is not something that just happens. Learning is a neuro-physiological phenomenon that occurs through biochemical processes in the brain and the growth and reorganization of neural connections. In the next section, we will examine teaching practices that can facilitate learning and aid in the creation of long-term memories, thereby helping learners master the content, skills, and concepts that are crucial for success in the classroom and workplace. Below, we see the importance of promoting long-term memory in the workplace as well as in schools.

From the Expert Practitioner

Long-Term Learning in the Business and Industry Workplace

The nuclear industry, like training in many other business and industry settings, has traditionally placed a heavy emphasis on helping learners to take in, or encode, new information. Often this encoding process has involved encouraging students to review information in study sessions on their own time or to

review content and objectives in the classroom. Although the encoding process is critical to getting information into long-term memory, it usually falls short of being sufficient to improve employee performance.

If the goal of workplace training is to create learning that transfers from the classroom to workplace application, then we must teach workers how to apply knowledge. To apply knowledge, however, assumes that learners can first recall the information that they need to apply. Though new learning may have been encoded into long-term memory, the learner must be able to flexibly recall and apply knowledge.

What does this mean for teaching and learning in the nuclear industry? We now know that we must teach students about these separate pathways and that for learning to last and be useful at work, we must practice recalling information if we want it to be available for critical thinking and problem-solving after training is completed. Recall practice can also be extended into the work environment to increase the probability that prior learning can be retrieved from long-term memory into working memory for workplace application.

Pamela Terry, EdD
Manager, Nuclear Industry Training

Arts Integration for Mastery of Content, Skills, and Concepts

Though rote learning certainly has been overemphasized in the past, the fact that students need to remember basic information related to what they are learning cannot be ignored. There is no way around the need for students to have at their disposal content knowledge ("knowing that . . .") and procedural skills ("knowing how . . ."). Though conceptual understanding is what practitioners are rightly striving for, facts and skills are often prerequisites to this deep understanding. It is impossible to understand subtraction, for instance, if you cannot count.

As previously noted, in order for information to be retained, it must make its way from short-term to long-term memory. In a review of research on factors known to improve long-term memory for information, I argue that arts integration, the use of the arts as a pedagogical method for enhancing and reinforcing learning goals, represents a powerful strategy for helping to make sure that information *sticks* in children's memories. The argument is based on the notion that many forms of artistic practice naturally incorporate activities that have been shown in research from the neuro- and cognitive sciences to aid retention of information (Rinne et al., 2011). Here we consider these research findings in some detail, as arts integration is at the core of the BTT Model and in particular of Brain-Target Four.

Arts integration, the use of the arts as a pedagogical method for enhancing and reinforcing learning goals, represents a powerful strategy for helping to make sure that information *sticks* in children's memories.

Before a deeper consideration of the research, though, it is important to first distinguish between arts education and arts integration. Arts education, including instruction in instrumental music, vocal music, visual arts, theater, dance, and creative writing must be recognized as an important area of study for students of all ages. Although arts advocates (myself included) agree that engaging in the arts *for its own sake* is important for every child, a growing body of research is also demonstrating that the arts are positively related to academic performance and promote the development of cognitive skills and capacities that transfer to core academic disciplines. Others argue that engagement with artistic activity still serves to cultivate *habits of mind* important for academic success. These include dispositions such as persistence in working on tasks over a sustained period, expression of one's personal voice, and reflective self-evaluation of work. Though these dispositions are not associated with any particular content area, they certainly lead to more effective learning.

All three of the arguments offered previously in favor of arts instruction—the arts *for its own sake*, as a means to enhancing academic and cognitive skills, and as a way of fostering useful dispositions—are good ones. Nonetheless, it needs to be recognized that there is yet another potential benefit of the arts that has often been overlooked; that is, integrating artistic activities into instruction is likely to enhance long-term memory for content. To test this theory, my team at Johns Hopkins University (Hardiman et al., 2014, 2019) conducted two randomized control trials testing the effects of arts-integrated instruction for long-term retention of academic content. We developed arts-integrated and conventional versions of four fifth-grade science units. Randomized groups of students received one body of content through an arts-integrated unit and a second body of content in a controlled unit that employed a traditional presentation. The units contained the same content but differed in the instructional delivery. For example, in the control condition, students displayed knowledge by completing a chart or presenting information orally; in the arts-integrated treatment condition, students sketched, sang, chanted a rap, or used body movement such as tableau to demonstrate the content or concept. Curriculum-based assessments conducted at the conclusion of each of the units showed that from pre-testing to post-testing, students learned approximately the same amount of information regardless of the way they were taught. However, approximately ten weeks later, delayed test scores were significantly better for the arts-integrated condition. The study found a differential benefit when comparing students according to levels of proficiency in reading: Students at the lower levels of achievement were the most likely to retain significantly more science content when given arts-integrated lessons than when given traditional science instruction. Could it be that the arts provided a different modality for learning that benefited students who struggle with traditional approaches to instruction? In summary, our work demonstrated how integrating the arts into content instruction produced better long-term retention of the content.

So how can the arts lead to better memory? Below, I review a variety of memory effects that have been the subject of considerable study over the last thirty years. Though conventional instruction could also be adapted to take advantage of these effects, I argue that arts-integrated instruction does the job *naturally,* guiding teachers' planning and implementation of instruction based on rigorous scientific research. Throughout the remainder of this chapter, you will hear from teachers who have experience in arts integration. The stories of these expert teachers further demonstrate the power of the arts in the classroom. They demonstrate activities that can be naturally incorporated into instruction without the need for specific training in arts instruction. Therefore, teachers who feel they are not *artistic* or are not highly trained in various forms of art need not worry; the process of using the arts in instruction does not require that one be a skilled artist. Rather, arts integration is about increasing learning through the promotion of artistic thinking and habits of working.

Arts integration is about increasing learning through the promotion of artistic thinking and habits of working.

Repeated Rehearsal

One of the most important strategies for establishing long-term retention is rehearsal, the process of repeating information to oneself or others in an effort to commit it to memory. Just as muscles are built through their repeated use, memories can be built through repeated rehearsals. It has long been known that repeated rehearsal improves recall of information, especially when rehearsals are spaced over time (e.g., Rundus, 1971). Effective rehearsal strategies help to form more elaborate memory traces that tie pieces of information together or connect them to other content or concepts (Baddeley, 2020).

Promoting rehearsal during instruction seems fairly intuitive. Teachers regularly give students multiple opportunities to rehearse information through classroom and independent assignments. Still, teachers (as well as corporate trainers) often find it challenging to provide enough variety in activities within a compressed learning cycle to promote repeated rehearsal of information without constantly resorting to the same (sometimes tedious) methods and modalities. Grounding activities in various forms of art motivates students to rehearse information in new and creative ways with each iteration. This allows teachers to keep students interested while reinforcing learning on multiple occasions with appropriate space between repetitions. In addition, teaching with and through the arts helps to motivate student learning and promotes sustained attention to tasks (Posner & Patoine, 2009).

Elaboration

As noted above, repeated rehearsal can create more elaborate memory traces and increase retention. Research has also shown that the act of elaboration by itself is an effective way to make information more memorable. In their work, *Make It Stick*, Brown et al. (2014) describe elaboration as the process of giving new material meaning. Learners express new knowledge in their own words and connect it to their prior knowledge. The authors explain how elaboration helps students draw on their prior knowledge to learn new information, which in turn helps with long-term retention of the new material. The arts provide students with numerous ways to elaborate on subject matter and relate it to their own lives. For example, students can elaborate on what they learn in any content area through the visual arts (e.g., drawing a scene from history or literature in which students place themselves), the performing arts (e.g., writing and acting out a skit that depicts a concept as it applies to them), creative writing (e.g., poetry or rap that demonstrates understanding and includes important facts and details), or tableau (e.g., assuming a body posture to represent a scene from a story or historical event).

The act of elaboration by itself is an effective way to make information more memorable.

From the Expert Practitioner

Eye of the Beholder

The arts can provide a new context in which students can apply their newly mastered knowledge. I design relevancy and personal agency into all my learning units. Through projects that require students to find and make personal meaning and examine real social issues, they can see that art has a place in their lives—offering them a chance to actively participate in the world around them.

For example, my eighth-grade students took part in a unit I called "EYE OF THE BEHOLDER." Students examined social ills beginning with questioning their lives and the world at large. They address questions such as the following: What have you seen that you wish you had not seen? What injustices have you encountered in your own life, your community, your school, or the world? What things do you wish you could change in the world? What things are wrong with life as we live it?

Students selected social justice topics based on a real experience, or ones that evoked strong feelings—something that enraged them. Through the use of printmaking and collage, students were to open our eyes—peers, teachers, the community—to a problem in the world. This project was about building public awareness and action around topics of social injustices and taking the classroom experience outside of the school. Students wrote to local organizations, and in the end donated their artwork to their organization of choice. Adam, for example, chose environmental degradation as his theme. He volunteered with various local organizations and was one of the founding members of the school's Environmental Club. His poster reflects the decay and destruction he experiences daily. Adam wrote a letter to the Chesapeake Bay Foundation to offer his artwork and his pledge to continue to work for the environment. Maggie chose homophobia as her theme. She researched the lives of various openly gay public figures and came across a Time *magazine article about Leonard P. Matlovich. She chose to use one of his quotes for her poster explaining that his words said it all. Her poster includes the quotation, "When I was in the military they gave me a medal for killing two men and a discharge for loving one."*

Vanessa Lopez-Sparaco
Artist, Arts Educator

Generation

Too often in traditional instructional programs, students are passive recipients of information and ideas—they listen to lectures, read texts, and reproduce information they have already received by completing worksheets, writing out short answers, or choosing responses from multiple-choice questions. There is well-established evidence, however, that when people are not just provided information in written or oral form, but rather generate that information themselves in response to some kind of prompt, their recall of that information is significantly improved (McCurdy et al., 2017; McCurdy et al., 2020; Zormpa et al., 2019).

Generating information requires active learning, which has been shown to produce better retention than passive information input. In general, if teachers identify content that is important and seek out ways to get students to generate relevant information, this will make content *stick* better. Although it may seem daunting to try and find ways to coax students into generating information, the arts can be a very useful tool for doing just this. For example, if students are asked to depict ideas visually, they will naturally generate details that they might otherwise simply be told to them, and these details will be retained better. Generating information through art also engages students in various forms of divergent thinking—thinking that leads to a variety of possible outputs or solutions. The topic of divergent thinking will be covered in greater depth when we consider creative problem-solving in conjunction with Brain-Target Five.

> When people are not just provided information in written or oral form, but rather generate that information themselves in response to some kind of prompt, their recall of that information is significantly improved. Generating information through art also engages students in various forms of divergent thinking—thinking that leads to a variety of possible outputs or solutions.

Enactment

Enactment involves physically acting out information or ideas and is naturally a part of activities such as role-playing or theatrical improvisation. Studies have demonstrated that retention of information is improved when participants actively perform an action phrase instead of merely reading that same information (Haverkamp et al., 2020; Makri & Jarrold, 2021). In a meta-analysis of studies on the enactment effect, Roberts and colleagues (2022) found a boost in memory when subjects performed a physical action compared to reading, watching others perform, or engaging in self-generated thoughts. They highlight two important factors that account for enhanced memory: planning the action and actually performing the action.

Acting usually involves some sort of motor activity that aids memory. In addition to enhancing memory for information, enactment also has the benefit, like generation, of engaging students in divergent thinking.

Using dramatic enactment as a teaching tool—from simple role-playing to staging full-fledged theatrical productions—has been shown to have positive effects on learning. Catterall (2009) outlines a compendium of studies that demonstrate how dramatic enactment in academic settings has a positive influence on both scholastic performance (e.g., story comprehension, character analysis, writing proficiency) and social skills (e.g., peer interactions, conflict resolution skills, self-concept). The physical and mental processes involved in acting out material instead of simply reading or listening to it have the power to cement targeted content into long-term memory. And it should not be forgotten that dramatic enactment is just plain fun, and activities that students find fun are obvious assets for teachers.

Using dramatic enactment as a teaching tool—from simple role-playing to staging full-fledged theatrical productions—has been shown to have positive effects on learning.

From the Expert Practitioner

Physics and the Arts—A Natural Fit

I am a high school physics teacher. I am a dancer. While those two professions may seem like polar opposites, to me they come together in how I teach every day. In dance I use body motions to convey the desired emotions to an audience; in the physics laboratory I use explorations and mathematics to convey the desired learning objectives to my students. In my classroom these two practices naturally merge in amazing ways.

This started my first year when I asked my students to explain Newton's three laws of motion to me in some art form. I was expecting a few songs, cartoons, and an overwhelming display of posters. While I did get a few

(Continued)

(Continued)

posters, I mostly got a vast array of art forms, and my students blew me away with their creativity. There was everything from rap songs complete with back-up vocals and a dance, to a play titled Three Laws: The Life and Physics of Sir Isaac Newton. *Most of my students wanted to demonstrate to their peers how they were able to make physics fun, and in the end I videotaped a number of student performances. The next few years, I even used the video clips in my teaching to help explain the ideas of inertia, acceleration, and action-reaction forces—leading off with a folk song called "Think Science."*

This project caused me to take my classes in whole new directions as often as I could. Previously I had been using the standard practice of lecture, lab, homework format of physics, but now I was including prerecorded clips of dancers and figure skaters spinning in circles to explain angular momentum. I was asking musicians to play their portable instruments to demonstrate the properties of waves and sounds. I was using photography to explain refraction, or the bending of light, in optics. Whenever I can within the physics content, I get the students involved in viewing and creating art. And their skills often exceed mine in so many artistic ways.

*Now as students come back to see me during alumni days, they are eager to tell me about physics in their daily lives and how topics we covered in class keep coming up in their experiences. Like why you bend your knees (pile) before or landing a jump—to store more elastic potential energy before the jump or to increase how long it takes to change your momentum thereby decreasing the force impacted to your body coming down. They may not remember the speed of light (c = 2.99*108 m/s), but they remember how a fish-eye camera lens bends the light to create the effect.*

Stephanie Rafferty
Teacher, High School Physics

Production

The production effect describes improvements in memory that arise when words are produced aloud rather than silently read (MacLeod & Bodner, 2017; Zormpa et al., 2019). In a context in which surrounding material is read, orally producing key words or phrases makes them distinct, and Ozubko and MacLeod (2010) argue that this is what causes them to be retained better. Teachers who emphasize multisensory learning, whether through materials based on multiple intelligences, formal programs for students with dyslexia, or simply through sheer instinct, have long recognized the value of using multiple modalities for expressive language tasks. The performing arts provide a natural way for students to orally produce key content in creative, elaborative ways. Art forms such as music, poetry, rap, and skits provide similarly powerful vehicles for oral production of content that teachers want students to remember over the long term.

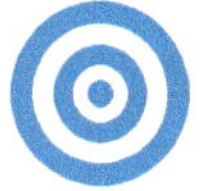

The production effect describes improvements in memory that arise when words are produced aloud rather than silently read.

Effort After Meaning

The concept of *effort after meaning* was first described by one of the pioneers of modern psychology, Frederic Bartlett (1932). Effort after meaning refers to the thinking that one engages in to make sense of stimuli in the environment—for example, sentences, images, and events. Effort after meaning is an important factor for memory; research has shown that when people must puzzle over a stimulus a bit in order to understand it, they end up remembering that stimulus better than they would if its meaning were made more obvious For example, in an early study of this effect, Auble and Franks (1978) presented study participants with ambiguous sentences, such as, "The man was hungry because the pole broke." Participants naturally struggled for a short time to make sense of that sentence. If they had been told immediately that "the man was a fisherman," they would not have had to exert as much effort to understand the text, and therefore would have had weaker long-term retention of the sentence. Zaromb and Roediger (2009) argue that the act of exerting special effort to understand information is a relatively unusual occurrence, and, as with generation and enactment, this leads to greater processing and better memory for content.

Effort after meaning is an important factor for memory; research has shown that when people must puzzle over a stimulus a bit in order to understand it, they end up remembering that stimulus better than they would if its meaning were made more obvious.

The exertion of effort after meaning is something that occurs naturally when people interpret art. In order to construct meaning of a painting or poem, for instance, students often must grapple with ideas before being able to demonstrate their own interpretation. If teachers embed the content they teach within a piece of visual art, students will need to make an effort in order to get at the underlying idea, and this will likely lead to better memory of that idea. There are ample opportunities to place educational content in artistic contexts. For example, visual art is full of geometry, and many poems and songs reference historical figures, cultural identities, and events. When this kind of information is presented to students through art rather than in isolation in a textbook or on a worksheet, students will naturally need to make an effort to understand the material they encounter. And this effort need not be an arduous one. With art, many students will make this effort joyfully, because they find art to be interesting and stimulating.

Exertion of effort after meaning is something that occurs naturally when people interpret art.

Pictorial Representation

The saying that "a picture is worth a thousand words" is not mere folklore. Studies have long shown that people often remember information better when it is presented in the form of pictures rather than words, even when the memory is assessed through verbal measures (e.g., Shepard, 1967). This *picture superiority effect* may occur at least in part because pictures are encoded both through visual and verbal mental processes while encoding words requires only verbal processing Moreover, pictures may require a greater level of conceptual processing than words, potentially leading to better retention of pictorial representations (McBride & Dosher, 2002; Zormpa et al., 2019).

The saying that "a picture is worth a thousand words" is not mere folklore.

Programs such as Artful Thinking (www.pz.harvard.edu), which originated from Harvard's Project Zero, use visual images such as works of art to encourage students to develop thinking processes and dispositions—such as curiosity, observation, comparison, and connection of ideas—that are important for learning. For example, students might view a painting and make observations about technical details of the painting, its relation to other genres from the historical period, or the painter's purpose in producing the work. Using pictorial representations helps to make students' thinking visible and promotes deeper conceptual processing through thoughtful questioning, consideration of subject matter from historical and social viewpoints, and exploration of new points of view.

Using pictorial representations helps to make students' thinking visible and promotes deeper conceptual processing through thoughtful questioning, consideration of subject matter from historical and social viewpoints, and exploration of new points of view.

Emotion and Memory

Most of us remember vivid details when we recall catastrophic events such as the terrorist attacks of September 11, 2001. We may have keen recollection of visual images from newscasts and remember where we were, who we were with, the exact time of day when hearing the news, and even the weather. For catastrophic events or even pleasant ones such as a birth or a wedding, our brains are capable of creating *flash-bulb memories* that last a lifetime.

Events producing flashbulb memories and ideas that carry emotional meaning can have lasting effects on learning. Research suggests that emotional arousal influences what we pay attention to (Immordino-Yang et al., 2018), and this can affect immediate as well as long-term memory (Tyng et al., 2017). Moreover, information that causes either positive or negative emotional arousal is remembered better over the long-term than that which is emotionally neutral (Cahill & McGaugh, 1995). As described in Chapter 4 on Brain-Target One, there is also evidence that positive emotions influence global understanding and promote better performance on cognition and creative thinking tasks.

Information that causes either positive or negative emotional arousal is remembered better over the long-term than that which is emotionally neutral.

Artistic activities provide the perfect way for students to explore what they are learning through emotional expression. Any form of artistic activity has the potential to forge emotional connections to content that are richer and more rewarding than those achieved using conventional teaching strategies. The arts encourage provocative questions, careful observations, exploration of multiple viewpoints, and new modes of interpretation.

Pedagogical Strategies for Forming Strong Memories

Mnemonics

Many of us have relied on mnemonics throughout our lives to remember information such as the order of notes on the treble clef (EGBDF—"Every Good Boy Does Fine"). For information that must be straightforwardly committed to memory, mnemonics clearly work (see Akpan et al., 2021). Mnemonics can take the form of acrostic sentences as in the example above. Acronyms are useful mnemonics too. Many of us learned, for example, "ROY G. BIV" to remember the order of the colors in the light spectrum (red, orange, yellow, green, blue, indigo, violet) and "Please Excuse My Dear Aunt Sally" for the order of operations in arithmetic (parenthesis, exponents, multiplication, division, addition, subtraction). Mnemonics can also take the form of rhymes and phrases such as "i before e except after c" or "In fourteen hundred ninety-two, Columbus sailed the ocean blue." Mnemonics may stick with us for life, remaining our primary means of recalling information. For instance, it may be difficult for many of us to recall which months have thirty days without reciting to ourselves "Thirty days hath September, April, June, and November."

For information that must be straightforwardly committed to memory, mnemonics clearly work.

A study conducted with high school students with learning disabilities shows that the use of mnemonics was significantly more effective in vocabulary acquisition compared to traditional methods (Whitescarver, 2018). Thus, it is clear that teachers should provide students with mnemonic devices to help them remember material. In addition, having students create mnemonic devices for themselves—while encouraging artistry and creativity—would surely make for a fun and effective class activity.

Desirable Difficulties

Teachers quite naturally spend a lot of time and effort to make learning easier for their students. In many cases, this is a good and useful instinct—if students are unable to understand or digest the material they're being taught, they're certainly not going to learn it to mastery. However, as was seen in the earlier section on how the arts engage students in *effort after meaning*, sometimes making things just a bit more *difficult* can actually lead to better learning. This is certainly not true in all (or even most) cases, and any effort to introduce difficulty must, of course, be undertaken with caution. Nonetheless, it is important to consider research indicating that increasing difficulty can sometimes aid memory. Diemand-Yauman et al. (2011) have shown that making written materials slightly more *disfluent*—that is, making it just a bit harder for our perceptual systems to deal with what we read—can lead to deeper processing and therefore better retention of material.

Sometimes making things just a bit more *difficult* can actually lead to better learning. It is important to consider recent research indicating that increasing difficulty can sometimes aid memory.

Everyone has likely had the experience when reading a book or article of glazing over a paragraph without really processing what's in it. When you get to the end of the paragraph, you inevitably ask yourself the question, "What did I just read?" This would seem to occur because one is perhaps reading a bit *too* fluently. That is, a good reader is likely capable of absent-mindedly reading text without really processing or understanding what that text is saying. Diemand-Yauman and colleagues (2011) showed—in a real-life high school setting—that simply changing printed materials to a slightly harder-to-read font led to substantial gains in course performance, likely due to an increase in processing of information (it is important to note that this increase in difficulty was not large enough to be noticeable to students). The lesson here is not that teachers should make learning tasks as hard as possible. Rather, as teachers are surely aware, sometimes students' level of attention and focus may slip, and therefore presenting information in formats that require students to process information more thoroughly can be a good idea. Of course, no one would want to make a task harder for a student who is already struggling. Research is showing, however, that teachers should perhaps think from time to time about how making tasks harder in certain ways, especially if the difference is not noticeable to students, can potentially lead to learning gains. Oftentimes, embedding information in the arts may do just this.

Simply changing printed materials to a slightly harder-to-read font led to substantial gains in course performance.

Chunking

Chunking aids memory by grouping items in an organized way so that they can be retrieved more easily than items in an unstructured list (see Gobet, 2022; Norris & Kalm, 2021; Thalmann et al., 2019). Phone numbers and social security numbers, for example, are made easier to remember by creating smaller groups of numbers that are separated with hyphens. One of the best known studies on the use of chunking was carried out by Chase and Ericsson (1981) with an undergraduate student, SF, who trained over a period of about two years to memorize long strings of digits. At first, SF had a digit span of about seven, which is comparable with that of the average person. Over the subsequent two years, however, SF was able to increase his digit span to around eighty digits. So how did he accomplish this feat? As it turns out, SF was an avid long-distance runner and began to chunk short strings of digits in such a way that they corresponded to running times for various distances. Over time, SF developed more interpretations that could be given to strings of numbers, such as ages or years, and eventually he could break extremely long strings into chunks that could be assigned distinct meanings and commit to memory the order of the chunks.

Chunking aids memory by grouping items in an organized way so that they can be retrieved more easily than items in an unstructured list.

Chunking information for students as well as teaching them to chunk information on their own is something all teachers should do when they present a large number of individual items that need to be retained and applied. As was discussed earlier, there's no one-size-fits-all prescription for the size and number of chunks. What's important is simply that each chunk be manageable enough for students to keep a few chunks in mind at any given time. As seen with the example of SF above, giving chunks meanings or interpretations can be a big help. Students can divide information into categories to help organize what they learn. For example, students could use a Venn diagram to categorize items based on shared and unshared properties. Color coding in visual displays such as a concept map can also assist in chunking information. Students, for instance, could use different colored pens to group similar items or create collages that visually demonstrate how chunks of information are related. If students can remember that there's a blue chunk, a red chunk, and a green chunk, and then can recall what each chunk is composed of, this will make it much easier for them to remember the entire set of information.

Interleaving

Interleaving refers to the process of intentionally ordering learning tasks so that the same task is not done several times in a row. In contrast to *blocked* structures (aaa, bbb, ccc), *interleaved* structures mix tasks together (abc, bca, cab). Interleaving practice sessions or presentations of material has been shown to increase task performance and retention over what is achieved using a blocked format (see Firth et al., 2021; Yan et al., 2020). For example, in a seminal study on interleaving, Kornell and Bjork (2008) found that subjects could better identify the artists of particular paintings when they were presented in an interleaved or random order rather than being blocked by the artist. Brunmair and Richter (2019) found similar results for mathematics tasks. Rohrer and Pashler (2010) posit that interleaving aids learning by helping the learner better discriminate differences in content. They point out that most mathematics textbooks tend to rely heavily on blocked sets of practice problems, despite the fact that this may not be as productive as doing mixed sets of problems requiring the application of a variety of different skills, as is common in cumulative reviews.

In contrast to *blocked* structures (aaa, bbb, ccc), *interleaved* structures mix tasks together (abc, bca, cab). Interleaving aids learning by helping the learner better discriminate differences in content.

Interleaving is not a difficult strategy to implement in the classroom, as it requires little more than a bit of forethought. Teachers can easily weave different kinds of tasks into a lesson if they plan, for example, to cover three topics over three days, rather than one topic each day. Alternatively, teachers could simply make a daily habit of reviewing selected material from previous lessons. Time on any given topic need not be lost—it just needs to be *spread around* a bit more. Although it may be simple and easy just to cover a section of the textbook each day, there is clear evidence that this is not the best way of delivering instruction. Instead, it's best to intersperse different forms of material and practice within each lesson. Here too, integration of the arts can be an asset. Students can be asked to create artistic products incorporating a variety of ideas that have been considered in conjunction with a given topic. The open-ended and generative nature of artistic activity allows for as many new and creative combinations of content as students can imagine. Thus, the visual and performing arts afford ample opportunity for students to revisit and think about material in an interleaved, as opposed to blocked, kind of way.

Although it may be simple and easy just to cover a section of the textbook each day, there is clear evidence that this is not the best way of delivering instruction.

Brain-Targeted Teaching® Learning Units

As this chapter illustrates, mastery of content, skills, and concepts requires that information be consolidated within long-term memory, and this happens when students actively produce or do something with what they are being taught. Though many educators talk about *active learning*, this means little unless one can say what this looks like in practice and can suggest pedagogical methods for engaging students in this kind of learning. As has been shown in this chapter, the arts represent a natural way to get students involved in activities that will lead to long-term retention and promote the kind of engagement that is required for deep conceptual learning.

From the Expert Practitioner

The Arts in Brain-Target Four

The arts offer varied modes of investigation and inquiry that deepen engagement and offer more opportunities of interpretation and application of knowledge. The following are a few examples of how memory effects are aligned with art processes.

As an example, in a chemistry unit for secondary grades, students learn chemistry concepts by experimenting with art processes and artists who think like scientists. Thinking as both artists and scientists, they explore—hands on—with artists' materials. Some of the science concepts they covered are molecular structure (exploring Pointillism and dot painting), solubility (painting on silk with soluble and insoluble materials), physical and chemical change (making clay sculptures and cyanotypes), and states of matter (choreographing dance sequences).

Generation

Design Thinking is an approach to learning through problem-solving and collaboration. Thinking like a designer includes a five-step process that includes discover, interpret, ideate, prototype, and test.

Enactment

Incorporating drama strategies in a daily routine is not hard. Emphasizing the low risk or no- audience performance builds confidence and allows for experimentation and collaboration. Living pictures, freeze frame, or tableaux capture a single moment. Bring the tableau to life by adding spoken word and movement using improvisation. Improvisation is defined as making or doing something that is not planned beforehand.

Effort After Meaning

Visual analysis uses the arts as a vehicle for teaching critical dispositions that include careful observation, asking deep questions, identifying connections, citing evidence, and generating explanations. To prepare to use visual analysis, ask these questions: What connections do you want your students to make by analyzing certain images? What are the images that will authentically connect with those concepts? What are the written/spoken prompts you will use that will lead to creative responses? There are many protocols for guiding rich discussions about visual images, but the common aspect with all is that the first step is observation.

Pictorial Representation

Drawing from observation is, of course, the fundamental way to use visual thinking. Looking with focused attention brings the mind/body connection together. Technique in realistic rendering is not the point—the focus is on knowing the subject, not the finished product.

How to make learners more comfortable with drawing:

- *Drawings can be simple yet communicative.*
- *Warm up with a page of scribbles to test materials and get used to holding a tool.*
- *Emphasize rough drafts, doodling, sketching, non-realism.*
- *Emphasize process over product.*
- *Draw to organize ideas and plan process.*
- *Organizational drawings are better for deep learning than representational drawings.*
- *Draw systems, diagrams, use stick figures, symbols.*
- *Sequence events or steps.*
- *Give the option to draw from 2-D resource images.*
- *Verbally describe or model the drawing process.*

(Continued)

(Continued)

- *Eliminate any sense of competition.*
- *Use sketches, maps, and diagrams as tools for assessment.*
- *Remind them that the goal is not realism but communication.*

Visualization—when we visualize we encode memory in a unique way. Seeing with the mind's eye involves making mental pictures in order to increase comprehension and deepen a connection with read or heard material.

Clare O'Malley Grizzard
Arts Educator, Arts Integration Specialist

Brain-Target Four - Strategies for Mastery of Content Map

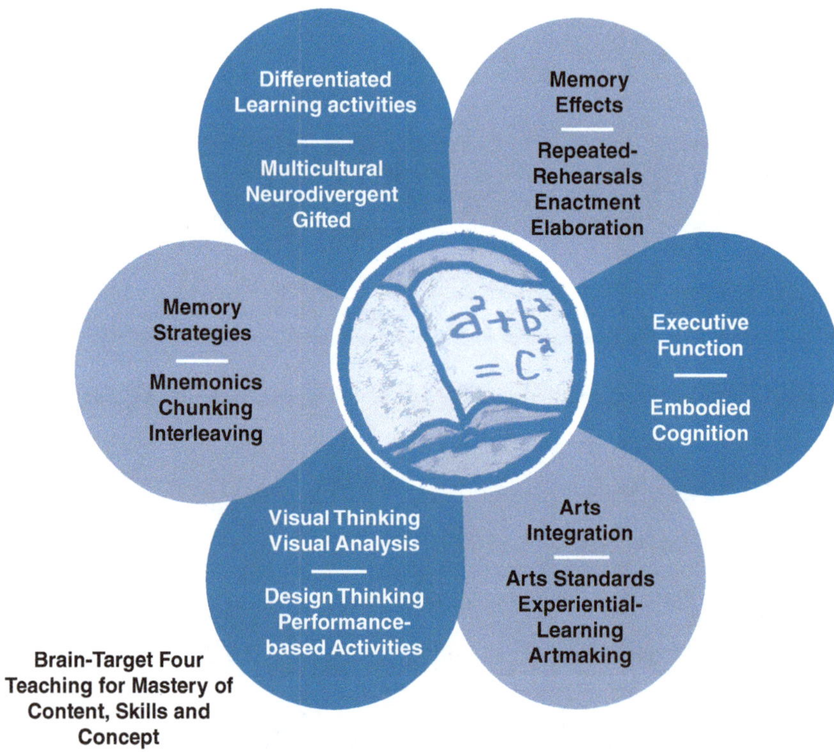

Brain-Target Four Teaching for Mastery of Content, Skills and Concept

Brain-Target Five

8

Teaching for the Extension and Application of Knowledge

Creativity and Innovation in Education

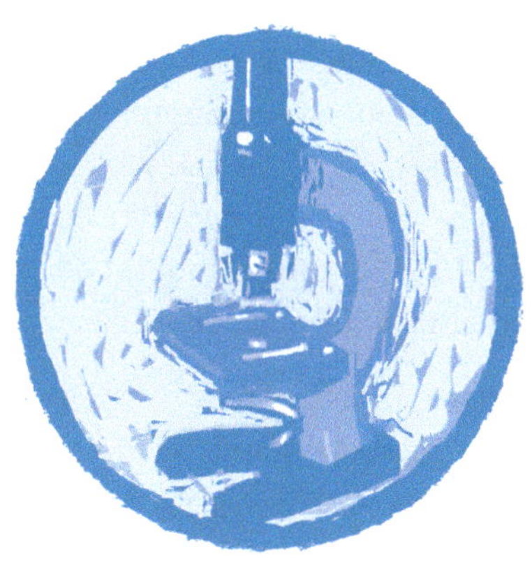

Brain-Target Five - Extension and Application of Knowledge Chapter Map

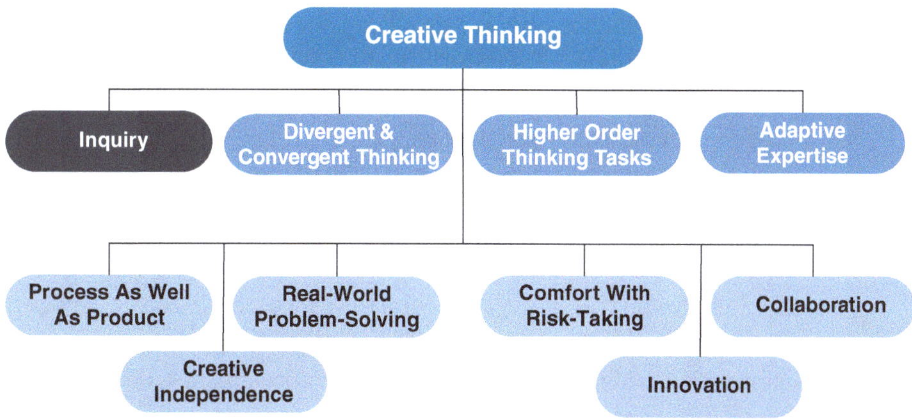

> *The principal goal of education in the schools should be creating men and women who are capable of doing new things, not simply repeating what other generations have done; men and women who are creative, inventive and discoverers, who can be critical and verify, and not accept, everything they are offered.*
>
> —Jean Piaget

We begin our study of Brain-Target Five with the words of Cory, a seventh-grade student from an urban school district. He states, "School is boring for me, and I mostly think it's a waste of time. It's usually the same thing all day long, like teachers talking at us and giving us lots of things to read from our textbooks and handouts, and then finding answers to questions and writing them on workbook sheets. The only time I think I really learn is when I get to do something real. Like last week we did something really cool. We made a survey to find out how people in the neighborhood felt about safety and community services. We then interviewed neighbors in stores and bus stops. We took all the answers and created charts and graphs. Then we wrote letters to city officials to explain improvements that could make the neighborhood better. I learned a lot, and I wish school was always this much fun."

Cory's frequent disinterest in school may be common for some students in our schools today and might be similar in any school and any location. Challenged by issues such as class size, lack of resources, classroom management, a dense array of topics to cover, administrative paperwork, test preparation requirements, and lack of time for collaborative and innovative lesson planning, teachers are forced to rely on teaching methods that not only fail to motivate students to learn but also make little attempt to promote creative thinking. With a steady diet of this kind of instruction, Cory may be poised to be one of the 2.1 million students who drop out every year across our nation's schools (National Center for Education Statistics, 2022 data; www.nces.ed.gov).

Luckily, although the many challenges teachers face seem insurmountable, teaching children to be creative thinkers is not. Brain-Targeted Teaching® Model (BTT) offers a framework for establishing creative strategies for all children. Recall that in the last chapter, we focused on teaching selected learning objectives to mastery—a notion that assumes that students retain information in long-term memory. Our *expert practitioners* demonstrated how to design arts-integrated activities to give students multiple, yet novel and creative ways to enhance retention of content. In most traditional teaching methods, when students have mastered the lesson objectives, teachers typically test students using an end-of-unit assessment and then move on to the next book chapter or unit of study. In the BTT Model, however, once students have acquired knowledge, an important next step must occur to foster deep understanding and true learning.

Brain-Target Five, the stage of the model described in the current chapter, focuses on this next step: expanding instruction so that students are given the opportunity to think creatively by applying skills and content in meaningful, active, real-world problem-solving tasks. As Cory describes above, this type of instruction allows students to see how instructional goals relate to their own lives in real-world problem-solving; this connection helps make the learning experience more meaningful and fun. The content presented in this chapter explores how instruction that leads to creative thinking might differ from conventional instruction. In addition, the discussion considers how theoretical notions and empirical findings can inform the design of instructional practices that promote creative thinking whether in classrooms or the workplace.

21st Century Skills

The aims of Brain-Target Five are closely aligned with the goals of the 21st century skills movement. Skills requiring sequential, literal, textual, and analytic modes of thinking are necessary for students but are not sufficient (Kennedy & Sundberg, 2020). Rather, for students to receive instruction consistent with the goals of the 21st century skills movement, they must be given ample opportunities to be inventive and to apply knowledge in ways that contribute to developing and fostering the creative mind. Moreover, the ability to think critically and the capacity to solve problems creatively are vital skills extending far beyond the classroom in that they have driven great discoveries and important changes in industry, health care, technology, environmental practices, and public policy.

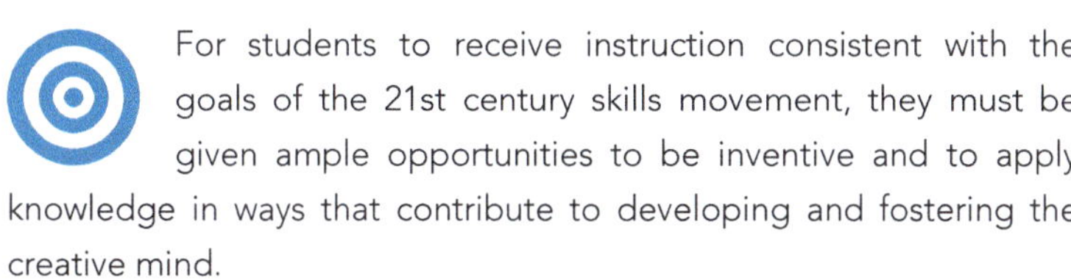
For students to receive instruction consistent with the goals of the 21st century skills movement, they must be given ample opportunities to be inventive and to apply knowledge in ways that contribute to developing and fostering the creative mind.

Unfortunately, as described above, practitioners are faced with a number of factors that prevent them from being able to provide every student with enough (or any) opportunities to develop such skills. With some exceptions, teaching that promotes creative thinking as the foundation of instruction is often hit or miss and is rarely institutionalized in curricular or instructional practices in school systems (Hardiman, 2017; Kennedy & Sundberg, 2020). Along these lines, Rotherham and Willingham (2009) warn that "we cannot afford a system in which receiving a high-quality education is akin to a game of bingo" (p. 16). So as this chapter unfolds, we consider ways that all students at any age can receive rigorous and meaningful instruction to engage the creative mind. This comes to life in considering the needs of neurodivergent children as told by our expert practitioner, Jackie Renfrow, as she describes her son's experiences in school.

From the Expert Practitioner

Neurodivergent Children: Applying Knowledge Through Declarative Memory and Creativity

A high level of creativity and problem-solving are valued traits in students entering the workforce. Today's organizations rely on employees' abilities to remember information and use this knowledge base to tackle problems, in other words, harness their declarative memory. And what my son, with Attention Deficit Hyperactivity Disorder (ADHD) and Autism Spectrum Disorder, lacks in social skills, he makes up for in a gifted memory. Therefore, my son often scores below average on standardized tests, but he succeeds when he can showcase his knowledge in unique ways. So he thrives in a classroom where the teacher works creatively to tap into his brain's big-picture thinking.

According to research by Boucher et al. (2012), declarative memory is a potentially powerful way for neurodiverse students to compensate for diverse deficits and disorders. For example, evidence suggests that divergent thinking is untouched in people with obsessive-compulsive disorder, Tourette syndrome, dyslexia, specific language impairment, and high- and low-functioning autism (Boucher et al., 2012). In fact, more recent studies revealed that having ADHD symptoms is associated with higher scores on all of the outcome measures for divergent thinking—fluency, flexibility, originality, and creativity (Kasirer et al., 2020).

So what happens when classroom teachers offer flexibility and allow students to obtain and present knowledge in a more creative and personalized way? You would be surprised by the enthusiasm and motivation that switching up a typical lesson plan can have on a student, specifically one who is neurodivergent.

At the elementary school level, the lesson plans routinely follow the same format: The students start the week with a theme, then they are given passages to read throughout the week that are linked to that theme. These passages can range from several paragraphs to up to two pages. Throughout the lesson, students interact with the content through worksheets, discussion groups, vocabulary building, and writing exercises. The curriculum holds a certain predictability.

My son, and many of his fifth-grade peers, find too much predictability boring and are more likely to refuse to work when not given control over assignments. So during a recent reading passage about the U.S. Transcontinental Railroad, my son asked the teacher to explore the topic further and requested help in finding additional reading. He was granted access to the school media center to check out books and the links to several school-district-approved websites. Ultimately, he was given the opportunity to present what he learned via a presentation to the class which included a diorama of a railroad, designed primarily out of Lego bricks. The results were a motivated student with a sense of pride in what he had produced. Plus, with the experience and presentation to the class, he was able to display and generate his understanding of the curriculum for long-term retention.

Jacqueline Renfrow
Parent and Adjunct Faculty in Higher Education

Creativity and Innovation in the Classroom

Brain-Target Five endorses the extension and application of knowledge through the promotion of creativity and innovative thinking (Hardiman, 2019). Before going further, we might consider "what is creativity?" While descriptions of creativity may vary, a common definition that is largely accepted in the creativity literature is offered by Plucker and colleagues (2004). They define creativity as "the interaction among *aptitude*, *process*, and *environment* by which an individual or group produces a *perceptible product* that is both *novel* and *useful* as defined within a *social context*" (p. 90).

Fostering creativity and similar skills presupposes that creativity is in fact an unfixed and impressionable quality; fortunately, many educators and scientists as well as a growing body of research support this assumption (e.g., Zhou, 2019). For example, Plucker (2017) discusses the importance of communication leading to exposure to other ideas, consistent with the argument that creativity processing can be influenced. Other findings demonstrate that individuals asked to find solutions to a problem can think of more ideas and more creative ideas when they consider the implications of the ideas as well as a plan for how to implement the idea (Byrne et al., 2010).

Despite the evidence, a common misconception in our culture is that creativity, innovative thinking, and problem-solving skills are traits bestowed only upon gifted individuals who demonstrate great intelligence or unusual talents. What is more, instructional practices and even educational systems more broadly are constrained by this notion. A striking example of how this misconception takes shape is the sharp differences one often finds in classes for gifted students compared to remedial classes. That is, most curricula and instruction provided in any "Gifted and Talented" program across the country include activities that tap into creative problem-solving such as complex science projects or interdisciplinary research assignments. These creativity-promoting activities may occur less frequently in more conventional classrooms, especially in instructional programs and curriculum offered for students with learning differences or those designed to prepare students for standardized testing. In these more conventional classrooms, students might instead be offered a limited menu of instructional strategies designed to promote skills and content necessary to succeed on tests. (Despite this challenge, it is heartwarming to witness the ingenuity of many educators and trainers as they embed their own creative activities into conventional instructional curricula.)

A common misconception in our culture is that creativity, innovative thinking, and problem-solving skills are traits bestowed only upon gifted individuals who demonstrate great intelligence or unusual talents.

Traditional instruction relies largely on *convergent thinking,* which encourages students to find the single, right solution to a problem. Most educators would agree that convergent-thinking tasks dominate educational practice and are the hallmark of accountability measures (Runco, 2004). In contrast, an activity that promotes *divergent thinking* leads students to generate multiple and varied solutions and approaches to finding solutions thereby enhancing creative problem-solving. The kind of teaching endorsed in Brain-Target Five (and in the BTT Model in general) supports both convergent and divergent thinking for students of all ability levels.

An activity that promotes *divergent thinking* leads students to generate multiple and varied solutions and approaches to finding solutions thereby enhancing creative problem-solving.

Before delving into theoretical frameworks and research involving creativity, it is important to make clear in what way—if any—creativity is related to intelligence. A high level of creativity capacity likely requires a strong knowledge base in a given area. This store of knowledge, often referred to as adaptive expertise, goes beyond a mere list of facts and incorporates the ability to process and understand patterns of information and to be able to flexibly apply the information in novel situations. Crawford and Brophy (2006) describe adaptive expertise as engaging "reasoning and problem-solving processes that enable experts to continue to learn and adapt to new situations" (p. 4). Although it is possiblc (and even likely) that one's level of adaptive expertise is related in some way to one's level of *intelligence*, many if not most educators and scientists agree that *creativity* encompasses more than just intelligence. The relationship of intelligence and creativity is not completely known; however, many researchers believe that the constructs overlap in some way (Esping, 2017; Zhou, 2019).

In a study using structural equation modeling, Plucker (1999) examined the relationship between adult creative achievement and scores on divergent thinking tasks and intelligence tests. Although scores for both types of tests contributed to the creative achievement, the divergent thinking test score contributed three times that of the intelligence test score. These findings among others have helped switch the focus of research on creativity from separating creativity and intelligence to understanding "the correlates, benefits, and conditions of creativity" (Runco, 2004, p. 679). Moreover, the evidence supports the idea that fostering creativity should not be associated solely with gifted education, and, because creativity is not essentially innate, it can and should be taught in our schools and encouraged in the workplace. Below is an example of how a creative teacher, Hennah, focuses on implementing Brain-Target Five in a chemistry class.

From the Expert Practitioner

Chemistry Comes Alive

In the middle of summer, after the lead chemistry teacher had resigned, I—the new hire—was assigned the role of chemistry lead teacher at a prestigious private school. I was told that the transition would be easy and that the curriculum had already been curated. I was also warned that most of the tenth-grade students who took chemistry absolutely hated it, and I should be ready for a high level of disinterest. Upon reviewing the curriculum, I could see why. Everything was taught out of a textbook and seemed, quite frankly, dull. That summer, I spent most of my time reworking the curriculum to include chemistry that my students would find exciting and relevant. I was ready for the challenge, especially after being exposed to the Brain-Targeted Teaching® Model in one of my EdD classes that semester.

In my first class, the buzz of excitement and nervousness filled the air, and I saw one student striding toward me; it looked like he was on a mission. As soon as he was in front of me, before introducing himself, he very matter-of-factly told me: "I don't do science, I'm not good at it, I never have been, I just need to pass this class. So before you think you can change my mind, I just wanted to let you know." With that, he turned around and sat as far away from my desk as possible. I wanted to speak to this student to understand his experience, but I also quickly recognized that our first class together would not be the time to do so. I went on to explain the course outline to the students, who quickly noticed that the syllabus was not arranged in units of study; instead, it was organized into the following themes: Smartphones and Our Bodies, Medicine and Research, Food, and Space Exploration. Several students asked if they were in tenth-grade chemistry, to which I responded yes. The young man who approached me at the start of the class said, "Well, the syllabus doesn't say anything about the periodic table and chemicals." I explained to the class that while the periodic table is essential in chemistry, it is not the entire course. We would learn chemistry as we see it in the world around us. A student asked, "Do we need to memorize the first fifty elements? My friends who took this class last year said that was their first test." I responded to a room full of skeptical students, "No, I will not require that. However, you will see these elements so often in our work that you may end up memorizing them as a by-product."

By the end of the first semester, my students were able to explain the emission spectra and how they could apply that understanding to the blue light their phones emit. They also learned to calculate concentrations of substances and why this is so important in medicine and research. Their assessments of knowledge were free choice. I allowed students to create anything they desired to demonstrate their understanding of specific learning outcomes, provided they accompanied their work with annotations that explained their understanding. Students were allowed to revise and resubmit work, which helped them get on board with the growth process. I wanted students to have agency and have the opportunity to take risks that were low stakes.

The student who came up to me on the first day of class to let me know he was not good at science produced a painting of his ADHD medication for his end-of-semester assessment. His painting was composed of several layers, and when you moved it in the light, you could see stoichiometric calculations of the medicine he took daily. He calculated the percent composition of each element that made up his medication and the molar mass of each component and converted the moles into grams. His complex calculations were 100% accurate. Not only was it a work of art that is so stunning that it hangs in my office to this day, but he also found how chemistry applies to his world. At the end of the school year, the same student asked me if I would write a recommendation for him to take AP Chemistry the following year. He shared how he had never learned why he needed to know certain things or be able to display his learning artistically. I began to wonder how many students, over the years, had walked into chemistry or any other science class and felt how this student felt and left feeling the same way because of how abstract and disconnected the class felt from their lives. Allowing students to be creative sparks a sense of innate confidence that all children benefit from. It also gets that investment into their students' learning that many educators hope for.

Hennah Abubaker
Educator and Teaching Consultant

What Do the Brain Sciences Tell Us About Creativity?

As applying information in novel, original, and useful ways relies on creative thinking, here we consider whether the ability to think creatively can be reflected in neural processes. As previously explained, extensive research on brain plasticity during the past two decades demonstrates that significant changes occur in the brain as the result of repeated sensory experience (see Fu & Zuo, 2011, for a review). For example, studies have shown that the brain strengthens existing networks when an individual is involved in multiple exposures to sensory stimuli (see Beaty et al., 2023).

In addition to considering how training or experience changes the brain, research has explored the differences in various modes of thought—for example, creative thinking versus more conventional thinking. In terms of cognitive processing, highly creative thinking is often differentiated from more conventional thought because it relies in part on divergent thinking, which, given the same input or content, generates multiple acceptable solutions. Although Zhou (2019) points out that studies investigating creativity training on behavioral and neural functions are limited, below are a sample of studies that exemplify how researchers are contributing to the understanding of neural mechanisms of creativity.

The seminal study of Limb and Braun (2008) contributed to our understanding of differentiated neural processing during the creative act of improvisation. Using fMRI technology, they observed brain activity of professional jazz pianists during the spontaneous playing of improvisational jazz. They compared this spontaneous playing condition with one in which the musicians played a previously memorized jazz score. The results indicated significant differences in brain activity between the two conditions. During improvisation, functional brain scans indicated a widespread deactivation of the dorsolateral prefrontal cortex, typically associated with self-regulation, self-monitoring, focused attention, and inhibition. Turning off this brain area may be associated with a type of "defocused, free-floating attention that permits spontaneous unplanned associations, and sudden insights or realizations" (p. 1,679). The researchers also found increased activity in the medial prefrontal cortex, a brain region that has been linked with actions of self-expression and individuality.

In a more recent FMRI study of scientific creative thinking, Beaty et al. (2023) focused on studying how the brain processes a divergent thinking activity compared to conventional thinking such as word naming. They focused on the three brain networks that support cognitive functions and behaviors. The executive or control network is responsible for high-level cognitive functions such as working memory and problem-solving. The default mode network is involved when a person is at rest, daydreaming, envisioning, or engaged in self-referential thought. The salience network plays a role in switching between the default and control networks. When performing a divergent thinking task, Beaty et al. found increased cooperation among the three brain networks compared to a conventional thinking task—a pattern similar to other studies of creative thinking. A study by Bartoli et al. (2024) found a strong relationship between the default mode network and spontaneous and divergent thought, suggesting the important role of the cognitive processes associated with the default mode network and creative thinking. Consistent with these findings, Hsu and Yeh (2024) report that creative performance is aligned with the default, control, and salience networks, and they also add that creativity is associated with not only generating novel ideas but also with the inhibition needed for suppressing non-original ideas and also executive decision-making necessary to recognize creative ideas.

Differences in brain structure and function have also been studied in individuals who take part in certain creative activities, such as a playing musical instrument. Hyde and colleagues (2009) sought to determine if those with musical training had anatomical changes as a result of this training or if they had been attracted to studying music because they already possessed preexisting brain structures that would make them more likely to continue to practice music. The researchers examined the effect of musical training in six-year-olds with no prior musical training. One group of children, the "instrumental" group, received an average of fifteen months of instrumental musical training in the form of weekly keyboarding lessons, and the remainder of the children, the "control" group, received fifteen months of weekly group music class in which they sang and played with drums and bells. The results demonstrated that compared with the control group, the instrumental group exhibited increased brain size in multiple areas of the brain, including the frontal lobe that controls higher-order thinking. The children in the instrumental group also showed increased motor control skills and auditory processing. These findings suggest that teaching children creative tasks results in changes not only in cognitive functions but also in brain structure. Studies on the effect of music on cognitive functions continue to show that music exposure improves various cognitive functions such as language and spatial-temporal skills (see Yazar, 2024).

Given the idea that experiences change the brain, it seems appropriate for educators to embrace the practice of embedding creative thinking into all aspects of instruction. Below we examine a model for teaching and measuring creativity—the 4 P model developed by Rhodes (1961) and further elucidated by Qian and Plucker (2017). This model views creativity through the perspective of the creative process, products, person, and press (environment).

Strategies for Embedding Creative Thinking in the Classroom

Creative Process

Creativity experts distinguish the *process* of creative thinking as distinctly different from the definition of creativity as a *product* (see Green et al., 2023 for in-depth review). A review of creativity literature suggests that the creative process begins with the identification of a specific problem that guides an internal inquiry and leads to the generation of novel approaches to a solution. Abdulla and Cramond (2017) and Bi et al. (2020) describe the creative process as one that includes not only thinking logically to arrive at a solution (convergent thinking) but also the important process of thinking in various directions to come to alternative solutions to a problem (divergent thinking).

The creative process involves internal visualization of a potential solution by imagining it in the "mind's eye" (Munro, 2019). Divergent thinking questions can ignite this creative thinking process. The motivated teacher can embed the creative process into instruction in myriad ways. One idea is for the teacher to pose a problem for students to solve, collect responses, and review students' ideas as a baseline for their creative thinking about the topic. The teacher later returns students' initial responses to them and encourages them to think of solutions that were not identified the first time. Visualization is one way to encourage "imagination in the mind's eye" to produce deeper exploration and more novel and innovative ideas. Using the power of visual thinking, as with mapping techniques like concept mapping or mind mapping, can encourage the interconnectedness of words, images, and visual-spatial awareness and creativity.

Creative Products

The outcome of creative processes are the products that students develop that are considered novel and useful. In a review of seventeen studies on scientific creative thinking, Bi et al. (2020) found that the product dimension of creative thinking was a most effective intervention for enhancing creativity in the classroom. Within classroom instruction, the product should align with content learning goals and may take multiple forms such as text, visual or performing arts activities, or mechanical models. A common assessment of the creative product is the Consensual Assessment Technique (CAT) that requires that a group of experts within a particular domain come to consensus on the creative aspects of the product. While this type of activity might be useful in a school or work setting for judging end-of-semester student portfolios or work products, it might not be feasible for use in daily instruction. Moreover, coming to consensus on ratings among groups of experts is often challenging (Qian & Plucker, 2017). Additionally, rubrics are often used to assess students' work and may be an effective way to communicate what is expected in a product that would be considered creative. Although the use of rubrics would guide students' work and allow for self-evaluation, they might also constrain creative thinking, as students focus on how to fulfill an extrinsic rating rather than enjoy their own creative spirit. One way to facilitate student agency and creativity would be to assign anonymous student-to-student peer reviews that would offer "glows" (praise of the product) and "grows" (ways to improve the work). By allowing the responsibility of creativity work to be put into students' hands, the teacher fosters students' ownership of their learning. The students' encouragement of one another would likely boost each other's self-efficacy and motivation to elaborate and expand upon their ideas.

Creative Person

In creativity literature, the creative person is described as one who displays special capacities or aptitudes for creative thinking. We support the belief that *all* students can engage in levels of creative thinking when given appropriate instruction and opportunities (Amabile, 1996; Kaufman & Beghetto, 2009). As previously discussed, accepting this notion requires that teachers believe in the creative potential of all students, not just some who might be identified for gifted programs. Whether in a classroom or work environment, students and workers must be freed from fears of failure, which then promotes greater levels of confidence in producing creative responses to problems. Still, one might encounter individuals who display unusual capacities for creative thinking within a content or context. For example, a student might regularly ask questions that extend beyond literal understanding in ways that are not typical of most other students. There are multiple ways to support and encourage those advanced creative students. For example, a student who stands out from others might be paired for a project with one who is less apt to take chances and typically seeks the "right" single solution. Both students may benefit from a stimulating exchange of ideas—combining divergent and convergent thinking that enhances the creativity of each of them. Nurturing this collaboration between the students by having them utilize concept maps to visually ideate on solutions together could foster the growth of both students. This type of activity also has the potential to increase content knowledge of each student. Similarly, the same strategy can be applied in a work environment in which the individual who demonstrates the ability to think of creative solutions to a problem is able to work with others to pollinate creativity in the organization.

Creative Press (Environment)

Environment refers to the relationship between individuals and the culture of the classroom or institution that supports the entire teaching and learning process. The environment consists of multiple variables that can either support or restrict creativity. Creative environments are those that invoke confidence and encourage individuals to imagine, envision, tinker, and create. A creative environment allows for choices in setting goals and flexibility in how to demonstrate understanding of a topic or a problem. Individuals should have opportunities to collaborate, to play with ideas in diverse and artistic ways, and to feel confident that errors are opportunities for learning. Teachers and leaders should assess the climate and culture, keeping in mind the emotional influence on learning and producing creative work. Reducing anxieties of novel learning experiences or work assignments can go a long way in fostering the creative mind.

Creativity and intelligence are related but separate entities. Creativity is not essentially innate, it can and should be taught in our schools.

Teaching children creative tasks results in changes not only in cognitive functions but also in brain structure.

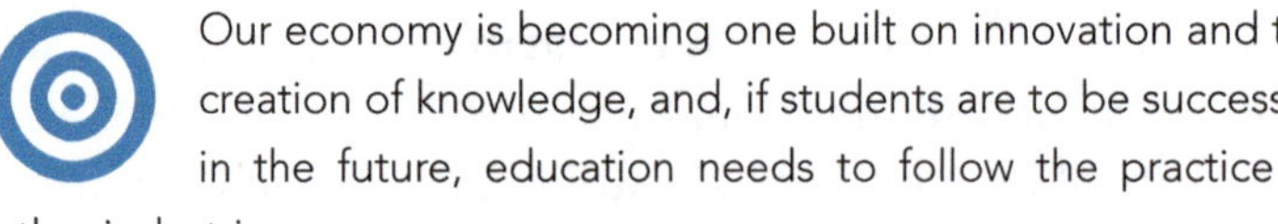

Our economy is becoming one built on innovation and the creation of knowledge, and, if students are to be successful in the future, education needs to follow the practice of other industries.

Content Versus Process in the 21st Century Skills Movement

Most scientists agree that creative thinking does not occur without having first mastered a body of content knowledge (e.g., Csikszentmihalyi, 1996; Heilman et al., 2003); this notion is consistent with the idea of adaptive expertise discussed earlier in the chapter. As Ulrich Kraft (2007) states, "Fresh solutions result from disassembling and reassembling the building blocks in an infinite number of ways. That means the problem-solver must thoroughly understand the blocks" (p.17). In other words, after having mastered a domain of knowledge, individuals are able to find solutions to novel problems by associating pieces of learned information in different ways. Such creative problem-solving raises acquired knowledge to a level far beyond basic mastery.

After having mastered a domain of knowledge, individuals are able to find solutions to novel problems by associating pieces of learned information in different ways.

Currently, educators and education policymakers debate whether curricula should focus on facts and content or on teaching critical thinking skills. But, given the perspectives described above, this dichotomy oversimplifies the teaching and learning process because teachers must address *both* parts. Along these lines, Rotherham and Willingham (2009) argue that knowledge and thinking skills should be interwoven within the school curriculum in all content areas. Without a strong body of content and skills, students will not have knowledge to apply creatively in real-world situations, and without creative-thinking skills, they would not be able to take learned concepts to new, untaught levels. Whether in a classroom or workspace, individuals need to have content knowledge and thinking skills applicable in multiple content areas so they can generate solutions to problems spanning disciplines.

Without a strong body of content and skills, students will not have knowledge to apply creatively in real-world situations. Below is an example of how social studies teacher Allisun Thompson combines content knowledge with a creative arts-integrated project.

From the Expert Practitioner

The Nigerian Mask Project: From Brain-Target Four to Five With Arts Integration

One of my Bran-Targeted Teaching® Units, The Nigerian Mask project, is designed to look at populations of cultures within political Nigerian borders. We would focus on how masks were historically used around the world. Students would connect to Halloween and Mardi Gras in the United States. After previewing five ethnic cultures, students would take a deep dive into one of their choices. They would look at the culture of the people, the geography of the land, as well as the characteristics and traditional uses of their ceremonial masks. In the end, researchers would write about the people and create a mask using the discovered attributes.

I have adapted the lesson a bit to include a study of European-imposed borders on the African continent, just so that the colonists could have the desired resource pillaged and shipped off to another continent. This usually gets the kids good and riled up. I have a mask from the Congo area displayed in the classroom so that I can use it as a model on how to research reputable websites and corroborate information found from primary and secondary resources.

I have also included our state Art Standards and mini lessons on sculpture such as symmetry and texture. This is what makes it Arts Integration! The rubric will cover research in addition to mastery of Social Studies standards.

Although the project starts with Nigerian cultural ethnicities, students are permitted to research a different modern-day country of their interest, thus enhancing their motivation and personal connection to the project. Using this lesson over the years, some students have brought into school images of family-owned masks, making the unit feel relevant to the class.

The culminating project encompasses a study of the Indigenous people, their land, and traditions, along with a short history of how and why they were colonized, which is further enhanced by the creation of the mask. Year after year, past students stop in to say hi and say "Hey, it's the mask project! I did the Igbo people of Nigeria and Cameroon!" There is nothing better than hearing a student remember the unit they completed years ago. They walk around to see what phase the students are on, exciting the younger generation.

Allisun Thompson
Social Studies Teacher, Grade 6

What Does This Mean for Teachers?

In most classrooms today, instruction is focused squarely on convergent thinking, and at least some scientists believe this kind of instruction is squeezing the creativity out of children. Kraft (2007), for example, argues that as we reinforce neural pathways through continuous repetition of the same type of convergent thinking activities, we may be diminishing the pathways that promote the creative mind. This brings us to the notion that creativity can and should be explicitly taught in our schools (see Lopata et al., 2022). The hope is that incorporating particular explicit instruction into the classroom can create new modes of thinking that children will implicitly employ not only in school but also in life.

Promoting creative thinking and more generally teaching for 21st century skills will require teachers not only to impart content but also to provide students with frequent opportunities to engage in activities that make possible and encourage divergent thinking, thus allowing for new and distinct free-flowing thoughts. Educators are likely in the habit of probing students for a solution to a problem; the challenge for educators, then, is to change the potential overreliance on seeking the one "right answer" to questions in class, on worksheets, and on curriculum assessments. Although this may come naturally for some teachers, others will feel uneasy moving away from the primary use of conventional teaching methods. And teachers' practices as well as their attitudes toward their practices are critical: Teachers' theories and concepts of how students should perform in class have been shown to either dampen or enhance creativity in the classroom (Beghetto, 2006), and few teachers feel that they are fully trained to design creative teaching activities (Kampylis et al., 2009).

Promoting creative thinking and more generally teaching for 21st century skills will require teachers not only to impart content but also to provide students with frequent opportunities to engage in activities that make possible and encourage divergent thinking, thus allowing for new and distinct free-flowing thoughts.

Overhauling traditional instructional methods is made more difficult because of what the students have come to know and expect. That is, from the time students enter school, they are rewarded for thinking logically and for providing the right answers on a multitude of standardized tests, from accountability assessments to college entry examinations. As a result, teachers not only have to adjust their practices but also have to teach students how to learn in new ways as they will ultimately face a world in which more than a single solution exists (Starko, 2018).

As we reflect on Cory's story at the beginning of this chapter, there is no question that our students deserve better than many receive in our classrooms today. Public policy, teacher training, and school practices must support teachers in designing and implementing instruction that fosters creative and engaging learning. And teacher preparation programs should explicitly show teachers how to facilitate creative behavior in their students. Only then will our schools produce the kind of creative thinkers that foster a creative, innovative society.

Strategies for Embedding Creative Thinking: Brain-Target Five Activities

As explained in the previous chapter, on Brain-Target Four, acquiring a body of knowledge and demonstrating mastery in traditional and nontraditional ways are important components of education. A teacher focuses on teaching content and skills to mastery through multiple exposures to key content, and the arts become a particularly useful vehicle for providing engaging learning activities to achieve that mastery. Here in Brain-Target Five, teachers encourage students to extend learning and move beyond the content through activities that require creative and critical thinking.

A number of creative thinking instructional models have been designed in recent years to improve school students' creative thinking skills. Saeed and Ramdane (2022) conducted a systematic review of models aimed at improving the creative thinking of secondary school students. They conclude that adopting creative thinking instruction resulted in drastic improvements in students' creative thinking, academic achievements, and conceptual understanding. Similar reviews (e.g., Yates & Twigg, 2017) focus on the development of creativity in early childhood studies. Explicit teaching of creative thinking skills should be a strong focus at all levels of educational programming. In the next section, we offer strategies to assist educators in embedding creativity strategies into instructional practices consistent with the Brain-Targeted Teaching® Model (Hardiman, 2003, 2012).

The suggestions that follow are not presented as a complete listing of teaching strategies. Instead, we focus on the following four components that might catalyze educators' own creative teaching repertoire:

- Reducing stress and encouraging risk-taking
- Inquiry
- Creative collaboration
- Intrinsic motivation

Reduce Stress and Encourage Risk-Taking

"In a supportive and socially engaged environment, not only are cortisol rates reduced, but the prefrontal cortex is engaged, and dopamine, serotonin, and oxytocin rates are increased, thus creating an optimal environment for promoting creative thinking" (Dow & Kozlowski, 2020, p. 8).

A learning environment that reduces stress produces both behavioral and biological benefits. Understanding factors that cause stress is important as educators seek to design creative learning environments. For example, a part of the creative process is ambiguity and uncertainty, which can also cause stress for some students (Kirschner et al., 2016). Exploring new possibilities and producing novel ideas and behaviors can build anxiety about possible failure (Runco & Jaeger, 2012). Further, fear of failure blocks perseverance and experimentation (Duckworth, 2016; Henriksen et al., 2019).

Strategies to Reduce Stress and Promote Creativity in the Classroom Environment:

- Model comfort with ambiguity and acceptance of failure as part of the creative act by sharing one's own personal experiences and the experiences of others.
- Encourage risk-taking by providing praise based on the learning process rather than on the final product.
- Demonstrate that risk-taking does not bring penalty for "wrong" answers.
- Provide classroom protocols that guide collaboration with well-articulated goals and scaffolded independence.

- Offer feedback that encourages students to want to express and share their ideas.
- Allow students to brainstorm and generate ideas with a single classmate or two rather than with a larger group.

Inquiry

"Creative ideation tasks are commonly called divergent-thinking tasks pointing to the notion that thought 'goes off in different directions'" (Guilford, 1959, p. 381).

Inquiry is a teaching approach that triggers curiosity and a hunger for exploration (Stumm et al., 2011). It encourages creativity because it provides a process in which students design their own questions, experiment, develop ideas, and reflect. This approach promotes student-centered learning, cooperation, and interdependence (Dole et al., 2016). Learning activities should scaffold relevant and motivating questions until students are able to take the responsibility of finding their own answers. Inquiry models are built upon divergent questioning strategies that spark curiosity; help students see beyond the obvious; and become a portal for deeper, creative thinking (Ritchhart et al., 2011). Another powerful approach is arts-based creative inquiry, known as arts integration. Through divergent thinking and student agency, arts integration is a catalyst for deeper thinking, understanding, exploring, and independent learning (Donahue & Marshall, 2014). Our own research has shown that teaching in and through the arts promotes memory for academic content, especially for students who struggle with traditional teaching (Hardiman et al., 2014, 2019; Hardiman, 2017, 2019).

Strategies to Promote Inquiry Within Instruction:

- Create questions and activities that allow for divergent thinking—encourage multiple responses that demonstrate flexibility, fluency, and novel ideas.
- Design learning tasks that include both associative and analytical thinking—include divergent and convergent responses within the lesson.
- Use generative and probing questions to move students beyond shallow responses into close observations and reflection.
- Embed inquiry-based approaches into the instructional program as in project-based learning, experiential learning, the maker-centered

approach, playful learning, design theory, as well as creative art-centered inquiry.

- Develop skills to use content knowledge flexibly, known as "adaptive expertise" (see Crawford & Brophy, 2006 and Gregory et al., 2013).
- Use portfolio-based journals for students to reflect and extend understanding.

Creative Collaboration

"I really like working with other students in my class on a project. Each of us takes a different part to investigate. Then all the different pieces come together like a really cool puzzle. For me, this makes learning fun."
Seventh-grade student, Baltimore, MD

Working in a collaborative group encourages observation, listening, and sharing ideas—all parts of the creative process (Chua et al., 2012). Collaboration allows for metacognition as one contrasts and values others' ideas. Bransford (2000) point out that collaborative groups help students to externalize their thinking, which supports metacognition and reflection. Research into individual and group creativity suggests that disciplined improvisation leads to constructivist learning for deep understanding, rather than rote memorization as assessed through standardized tests (Sawyer, 2006, 2011).

Strategies to Promote Creative Collaboration:

- Present student groups with rigorous, multifaceted problems that benefit from multiple points of view.
- Design protocols for engaging in debate and discussion within small groups and the whole class to encourage extended elaboration and negotiation.
- Introduce external mediators such as checklists, basic literal guides, and other resources such as works of visual art or music.
- Provide support for collective improvisational discussions through inquiry-based designs, project-based designs, and arts integration.
- Create assessments (including self-assessments) for students, both individually and as a group, to ensure a high degree of individual accountability.

Intrinsic Motivation

"People are most creative when they feel motivated primarily by the interest, enjoyment, satisfaction, and challenge of the work itself—and not by extrinsic motivators." (Amabile, 2012, p. 1)

Students' creativity thrives in environments that provide intrinsic motivations that stimulate personal interests and enjoyment in their work (Amabile, 1996). Grohman and Snyder (2017) suggest that intrinsic motivation that leads to creative thinking is influenced by students' feeling of autonomy and confidence in their ability to accomplish a task. Moreover, feeling a sense of passion for the work significantly contributes to intrinsic motivation and creative flow (Csikszentmihalyi, 1996). While extrinsic or external motivation may also produce creative work, it is likely to be less effective if students work for external rewards such as grades, praise, or a type of compensation for task completion. Ryan and Deci (2000) identify three essential components for positive self-determination and natural propensities for growth and well-being: competence, autonomy, and relatedness.

Strategies to Promote Intrinsic Motivation Within the Learning Experience:

- Allow for choice in how students acquire or demonstrate learning goals to give them a sense of autonomy and control.
- Promote a growth mindset for creative tasks by encouraging success in task process over product.
- Scaffold learning tasks and provide meaningful feedback at regular intervals.
- Group students for projects based on shared interests and passion, not extrinsic factors such as competitive awards.
- Provide positive and constructive criticism and time for student reflection and action.
- Create open and growth-based environments. Novel environments with meaningful activity, such as gardening, offer bold intrinsic motivation (Skinner et al., 2012).

Brain-Target Five Summary

As our expert teachers explained, high quality classroom instruction requires students to be innovative and creative thinkers. Research from the learning sciences demonstrates that this kind of thinking engages neural processes that are distinct from those that support other sorts of thinking; studies in plasticity tell us that repeated experiences sculpt the brain. Thus, developing students' cognitive and academic skills and preparing them for work and life demands that classroom instruction include activities that encourage and support creative and innovative thinking, which are just the types of activities that Brain-Target Five promotes at all levels from early childhood programs to adult learners. Below we see how Bob Lessick uses the strategies of BTT in his higher education bioinformatics course and end with our continued study from Clare O'Malley Grizzard who shares how the arts inform Brain-Target Five.

From the Expert Practitioner

BTT Meets Higher Education

I recently attended a conference on undergraduate biology education and found that some of the most successful professors are using techniques that fit in well with Brain-Targeted Teaching® Model. One award-winning instructor stressed activity and movement. She devised a game to help teach her students the nitrogen cycle. Her students enjoyed it and showed a dramatic increase in meeting higher-level learning outcomes.

I have been teaching university-level bioinformatics and molecular biology for quite some time, and I am realizing that some of my more successful teaching techniques are grounded in the tenets of Brain-Targeted Teaching®. I have used a belt and telephone wire to explain higher-order supercoiling of DNA, and how specific enzymes relieve that supercoiling. The visuals and the students' use of those manipulatives really help them to conceptualize the problem. Moving forward in that course, my students have been able to recognize supercoiling as a crucial issue when they studied DNA replication, gene expression, and cell division.

After many stimulating discussions with peer instructors who are really pushing to improve science education, I can really see how I can apply the Brain-Targeted Teaching® Model even more extensively. After

(Continued)

(Continued)

attending the workshop on BTT, I was inspired to replace the standard cookbook laboratory exercises with lab projects where the students are given materials and a goal to design the experiments themselves. It occurred to me that while lab exercises are hands-on activities, students are really just following a recipe. If they design the experiments, they are developing creativity and understanding the process on a higher level, much like the chef who knows how to improvise.

I am finding that it works in the computer lab. I teach a hands-on bioinformatics course, where students use computers to analyze DNA and protein sequences. I have always found that the best way to learn bioinformatics is to do it, and students have usually appreciated the grueling exercises that I design for them. I am finding that a slight redesign of some of those structured activities to allow for students to "help write the recipe" seems to improve conceptual understanding of some difficult issues. I really see students who now seem more willing to engage other students in discussing the problems and how to approach them, and their thinking definitely becomes more creative.

Bob Lessick, PhD
Undergraduate and Graduate Bioinformatics

From the Expert Practitioner

The Arts in Brain-Target Five

How do we find "Big Ideas" for creative application? Brain-Target Five employs artistic thinking to go beyond the acquisition of knowledge (BT4) to creative, active application of knowledge in new ways. Learning goals are derived from underlying enduring ideas or essential questions; these are broad foundational concepts that transcend any one content area and link ideas in subject matter with other disciplines: in this case, the arts.

Some examples of generative big ideas are change, power, conflict, interdependence, life cycles, etc. The identification of global ideas guides purposeful and cohesive design—whether in a classroom or workspace. A strategy for finding big ideas for the classroom is mining the broad themes of the National Standards. In Science, for instance, the Cross Cutting Concepts (CCC) cited in the Next Generation Science Standards (NGSS) presents authentic connections between disciplines. Some of the CCCs are Pattern, Cause and Effect, Scale, Proportion, and Quantity. (Isn't it intriguing how many Cross Cutting Concepts mirror concepts in artistic practice?)

The best Brain-Target Five activities encompass several of the brain targets. They are complex and call on higher-level thinking skills. Here's an example using the cross-cutting concept of Stability and Change, in a fifth-grade Earth Science arts overlay. While fifth graders were studying the environmental impact of the spheres that surround the Earth, they researched contemporary iconic land artists and then created their own collaborative land sculpture on school grounds. Students predicted outcomes based on the materials they used; documented the effect of their environment over time on the sculptures; and ultimately, designed sustainability techniques based on their collected data and observations.

Brain-Target Five embodies a deeper engagement by learners in layered tasks that apply and extend the concepts they have been studying. In the following example, in a middle school Social Studies unit on the Civil War, the focus was on the impact of photography on the documentation of the war. Students focused on the impact on civilian life, in terms of the suffering as well as the creation of new opportunities. Brain-Target Four activities included the study of Civil War portraiture and poetry. Based on primary-source photographs, students wrote poems as a first-person narrative of a young person living through the war. The Brain-Target Five project used real-world and relevant subjects in the creation of a photo essay of people working in their school and first-person narrative poems based on interviews with their subjects.

Creative Conceptual Strategies for Brain-Target Five:

- *Collage: juxtapose imagery, movement, and/or text to reveal new meaning*
- *Metaphor: cast one thing as another*
- *Visual analogy: compare one thing to another*

(Continued)

(Continued)

- *Format: present an idea or concept in graphic terms*
- *Reformat: present an idea in an unusual mode that reveals its inherent meaning*
- *Mimicking: use the methods of a non-art discipline*
- *Enact: take on the persona of a figure in a non-art discipline*

Clare O'Malley Grizzard
Arts Education, Arts Integration Specialist

Brain-Target Five - Strategies for Creative Thinking

divergent thinking + convergent thinking

encourage multiple and novel responses
real-world context activities
investigations + experiments
metaphors + analogies
perspective taking
visual and performing arts
comparisons, classifications, analysis

embodied cognition + executive function

Creativity
&
Innovation

Brain-Target Six

9

Evaluating Learning: Evaluation of and for Learning

Creativity becomes more visible when adults try to be more attentive to the cognitive processes of children than to the results they achieve in various fields of doing and understanding.

—Loris Malaguzzi, Founder of the Reggio Emilia Approach

Brain-Target Six - Evaluation *of* and *for* Learning Chapter Map

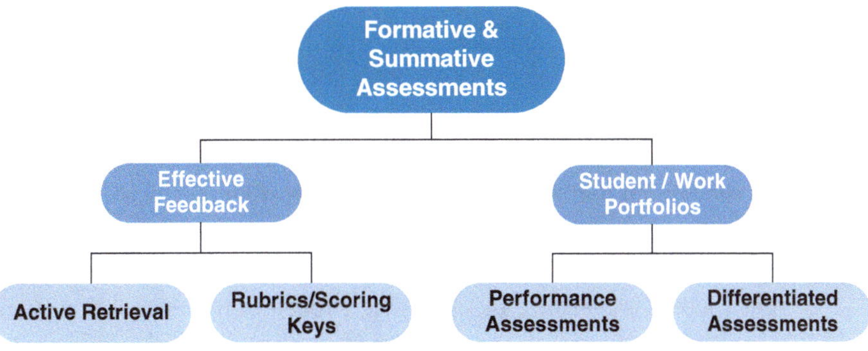

Brain-Target Six, which focuses on evaluating learning, is the final element of the Brain-Targeted Teaching® (BTT) Model. However, it is important to keep in mind that all six brain targets apply to all stages of the teaching and learning process and that evaluation does not occur only at the completion of a learning unit or work project. Rather, evaluation in various forms should be happening during every phase of the teaching, learning, and work process in order to provide guideposts to help assess progress and foster continual improvement. In addition to offering formative feedback for documenting the attainment of learning goals, the impact of assessment on memory is equally important to Brain-Target Six.

In this chapter, we consider research that demonstrates how feedback can be a powerful tool for enhancing learning and memory. We then look at how traditional types of assessment in schools such as tests, quizzes, mid-chapter reviews, and benchmark assessments can be supplemented or supplanted by alternatives such as arts-integrated activities, portfolio assessments, and performance assessments. Alternative assessments help all learners improve academic competence, allowing for cultural differences, providing alternate means to assess learning for those who struggle with traditional forms of assessments, and addressing achievement gaps for traditionally marginalized students (see Darling-Hammond et al., 2020). Similarly, in the workspace, traditional performance evaluations also can be supplemented with portfolios that track, refine, and celebrate work progress. Ideal evaluations reap benefits for retention and understanding while also engaging individuals in critical and creative thinking. In short, in Brain-Target Six, we emphasize that evaluation is not only *of* learning, evaluation also is *for* learning.

Evaluation in various forms should happen during every phase of the teaching and learning process.

Research To Practice: Evaluation to Enhance Learning

Over time, research from education, psychology, and cognitive science has shown that tests and other assessments do much more than simply tell how much learning has occurred. Assessments provide feedback that informs and motivates individuals while enhancing memory for material in specific ways. First, assessments provide useful feedback that increases learning by clarifying expectations, reinforcing work done well, and guiding areas for improvement. Second, assessments promote active retrieval, which by itself has been shown to improve retention. Third, intentionally *spacing* multiple assessments of the same material over specified time intervals can prompt students to engage in patterns of study and active retrieval that further increase retention (e.g., Kornell et al., 2010). These techniques support a wider view of assessment that allows *all* learners to successfully demonstrate what they know and can do as a result of instruction.

Assessments provide feedback that informs and motivates individuals while enhancing memory for material in specific ways.

Effective, Frequent, and Timely Feedback

This section addresses various ways to provide feedback and how effective feedback leads to positive learning outcomes. For example, Shen et al. (2021) examined how creativity could be enhanced based on type of feedback provided within Science, Technology, Engineering, Art, Mathematics (STEAM) education. One group of college-aged participants received feedback based on *teacher opinions*, while the second group received *teacher suggestions*, and the third did not receive feedback. Scores on a creativity assessment showed that participants who received suggestions from the teacher scored significantly higher on the creativity scale than the other two groups. Similarly, Wondim et al. (2024) found that written corrective feedback significantly improved writing skills of second language learners. The feedback was more effective when it was clear and direct, rather than indirect and generalized. Similar results were found in a meta-analysis of timely corrective feedback that explains *why* responses are accurate or inaccurate and then asking students to continue working on a task until they have attained success (see Marzano et al., 2001).

Effects of corrective feedback appear to be strongest when teachers explain why responses are accurate or inaccurate and/or ask students to continue working on tasks until they have attained success.

Consistent with the findings of the meta-analysis cited above, Pashler and colleagues (2005) found in a study of memory for native/foreign language word pairs that giving participants only right/wrong feedback produced the same results on subsequent tests as giving no feedback at all. In contrast, participants who were provided the correct response after they had produced an incorrect answer exhibited the greatest improvement on the final free-recall assessment—retention of the material increased by 494%. Fazio et al. (2010) also found that when responses are incorrect, giving only right/wrong feedback conveys little helpful information to the learner. Further, Finn and Metcalfe (2010) have shown that feedback can be effectively *scaffolded* by providing hints incrementally rather than just giving students the correct answer. This way, students receive helpful feedback but arrive at the correct responses themselves. Scaffolded feedback produced better long-term retention than did other types of feedback (traditional corrective feedback, minimal feedback, or answer-until-correct multiple-choice feedback).

The kind of feedback that a teacher provides also influences students' social acceptance. In a longitudinal study with early elementary students, Wullschleger et al. (2020) found that public feedback targeting incorrect social behavior resulted in lower social ratings of the involved students by their peers. Positive feedback on academic performance was associated with higher social acceptance. The authors conclude that teacher feedback behavior influences how students perceive one another and affects how they collaborate during classroom activities.

Feedback can be effectively *scaffolded* by providing hints incrementally rather than just giving students the correct answer.

Effective feedback depends not only on the *kind* of feedback but also on its *timing*—and students' awareness of the timing—which may be particularly important for student motivation. When students know that they won't receive feedback for a while, they (perhaps unconsciously) make less of an effort to perform well. Kettle and Häubl (2010) conducted an experiment to investigate the effects of timing on performance feedback in an academic setting. Students knew ahead of time when they would receive grades on a presentation they were giving. The proximity of feedback ranged between zero (same day) and seventeen days after the presentation. The results of the study revealed that performance increased linearly in direct relation to the proximity of feedback. In other words, students who knew they would receive feedback sooner tended to perform better than students who knew they would receive grades after a greater delay. The researchers concluded that the anticipation of timely feedback likely motivated participants' performance.

Students who knew they would receive feedback sooner tended to perform better than students who knew they would receive grades after a greater delay.

The above findings have important implications for the busy educator or leader who might be tempted to provide minimal and/or delayed feedback. Students will likely fail to benefit from practice tests or benchmark assessments that tell them only the percentage of responses they got correct. In addition to drawing attention to incorrect responses, we should be sure that students learn the correct answers when they are wrong and also attend to what they got *right*. A good way to get students to attend to correct responses is to have them correct their own work using an answer key (knowing the score will be checked by the teacher). This strategy also allows students to get prompt feedback soon after completing an assessment, taking advantage of the link between the timing of feedback and student motivation.

To summarize, useful and important evaluation strategies for teachers and leaders include the following: (a) ensuring timely feedback, (b) communicating beforehand when feedback will be offered, (c) scaffolding feedback by incrementally providing hints that allow individuals to self-correct, (d) allowing continual work on learning tasks until demonstrating full understanding of the material or work product, and (e) monitoring corrective public feedback that might negatively influence peer social acceptance.

Students will likely fail to benefit from practice tests or benchmark assessments that tell them only the percentage of responses they got correct.

Although direct feedback from the teacher or leader is powerful, this is not the only approach. Another simple strategy for getting students feedback quickly is peer review. This can be done by assigning students to partners with whom they have developed a trusting and supportive relationship, by instituting more formal class wide peer tutoring programs, or by implementing team-guided student performance reviews. Sun et al. (2023) studied the effects of peer feedback compared to teacher feedback within a writing assignment. Findings showed that both peer and teacher feedback were effective in offering recommendations for revisions of writing drafts. However, teacher feedback tended to provide more solutions and constructive comments for identified writing problems. That said, in general, peer feedback is an effective strategy to provide prompt feedback while helping all students learn skills in analysis and synthesis as they offer suggestions to peers.

Finally, a plethora of computer-assisted programs exist to provide students with immediate feedback and scaffold learning based on the type and frequency of errors. Gamification is one way to use technology to enhance learning goals. Serice (2023) describes gamification as fundamental to the teaching and learning process. She highlights how the goal of gamification is to promote learning, not merely to entertain (as most games are designed to do). She argues that gamification offers novelty in learning tasks, fosters positive emotions and motivation, enhances memory, and facilitates creative thinking. Below are examples of how gamification has been used in higher education and in other contexts.

From the Expert Practitioner

Gamification for Learning

I have observed firsthand the power of using game principles and gamification in higher education settings. Unlike traditional educational games, which often involve straightforward game playing, gamification involves applying game-like elements. This method is utilized to enhance learning and engagement in my courses. In my course, students are not merely learning about business and entrepreneurship in the traditional sense; they participate in a series of game-like scenarios that mimic real-world business challenges. These scenarios are designed to cultivate resilience, strategic thinking and innovation. Students must navigate these obstacles as they develop their own business plans, much like players in a complex game setting out to achieve high scores or complete quests. The culmination of this process is a Shark Tank style presentation, where students pitch their business ideas to a panel of potential investors. This not only serves as a final project but also as a practical assessment of their ability to apply what they've learned in a high-pressure, real-world environment. By implementing these practices into my classroom, it creates a learning environment that informs and fosters a classroom atmosphere that radiates excitement, challenge, and personal growth.

> *Human beings are naturally wired for play, and as a result, the emotions experienced during gameplay are undeniable. The desire to play is a superpower for both children and adult learners. Harnessing this superpower through gamification can open doors for teaching content, evaluating knowledge, and tuning the emotional climate. Using games makes the learning environment or workspace fun on demand. In this positive, energized atmosphere your students feel valued, emotionally supported, and ready to learn.*
>
> Aisha Austin
> Educational Consultant, Higher Education Instructor

Active Retrieval of Information

Prior research has demonstrated that actively retrieving information from memory appears to benefit long-term retention much more than does simply studying. In the seminal study, Karpicke and Roediger (2008) compared the effect of repeated testing with that of repeated studying for long-term retention of foreign language vocabulary. They found that repeated testing of English/foreign language word-pairs produced significantly greater retention than did repeated studying. This has commonly been referred to as the *testing effect*, though in theory any activity that would cause students to retrieve information (not just tests) would yield the effect. When students have to retrieve information actively, as occurs when they are tested, this appears to play a role in reinforcing memory for that information. Standard studying relies on the more passive receipt of information and does not seem to have the same effect. Although studying is surely better than nothing, it does not recruit memory systems in the same way as retrieval of information. Since time for schoolwork is always limited, students will often be better served by retrieval practice (e.g., self-quizzing) than by studying alone (e.g., rereading). It is important to model retrieval practice for students so that they understand what this means (e.g., "no looking at the answers") and to encourage students to engage in retrieval practice as a strategy for remembering information. Students tend to believe (incorrectly) that studying is more effective than retrieval practice (Kornell & Son, 2009). The old standard practice of flashcards can help students understand what retrieval entails (and effects of active retrieval explain why flashcards are so effective).

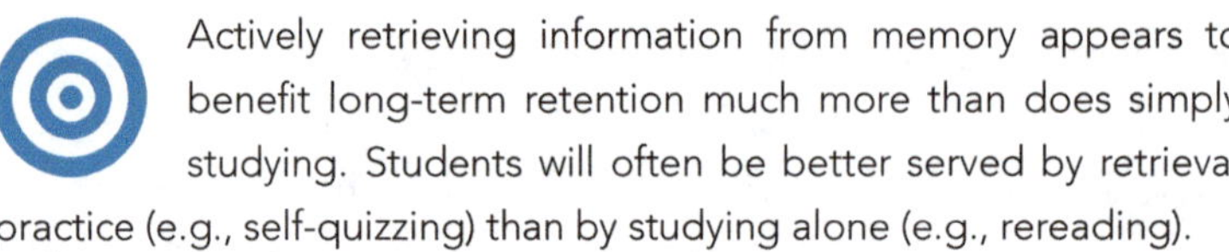

Actively retrieving information from memory appears to benefit long-term retention much more than does simply studying. Students will often be better served by retrieval practice (e.g., self-quizzing) than by studying alone (e.g., rereading).

Karpicke and Blunt (2011) argue that educators intuitively provide students with activities that focus too heavily on acquiring and studying information and not enough on having them practice retrieval of information to reconstruct what they know. But how might retrieval practice stack up against a more elaborative form of studying? In a pair of experiments, Karpicke and Blunt investigated the relative benefits of retrieval practice versus elaborative studying for learning of science content. Learning was measured both by verbatim recall of concepts and by the ability of students to draw inferences involving multiple concepts—a measure of *deeper* understanding. The results indicated that active retrieval of information consolidates learning in a more powerful way than even elaborative forms of studying. Karpicke and Blunt posit that, because the act of retrieval itself strengthens memories in a unique and specific way, retrieval practice should be recognized as critical to the learning process.

Educators would be remiss if they view testing only as a way to *measure* learning; as the research discussed above shows, testing also has the power to *cause* learning. It is important to note that testing as understood here should not be equated with the kind of standardized testing commonly associated with accountability measures. Rather, the idea is that students should frequently test their knowledge on their own, or in response to teacher prompts, with the goal of consolidating learning. As will be seen later in this chapter, knowledge can be tested in creative ways through arts-integrated activities that eliminate all of the negative connotations accompanying the word *test*. Providing multiple ways of assessment and allowing for choice is an effective way to capture the knowledge of atypical learners. Neurodiverse learners, second language learners, and any student who struggles with traditional testing techniques would benefit from the strategy described below by Kristen McGinness. Testing also has the power to *cause* learning.

Spacing Effects

We have discussed in previous chapters the growing practice in our schools of trying to teach too much subject matter in too little time in order to cover all required material. This practice leads to a *teach, test, and move on* approach that is not amenable to deeper, more protracted interactions with content. It also discourages review and retesting of

From the Expert Practitioner

Tic-Tac-Toe Assessment

As part of my Native Americans unit, I use projects to assess the students' mastery of the content and give them a choice of how they want to display learning. Each student receives a Tic-Tac-Toe board that describes nine different small projects. Students then choose three assessment methods in a row, going any direction. The students enjoy the challenge of picking their desired projects and feel empowered by having choices in how to assess learning. I designed the game board to ensure variety in the methods of assessment. Some projects involved writing and researching while others included more hands-on activities.

For example, one row requires students to write two paragraphs explaining why cultures of Native Americans developed differently, then follow a recipe containing some of the main ingredients that Native Americans often used, and finally build a model of one type of Native American home along with a paragraph describing it. Each row included projects that would help me to assess what they had learned while also letting them have fun and use their different strengths and interests. I was amazed at the effort and excitement that they put into their projects. One student became so engaged that she built a life-size tepee!

Kristen McGinness
Teacher, Leader, Elementary School

previously mastered material at later points in time. Researchers have long recognized the efficacy of introducing delays between learning events (Cepeda et al., 2006, 2008); this is commonly called the *spacing effect*, which refers to spacing out learning events over time rather than massing learning into one or only a few sessions within a short timeframe. Ongoing research continues to demonstrate the potential of spacing repeated studies as an effective way to promote retention of information (e.g., Carpenter et al., 2022; Kim & Webb, 2022; Knabe & Vlach, 2020; Lyle et al., 2020; Rogers, 2023). Massing learning practice such as cramming for a test or learning material in one sitting might produce short-term retention, but the information will more likely be forgotten. When learning sessions are interspersed with other activities, learned information can consolidate into longer-term memory.

Research has found the neurological mechanism that explains why the spacing effect is important for the consolidation of memory. In animal studies, Okamoto et al. (2011) observed specific protein synthesis occurring in the cerebellum when learning was spaced but not when it was massed (learning occurred all at once). The researchers suggest that this study adds a biological explanation to the well-known advantages of spacing multiple exposures over time to learning particular tasks.

Researchers have long recognized the efficacy of introducing delays between learning events.

What does this mean for classroom instruction? If the goal is for students to remember information for an upcoming unit test four to six weeks after content is initially taught, then content should be revisited with a follow-up study/test session after about a week. Conversely, if teachers need students to retain information longer (e.g., up to a full school year for final exams or standardized tests), then content should be revisited only after a month or more has passed. Though Cepeda and colleagues (2008) did not investigate intervals longer than a year, if the goal is retention for many years or a lifetime, it is likely that content will need to be revisited multiple times over several years with large gaps in between. The biggest take-away from this research for teachers and trainers is this: *Make it a priority to revisit previously taught content after a significant delay and have students study/test their knowledge.*

Research on the effects of feedback, active retrieval of information, and spacing of learning events has strong implications for many aspects of learning, whether in formal education or in the workspace. This research can inform the work of individuals who make important educational decisions, from policymakers who set standards and testing policies, to textbook publishers who sequence content and curriculum reviews, to classroom teachers and corporate trainers who ultimately make the day-to-day decisions regarding content and assessments.

Multiple Kinds of Assessments

As was discussed in previous chapters, quality teaching involves the interplay of a variety of pedagogical methods, from conventional direct instruction to highly student-centered instruction that fosters creative, divergent thinking through student-generated products. Similarly, the challenge of effective evaluation is to balance the use of assessments that require selection of the correct answer with those that call for students to construct open-ended responses, solve problems, and apply knowledge.

The challenge of effective evaluation is to balance the use of assessments that require selection of the correct answer with those that call for students to construct open-ended responses, solve problems, and apply knowledge.

Few educators would deny that testing drives teaching—that is, the way we test and what we test largely affects the way we teach and what we teach. Therefore, teachers might feel compelled to match teaching techniques and student assessments to the current format of achievement tests so that students are prepared to be savvy test-takers. Fortunately, however, some policymakers and the general public are calling for assessments that provide broader measures of educational attainment (including better multiple-choice tests), addressing areas such as thinking skills and problem-solving abilities. As we look to educate students to think creatively, our teaching as well as our testing must reflect this challenge. In this spirit, assessments provide opportunities for promoting learning rather than ranking students against each other (Darling-Hammond et al., 2020).

As we look to educate students to think creatively, our teaching as well as our testing must reflect this challenge.

In contrast to current standardized achievement tests that too often measure low-level recall of factual information rather than higher order thinking (Brookhart, 2010), *this chapter* describes some forms of alternative assessment that change what teachers focus on and what children learn in response. These assessments make it possible to gauge important critical thinking skills: investigation, synthesis of disparate ideas, exploration of multiple points of view, problem-solving, metacognition, and demonstration of global understanding through metaphorical thinking.

Portfolio Assessments

Portfolio assessments are collections of student work that track progress over time. Portfolios often combine both student-selected and teacher-selected work and include not merely traditional assessments (worksheets, quizzes, and tests) but also samples of audio-visual work, poster displays, technology apps, and arts-integrated content projects. For some students, a collection of this kind of work may present a fuller and more accurate picture of progress and understanding than do tests that focus almost solely on memorized information. Portfolios are a powerful tool to demonstrate progress in attaining learning objectives, and such visible progress can be a strong motivator for students and teachers alike. Likewise, the same method can be used when evaluating a worker's performance in a corporate setting. A portfolio of work selected by the worker and leader is empowering and motivating for both young children and adult learners in multiple contexts.

Portfolios are a powerful tool to demonstrate progress in attaining learning objectives, and such visible progress can be a strong motivator for all individuals.

From the Expert Practitioner

The Power of Student Portfolios

Feedback through portfolios is an especially informative way to teach my students. I select items that students will include in the portfolio and allow the students to choose the work they want to show me, peers, and parents. I ask that they include some writing that analyzes how they are learning. I scaffold their writing by giving students sentence threads that they complete such as, "This math unit was hard because . . ." or "The part I liked the most about this science unit was . . ." or "Something new that I learned was . . ." or "The problems I'm still not sure of are. . . ." During the unit, I ask students to meet with me individually and with peers to demonstrate what they have learned and which activities helped them learn best.

Students not only like being able to analyze their own learning but also to evaluate my creative thinking in crafting activities for them. We all acknowledge that teaching basic skills can be rote and dry, but I feel challenged everyday to make learning exciting and relevant to their lives.

Robin Melanson
Teacher, Middle School Science and Mathematics

Portfolio assessment can also encourage metacognition (awareness of one's own thought processes) that permits individuals to set their own learning goals and then track their progress. Even for traditional forms of assessment, students can use the process of building a portfolio to gain a deeper understanding as they review and write about what questions they found to be challenging, which items they got wrong on a test, why they came up with the wrong response, how they would correct the response, and how they might prepare differently for the next assessment. In questions with multiple solutions to a problem (divergent thinking), students can assess how they can expand their thinking beyond the prompt to enhance their creative thinking. For project-based learning tasks, students can showcase their learning in ways that might include how they constructed models and how the use of the arts enhanced their work.

Journals

Journals are another powerful tool for evaluating and enhancing learning. Though journal writing may take a number of different forms, two seem particularly useful: *reflective journals* and *learning logs*. When individuals create reflective journal entries, their aim is to contemplate what they have learned and explore in a relatively freeform fashion potential connections to other ideas and applications to their own lives or those of others around them. Reflective journal writing has been shown to encourage more metacognition and the use of more sophisticated cognitive strategies during learning tasks. As Dyment and O'Connell (2010) point out, however, it is important that reflective journal writing engage in critical, creative thinking and not lead to mere descriptive accounts of events. Without sufficient guidance, students are prone to slipping into this purely descriptive form of writing, the benefits of which for learning are probably minimal. Thus, teachers and leaders should be sure to model the practice of critical reflection and creative, divergent thinking through journal writing to maximize benefits.

Reflective journal writing has been shown to encourage more metacognition and the use of more sophisticated cognitive strategies during learning tasks.

Learning logs represent a somewhat more constrained and objective kind of writing task. When students create learning logs, they work to explicitly recount the important ideas they have come to understand as a result of instruction. For example, students might be prompted to respond to questions like "What are three important ideas I learned today" or "Are there any ideas that I would like to understand better." This more constrained style of journal writing may be more efficient and easier to engage in for many students (especially younger ones), as students are provided with a more specific focus and a clear starting point. Learning logs may also be especially useful for teachers who are trying to keep track of progress for each of the individual students in the class. Students may oftentimes be more willing to candidly describe what they do and don't understand if they can avoid doing so in front of the class. In addition, learning logs provide an opportunity to use non-textual forms of expression such as creating a sketch, icon, concept map, or other forms of pictorial representations.

Teachers should consider the benefits of both learning logs and reflective journals for their students and utilize whatever combination seems most appropriate for the particular population of students they serve. Leaders can also encourage a version of learning logs described above as part of a process that documents work attainment or identifies needs for further engagement or mentoring.

Learning logs may also be especially useful for teachers who are trying to keep track of progress for each of the individual students in the class.

Performance Assessments

Performance assessment measures a student's ability to apply knowledge through the performance of activities such as experimenting, weighing evidence, evaluating sources, designing a plan of action to solve a real-world problem, developing multiple points of view, and demonstrating through artistic expression an understanding and interpretation of content.

Performance assessments are often graded through the use of a rubric, which makes it possible to assess performance on several different criteria. If using a rubric, it should be given to students at the start of a project or (better still) at the beginning of the learning unit to give students the *big picture* of what they will be expected to do to demonstrate understanding (see Chapter 6 on Brain-Target Three). Rubrics can be holistic, providing students with an overall score derived from a subjective combination of multiple criteria, or they can be analytic, specifying precisely how points should be assigned for each criterion and how different criteria are weighted (see the following for a sample analytic rubric).

Example Performance Assessment Activity and Rubrics

Learning objective: Demonstrate how the geographical features in the environment influence the cultural beliefs, government, religion, and education of a civilization.

Content: Students are presented with major features of geography and culture of early civilizations. Next, using Mesopotamia as an example, the students are shown how particular features might constrain the culture—the knowledge, beliefs, and behaviors—as well as the government, religion, and education of a Mesopotamian culture.

Activity: Students will be directed to apply the knowledge they have learned about the workings of a civilization to create their own primitive culture. They will identify the geography of the region in which the civilization can be found and various features of the civilization: the cultural or belief system, government, religion, and education. They will then describe *why* the geography supports each of the particular features you describe.

Grading Criteria Given to Students (Holistic Rubric):

1. Content: Recognize and specify all of the major parts of a civilization.
   a. Have you identified a geography as well as the four features (government, religion, education, culture) of your civilization?
2. Critical Thinking: Plausible explanations for why the geography supports each feature.
   a. Are your explanations comprehensible and logically sound? That is, is each identified feature possible given the geography you describe? For example, a nomadic community would likely not have a goddess of agriculture.
3. Originality: How do your identified geography and features compare to the example given by the teacher and to the other groups?
   a. How different is your set of features relative to those in the example described by the teacher?

(Continued)

(Continued)

4. Extension: Are you including new information beyond what was presented by the teacher?
    a. Does your civilization reflect additional experiences or knowledge that was not taught in this lesson but that you have, from your own culture or from other lessons, taught in school?

Grading Criteria (Analytic Rubric):

	CONTENT KNOWLEDGE	CRITICAL THINKING	ORIGINALITY OF FEATURES	EXTENSION OF INFORMATION
WEIGHT:	X 1	X 1	X 2	X 2
TOTAL SCORE:				
3 Points	Precisely identifies the geography and each feature of the civilization: government, religion, education, and culture.	Provides reasonable and thorough explanation for why each feature could be found in a civilization with a particular geography.	Identified geography and features are unique: They are all different from those used in the Mesopotamia example and mostly different from those described by other groups.	Most of your civilization reflects your knowledge from other disciplines or personal experiences that are unrelated to what was taught.
2 Points	Partly or vaguely identifies (some or all) geography and features of the civilization.	Provides reasonable, but possibly limited explanation for why some or all of the features could be found in a civilization with a particular geography.	Identified geography and features are somewhat original: Some are different than those used in the Mesopotamia example, and some differ from those described by other groups.	Some of your civilization reflects your knowledge from other disciplines or personal experiences that are unrelated to what was taught.
1 Point	Incompletely identifies elements for some features of the civilization. Some features may be left unspecified.	Provides unlikely and/or possibly vague explanation for why some of the features could be found in a civilization with a particular geography.	Identified geography and features are mostly the same as those used in the Mesopotamia example, and most features overlap with those described by the teacher in class.	Very little of your civilization reflects your knowledge from other disciplines or personal experiences that are unrelated to what was taught.

Assessing creative thinking and problem-solving through rubrics represents a helpful way for teachers to evaluate student learning by using dimensions that are not accessible to more traditional measures. Debates continue, however, about how (or whether it's even possible) to *grade* creativity. Moreover, Brookhart (2010) points out that it is common in educational practice for teachers to reduce assessments of creativity in student work to mere judgments of aesthetic or artistic appeal (e.g., a neat design drawn on the cover of a report). Effective assessment of creative thinking must involve a deeper understanding of the creative process (see Chapter 9 on Creative Thinking). Rubrics intended to guide teachers and students with respect to what counts as creative thinking should be one tool to assess the student's ability to combine disparate elements of learned content to formulate unique and original ideas.

> Rubrics intended to guide teachers and students with respect to what counts as creative thinking should assess the student's ability to combine disparate elements of learned content to formulate unique and original ideas.

From the Expert Practitioner

Creativity in Mathematics

As a second-grade teacher who enjoys teaching through the arts, evaluating learning in alternative ways speaks to my natural way of teaching. I use the principles of the arts to teach and measure students' divergent thinking and their ability to solve open-ended mathematics problems. I also encourage students to include an expression of a personal connection to the real-world application of the math unit.

While I still use traditional methods of assessment, much of the evaluation is based on projects that allow students to be creative, such as making a product to demonstrate a mathematics concept. For example, when studying measurement, I administered the typical mid-chapter review. Then I decided that a more creative way to assess student learning would be to ask them to draw a map of a farm. They had the choices of which animals and physical features they would include. They then had to determine the

(Continued)

(Continued)

area and perimeter of the pens for each group of animals based on the size and number of animals they chose. I gave the students a scoring key to determine what elements will be graded and allowed them to self-assess before I scored their work. Students had this rubric at the start of the unit so there were no surprises for them. The only surprise came to me when I saw the amazing work they had done and how proud they were of their learning.

Rebecca Singer
Teacher, Elementary Mathematics

Name

Midchapter Review

Good!

Do your best!

Estimate. Then measure.

	Estimate	Measure
1	about ___ inches	about ___ inches
2	about ___ inches	about ___ inches
3	about ___ cm	about ___ cm
4	about ___ cm	about ___ cm

Measure each path.

5 about ___ inches

6 about ___ cm

Measure. Add to find the perimeter.

7 ___ cm

8 ___ cm

Draw a diagram to solve.

Use your own paper.

9 A map shows a square garden. There is a big tree in each corner. There are 2 small trees between each big tree. How many trees are in the garden? ___ trees

10 How did you solve problem 9? ___

Journal How do you estimate the length of an object?

CHAPTER 10 Midchapter Review three hundred sixty-three • 363

P=26
A=26 sq units
Barn

P=16
A=16 sq. units
pigs

P=25
A=26 sq. units
farm house

A=26 sq units
P=24 sq. units
horses

A=6 sq. units
P=10
chikens

cows
A=45 sq. units
P=28

Lake

Area and Perimeter on a Farm Rubric

Give yourself one ☺ for each item you included in your drawing.

______I drew pens for at least 4 animals.

______I found the perimeter of each pen.

______I found the area of each pen.

______I remembered to record the perimeter and area for each pen on my map.

_____I added details to my map.

I gave myself________☺'s.

Your teacher will check your work and give you one ☺ for each item you included.

______You drew pens for at least 4 animals.

______You found the perimeter of each pen.

______You found the area of each pen.

______You remembered to record the perimeter and area for each pen on your map.

_____You added details to your map.

Your teacher gave you _____☺'s.

As we have reviewed in this chapter, effective teaching and effective testing are two sides of the same coin. Evaluation of learning is an ongoing process that begins as soon as one starts teaching and continues indefinitely in order to sustain what has been learned. Evaluation and feedback are essential to making learning efficient, and assessments—insofar as they prompt students to test their knowledge—can be a powerful catalyst for lifelong retention.

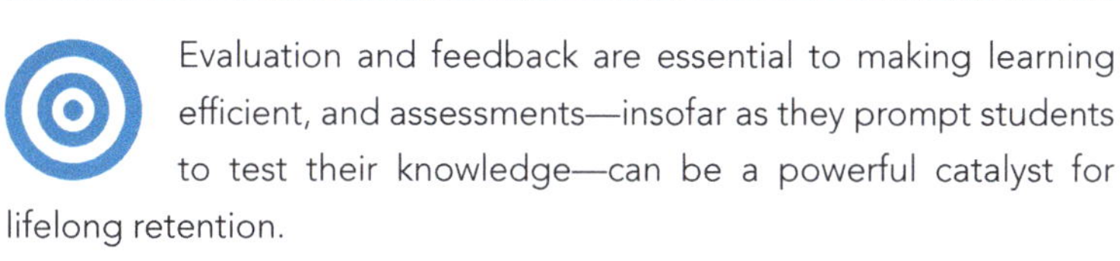

Evaluation and feedback are essential to making learning efficient, and assessments—insofar as they prompt students to test their knowledge—can be a powerful catalyst for lifelong retention.

We now return to the expert advice for how the arts are used in evaluating learning by Clare O'Malley Grizzard.

From the Expert Practitioner

The Arts in Brain-Target Six

Teachers who want to include creativity strategies in their practice are deterred by uncertainty about how to assess creative work. Creative work in arts integration is a purposeful, examined process, so ongoing feedback is essential and can

(Continued)

(Continued)

be through quick drawing prompts; sketchnoting; generative discussions through visual analysis; student-created video shorts; peer and self assessment; gallery walks, admit/exit tickets, and digital response tools.

Process portfolio formats, rather than summative work portfolios, offer evidence of thinking and learning. Take the research workbook described by Julia Marshall (2019), which is as much a science field study guide as a sketchbook. It is a collection of exit tickets, sketches, quizzes, experiments with materials, brainstorming maps, and reflection notes that, together, provide a comprehensive documentation for assessment. In addition to the suggestions above for designing a rubric, another similar approach might use the following: diversity or variety of ideas and contexts, a variety of source material, novel combination of ideas to make something new, communication of something interesting and relevant.

Artist statements are written reflection pieces that explain the artist's thinking—What were the big ideas behind this work? What resources did you use? What do you want the viewer to notice or understand? What challenges or surprises did you experience? How does this artwork connect with the concepts of the subject? What would your next steps be in exploring these ideas further?

In this example unit, middle school students are studying the novel Animal Farm *and the power of language and images to inspire, persuade, and control. After a visual analysis of propaganda posters used throughout modern history, as well as the study of elements of good poster design, students design propaganda posters that accurately portray events and characters from the novel. A second task follows with students composing their own advocacy posters for an issue of personal and/or civic concern. Ultimately, they are employing the design skills they have learned as well as demonstrating their understanding of the main concepts of the unit.*

A rubric for these tasks includes the following:

- *Audience of the poster is clearly identifiable*
- *Graphic images and concise text communicate message*
- *The poster uses a propaganda technique*
- *Grammar and spelling are correct and legible*

Clare O'Malley Grizzard
Arts Educator, Arts Integration Specialist

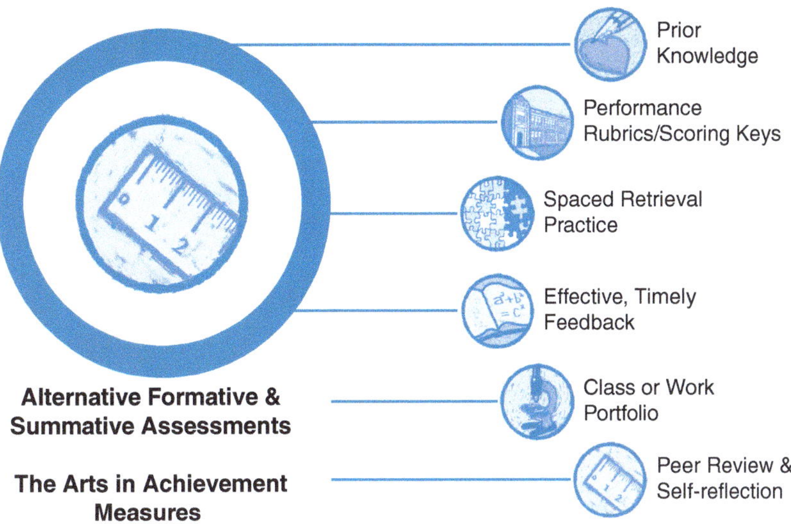
Brain-Target Six - Strategies for Evaluation & Assessment
Prior Knowledge
Performance Rubrics/Scoring Keys
Spaced Retrieval Practice
Effective, Timely Feedback
Class or Work Portfolio
Peer Review & Self-reflection
Alternative Formative & Summative Assessments
The Arts in Achievement Measures

10 Implementing the Brain-Targeted Teaching® Model in Schools, Workspaces, and Beyond

The Brain-Targeted Teaching® Model

It is the supreme art of the teacher to awaken joy in creative expression and knowledge.

—Albert Einstein

I believe that many practitioners, leaders, and parents already use strategies consistent with some or even all of the components of the Brain-Targeted Teaching® (BTT) Model. Beyond recognition of their use of good strategies, readers may find that the model offers a deep research base and a rationale for these best practices. The model can also provide support to those who continually seek out new ways to enhance learning; the model provides guidance and direction in the form of a unified framework for understanding how learning occurs and for identifying additional strategies that are most effective. In thinking about applying the model not only in the classroom but also in schools, workspaces, or in the home, the model provides a vision of learning focused on the acquisition of deep content knowledge as well as creative thinking and problem-solving. This vision leads to deep and rigorous learning and working in a joyful and engaging environment. Finally, and possibly most important, the model provides a common language that helps to unify all members of a community around evidence-based best practices.

While sharing the model with practitioners and others in schools and conferences nationally and internationally and learning of their experiences in implementing Brain-Targeted Teaching®, I have been enlightened as to how the model influences teaching practices from early childhood through higher education, in the workplace, and in the home. I have also been amazed at how those working in professions outside of education have adapted the model to their organizational structure through activities such as strategic planning, content development, and corporate training. I have also loved hearing from parents about how they learned of the model and use strategies in their homes and how athletic coaches use the model as they develop players in multiple sports. It has been exciting for me to be the learner! As the words of expert practitioners have demonstrated throughout this book, the model can take on many shapes and forms. In short, I have learned the power that can be gained when one understands the ways in which research from the learning sciences can inform and guide effective learning. In this chapter, I share how the model can be implemented in multiple settings including schools, the workplace, and the home.

Brain-Targeted Teaching® Model in Schools and the Workplace: Getting Started

Although there is no single approach to implementing the BTT Model, I will offer strategies that have been successful, emphasizing the importance of supportive leadership and collaborative planning.

Instructional Leadership and Support

An organizational leader—principal, head of school, team leader, corporate trainer, athletic coach, CEO—must have deep knowledge of any program, initiative, or process and must not only support but also guide its implementation. This entails communicating to all stakeholders how this (or any program or initiative) furthers the organization's vision and mission. An effective way to implement the BTT Model from a leadership perspective is to embed its principles in broad-based expectations for climate, planning, educating the workforce, leading practices, and evaluating goals. The targets set forth in the model can become part of a yearly or long-range plan for creating a successful school or organization that meets benchmarks while simultaneously offering a well-rounded and challenging, yet joyful educational and work experience.

I open this chapter by first observing how the BTT Model has influenced a successful and joyful school. Next I show how the model has been used in business and industry. Whether your work is in a school or office, you might relate to the section below offered by Connie Coker, Head of School, and Pamela Terry, a Corporate Trainer in the nuclear industry. Then, we look at how the BTT Model can be implemented broadly within educational environments.

From the Expert Practitioner

Leading and Learning With Joy

It was late August—still sweltering outside, and one by one, familiar colleagues and some newly-hired friends rolled into the Multipurpose Room for the Opening Faculty and Staff Meeting. There was a buzz of excitement in seeing dear friends again after a summer respite. There was also palpable anticipation of classroom setup combined with meeting students and families this group of teachers would soon wrap in their figurative arms

(Continued)

(Continued)

for the upcoming school year. I had asked faculty to bring pictures to the meeting which represented a moment of joy for them over the summer. They laughed and reminisced as they shared these pictures and joyful summer memories with one another. After this moment of connection, I bravely asked this group of extraordinary educators to close their eyes. Every single person then willingly trusted me to lead them through a body scan meditation. For three minutes, these loving, dedicated teachers who had quite a bit to do to prepare for their students' first day, quieted their hearts, their minds, and their bodies to connect deeply with themselves to be able to connect deeply with others. Establishing an emotional climate for the school year was priority number one.

As the Head of an independent school, neuroeducation research and the Brain-Targeted Teaching® Model not only guide our educators to improve student outcomes in classrooms but it also guides my leadership and the school's collective success. Leaders set the tone for a positive (or negative) culture and climate. Just as our teachers intently establish an emotional climate for learning, create a nurturing and organized learning environment, and design the learning experience to authentically assess learning outcomes, leaders must also establish an aesthetically and psychologically supportive environment while helping their colleagues understand and leverage their unique strengths and talents for the benefit of the organization's mission and priorities. This supportive environment includes classrooms and offices with soft lighting, plants, and natural daylight; a "good morning" alongside a smile, eye contact, and an acknowledgement of one another every single day; opportunities for adult fun and creative expression; and Teacher Learning Walks and professional portfolios to demonstrate teaching and learning outcomes. If we want brain-targeted outcomes for our students, we must also holistically approach teachers and schools from this evidence-based model.

Not surprisingly, our theme for the school year became Cultivating Connections. The summer photos referenced above are now on the bulletin board in our entry foyer–alongside joyful photos of our students and families. In addition to providing a joyful learning experience for every student who walks into the school each day, it is my hope that every teacher also engages in deep, joyful, and lasting learning and connections. The research and practical applications of the Brain-Targeted Teaching® Model provide the foundation for this outcome.

Connie Coker
Head of School

From the Expert Practitioner

Implementing BTT in the Workplace

Companies invest millions of dollars each year into workforce training, yet little of what is taught in business and industry classrooms transfers to real workplace application. To improve corporate returns on training investment requires that we consider not only what happens in business and industry classrooms but, just as importantly, what happens in the workplace before and after training.

Workplace culture, peer and leadership support, and opportunity to apply new knowledge and skills after training all influence whether training improves individual and organizational performance or is a wasted investment. Before employees set foot in the classroom their perception of whether they will apply content on the job affects their attention and learning effort. Leaders can improve learning outcomes by simply discussing the importance of upcoming training events with their employees before they occur. Alternatively, leaders may kick off a training event by describing expectations for how knowledge gained will be used and why the training is important. With this foundation established, students are much more likely to engage in learning and make connections between the content and how it can be applied on the job.

After completion of a training event, supervisor and peer support for workplace application of knowledge is another driving factor toward transfer. When learners have supervisor and peer support in implementing changes and making improvement based on their learning, they are more likely to apply their new skills and knowledge. When employees are not supported to make improvements, use new skills, or are not given time to do so, transfer will be limited.

Finally, transfer implies that workers are given the opportunity to apply new knowledge and skills when they return to work—and sooner is better. When training content isn't immediately relevant to workplace application, new knowledge remains unused, new skills remain unpracticed, and the ability to recall and apply the information decreases over time. Leaders can be purposeful about providing new assignments, or even holding recall practice sessions for infrequently used knowledge, to improve the likelihood of the transfer of learning to the workplace.

(Continued)

(Continued)

If, on the other hand, leaders do not have an expectation or do not believe there are opportunities to apply learning after completion of training, we must then ask whether the training event is a good use of scarce financial resources and employee effort.

Pamela Terry, EdD
Manager, Nuclear Industry Training

Curricular Decisions and Instructional Planning

Similar to the description of the importance of leadership in schools and corporations, the role of the leader in educational settings is critical to successful teaching and learning. Every component of the BTT Model is dependent upon the support that educators are given in learning, practicing, implementing, and evaluating instruction for continuous improvement. Whether considering the school's climate, its environment, student learning, or student and teacher wellness, the role of the leader is key to the mission and vision of the institution.

Ongoing professional learning experiences are critical for understanding new ways of teaching and learning and essential for teacher efficacy (see JohnBull & Hardiman, 2023). Next, leaders can support practitioners by providing regular opportunities for collaboration in sharing strategies and planning art-integrated learning units.

A strong recommendation for school leaders is to facilitate regular opportunities for teachers to engage in collaborative planning. As teachers in elementary grades design learning units, those who teach the same grade in self-contained classrooms benefit from sharing ideas and materials. In addition, collaborating with teachers from other grades helps in coordinating content and scaffolding activities to help students progress to ever-increasing levels of complexity in concept and skill acquisition. Likewise, teachers at the secondary level benefit from collaborative planning, whether through content departments or in interdisciplinary planning teams with teachers representing various content areas. Also, as arts integration is a central component of the model, engaging school-based arts educators as well as practicing artists from the community is valuable at all levels.

As the chapter on Brain-Target Three explains, the approach to writing a learning unit is holistic as well as analytical. That is, learning unit design begins by choosing the standards, content, skills, and concepts to be taught and mapping connections among the unit's elements through visual representations. Only then does one specify learning objectives and activities that will provide multiple exposures to the content (especially through arts integration), promote creative problem-solving, and provide multiple approaches for measuring achievement.

Although writing the entire unit *up front* takes more time in the beginning than planning day-by-day, ultimately the benefits of having a well-thought-out learning unit reap rewards for the teacher and students alike. In addition to benefiting the teacher and students in the classroom where the unit is taught, the upfront writing and planning leads to a heightened spirit of collaboration among faculty as they brainstorm activities and share outcomes. In addition, teachers who are often viewed as *special subject* teachers (visual and performing arts, physical education, technology, and foreign language) take on new roles in the school; their expertise in active learning helps content teachers design creative learning tasks.

All at Once or Little by Little?

School leaders must decide whether to implement the model schoolwide initially, or rather to develop and support a smaller group of faculty who write and demonstrate units to peers, with the eventual goal of having the model adopted by all teachers. Both approaches are useful depending on the school's readiness and need. The latter is the approach I took as a school principal when the model was first being developed. After training faculty in the background and components of the model, I facilitated collaborative planning time for several groups of teachers to plan and *field test* interdisciplinary units. These teachers made observations related to the effectiveness of the model and its overall success in achieving learning goals. They then prepared a PowerPoint presentation to demonstrate the units at professional development sessions and faculty meetings. Throughout the school year, more and more teachers participated in the process. I found that teachers enjoyed learning from each other; many wanted to participate after hearing their students enthusiastically sharing activities from other classes where teachers were implementing the model.

This approach is also useful in higher education or any work structure. Leaders may choose to adopt all components of the model or to focus on a particular brain target. For example, if the climate of the organization needs to improve, focus on the emotional climate for learning (Brain-Target One). Or if the need for better workforce training is a priority, focus on the strategies in Brain-Target Four. If creative thinking and problem-solving are important skills to develop in the workforce, focus on the information presented in Brain-Target Five. In short, there is no one right way to use the information presented in this book. My only hope is that both children and adults benefit from a focus on a wholistic approach to teaching, leading, and learning.

What Does Implementation of the Brain-Targeted Teaching® Model Look Like?

Implementation of the model should garner observable rewards. Below, is a quick listing of indicators of successful implementation through the lens of each brain target:

Brain-Target One—Emotional Climate for Learning

- Conversations between adults–including practitioners, support personnel, leadership, and parents–and children demonstrate mutual respect
- Behavior-specific praise for effort is freely given to both children and adults
- Cultural inclusiveness occurs regularly via recognition and respect of cultural differences and experiences
- Routines and rules are clearly evident and fairly applied; they focus on respect and the elimination of any form of discrimination
- Rituals provide quick and enjoyable ways to motivate and engage learners
- Celebrations are offered to recognize growth in attaining goals
- In schools, every child is able to identify caring adults within the school and classroom; in work environments, mentors are available to assist and support personnel
- Multicultural themes are evident throughout the school, in every classroom and in the workplace
- Every learning unit or work project includes activities that foster personal connection to the content
- Learners are given choices in learning and evaluation activities
- Students and employees are treated with warmth and empathy to create a trusting environment
- Humor is used frequently and appropriately to provide a relaxed environment

Brain-Target Two—Physical Environment

- The physical space, including halls, meeting spaces, and classrooms, reflects a clean and orderly environment
- Multicultural themes are evident in visual displays in classrooms and the workspace

- Classroom displays reflect the current unit of study and exhibit students' work rather than only commercially made products
- Lighting and sound are optimal in classrooms and workspaces
- Seating arrangements are flexible as space allows for movement
- Soft music and suitable scents are evident in classrooms and workspaces when appropriate
- Time is available for quiet reflection

Brain-Target Three—Learning Design

- Content standards are used in curriculum planning; the scope is multidisciplinary and the curriculum spirals through important content, skills, and concepts in each grade; multicultural themes are clearly evident in curriculum planning
- Learning goals are clearly displayed
- Concept maps and other visual representations are evident in classrooms and workspaces to depict *big-picture* learning or work goals
- Collaborative planning is prioritized in schools and the workplace
- Ongoing professional development, mentoring, and coaching support curricular and instructional decisions
- Learning goals and activities are readily accessible to parents and the community though multiple means, including concept maps
- Teachers share learning units in a professional library

Brain-Target Four—Teaching for Mastery of Content, Skills, and Concepts

- Observable activities provide a range of experiences to reinforce learning
- The visual and performing arts are evident in instructional activities
- Activities reflect the needs of all students, including typical and atypical learners
- Technology is meaningfully integrated into instructional activities
- Student work shown in the classroom and halls displays arts-based projects that show acquisition of content and multicultural themes
- Benchmark assessments and other testing programs document student mastery of content, skills, and concepts

- Learning activities build on prior knowledge
- Homework and out-of-school activities reinforce learning goals

Brain-Target Five—Teaching for the Extension and Application of Knowledge: Creativity and Innovation in Education

- Students are provided with opportunities for divergent thinking within classroom discussions, class activities, and projects
- Critical thinking and problem-solving activities are visible in lesson activities and work projects
- Real-world application of content is incorporated into each learning unit
- Students are given multiple opportunities to extend knowledge beyond presented material and to display creative thinking through novel projects, assignments, and performance tasks
- Arts are integrated into activities to extend learning such as role-play, song writing, play writing, mix-media presentations (podcasts, blogs, digital art)

Brain-Target Six—Evaluating Learning

- Assessments of learning goals are provided at regular intervals and used to extend thinking and learning
- Assessments are varied to accommodate neurodiverse learners and second language learners
- Students are given regular opportunities for active retrieval of information
- Feedback on performance is timely and students are told in advance when to anticipate feedback
- *Scaffolded feedback* is provided to allow students to arrive at correct responses
- Portfolios are used to demonstrate learning and work goals and include arts-related projects
- Performance assessments are used to demonstrate learning and work products
- Assessments are spaced to provide regular review of content
- Holistic and analytic scoring rubrics are used liberally to assess learning

We have reviewed above how the Brain-Targeted Teaching® Model has been used in schools and the workplace. I end this chapter by sharing the words of multiple individuals who describe how they use the model. You will see many examples from artists, professional developers, educators, and leaders in higher education and K–12. I hope their voices spark ideas and add to your repertoire of learning activities through the BTT Model for children and adults.

From Expert Practitioners in Many Fields

Beyond the Syllabus

I have been using Brain-Targeted Teaching® as a foundation of my pedagogy since its inception. I have used it in K–12 in regular ed, special ed, and arts education learning spaces.

When I transitioned to higher ed, I was surprised to see that the best practices for K–12 weren't being adapted and utilized for college-aged learners.

I came to teaching as a second career, after having received a BFA in Acting. When I was in school, the conservatory approach absolutely (and confoundingly) did not consider social-emotional health. The goals and objectives were not mapped out in any way that seemed scaffolded for deeper understanding. Foundational concepts were inconsistent between instructors, and of course, assessments were highly subjective. When I became a professor thirty-five years later, little seemed to have changed.

It is uncomfortable to learn new approaches, but it is imperative that we not teach the same way we were taught. The learning brain needs more care and consideration. Here are some of the methods and practices I employ:

- *A carefully crafted* **syllabus** *that I use as a guide in every class session. It is our road map and includes the rationale behind the progression of skills, concepts, and activities.*
- *I start each class session with ninety seconds of* **meditation** *breathing, prompting students to* **set an intention** *for the class.*

(Continued)

(Continued)

Sometimes I use a metallic "singing bowl." After a few weeks, I ask for a volunteer to lead the meditation.

- *As a former K–12 teacher, I know the value in writing and reviewing* ***objectives*** *on the board. Additionally, I write out the Key Skills & Concepts and discuss how they relate to what we've already covered.*
- ***Novelty****. Using minimal technology or unexpected props in a studio/class session to engage students always leads to creativity and innovation. "A playful approach to an earnest endeavor" is my motto!*
- ***Closure****. Building reflection time into the schedule allows for a contemporaneous record of breakthroughs, questions, and concerns. I often journal my reflections while the students are writing as well. It helps with narrative accounts of their progress and my own efficacy.*

This is all part of a deeper change in how our creative spaces, our rehearsal studios, our classrooms need to decolonize and become more inclusive. Fostering curiosity and acknowledging that learning can be as exhausting as it is exhilarating can unlock the mind's potential for profound understanding.

Susan Rome
Actress, Teacher, Higher Education Instructor

Brain-Targeted Teaching® Model Through a School Leadership Lens

Imagine walking into a school building where the floors are shiny, the walls are freshly painted reflecting the school's colors, and student-created artwork is displayed throughout the building. The front entrance smells clean and is brightly lit and there is a large colorful welcome banner to greet you. Front office staff is friendly and welcoming, and as you walk to your classroom, the staff greets you with a kind "good morning," or "hello, it's good to see you."

Classrooms are softly lit with floor lamps and natural light; are clutter free and organized with bins, baskets, and shelves; and current student work is displayed on bulletin boards and throughout the hallways. Student desks are arranged to support group learning, and teachers circulate the groups to check in and provide feedback. Learning goals and objectives are clearly posted, and instructional activities are aligned with content standards. Concept maps are on display that provide a visual representation of the learning unit. You can hear students discussing the work and explaining the how and why of the work. Teachers use their data to reflect and adjust instruction to meet the needs of all students.

Our leadership team meets bi-weekly to discuss instructional trends by reflecting on previous and current assessments, attendance, behavioral data, and informal/formal teacher observations. The data is then used to develop "look fors" during learning walks and is shared with staff and is aligned with the school's goals, mission, and vision.

Stephanies Bass
Educational Leadership Team

Using BTT in Gifted and Twice-Exceptional Learners

I began working with the Brain-Targeted Teaching® Model as a third-grade teacher in the early 2000s. Many years and grade levels later, it is still at the forefront as I plan. I am currently a Gifted and Talented Coordinator with over five hundred students in grades K–8 on my caseload. Since I cannot service all of these students individually, it is important for me to work with other content leads and support classroom teachers in planning to ensure students are getting what they need in mixed-ability classrooms.

Our school district requires all gifted and advanced students to have an Individualized Learning Plan, or ILP. Work can be compacted or accelerated as part of this plan, but most importantly, students are to create an interest-based project. Many gifted students develop asynchronously or struggle with executive functioning skills.

(Continued)

(Continued)

When faced with a challenge, I find that many of our most gifted students cannot persevere. Work is so easy for them in early elementary that the first time they can't do something right away, they avoid the task or shut down. Eventually, this can lead to failure. I work with our teachers to challenge their students early and risk-free. We plan activities that push students to think, not just do. When students see me for small-group instruction at any grade level, I encourage risk-taking where no grades are tied to their work. I tell them what they do with me can only help them, never hurt them. By creating this emotional climate of safety, students are able to reach outside of their comfort zone and grow. The earlier our students are faced with divergent questions and activities where there is not just one perfect answer, the earlier we build resilience. Even our kindergarten students are working on activities to cultivate higher order thinking skills!

Our twice-exceptional students (students who are gifted but also have a learning disability such as ADHD or autism spectrum disorder) are just as capable as their peers but may struggle with the organization of materials or information. Their pencil or computer keys often do not keep up with the speed of their thoughts or ideas. They can get frustrated or produce work that does not show their full capability of thought and creativity. I encourage our teachers to allow alternative methods of evaluation when possible. Can they draw it, act it out, or sing a song about it? By using a strengths-based approach, we hope to keep our brightest shining.

One of the important ways we meet our gifted and advanced learners is through Brain-Target Five. Gifted children typically master material at a quicker rate than their peers. Giving them a chance to apply or extend their knowledge is so important. The way most educational institutions are set up, we can actually do a disservice to our gifted and advanced students by just giving them "harder work" from grade levels above. They don't get the chance to "go deeper" and apply critical thought. I keep a shared drive where every grade level has small group activities and projects to use with their gifted and advanced students for each math and ELA module. For example, where all fourth-grade students complete a Myth Making unit, our GT students are given the extension to read a "challenge novel." Students are given a choice of novel and choice of project to complete along with it. Most students chose Percy Jackson books. Projects included using the themes and characters to create a performance or game board. It is so exciting to see them using higher order thinking to make sure that all board spaces, questions, and moves work like any board game you might buy!

As students gain more independence in middle school, we require more in-depth projects from our gifted and advanced learners such as the Science and Engineering Fair and National History Day, where students must research primary and secondary sources related to the yearly theme. They can choose whether to create a performance, documentary, website, exhibit, or paper as part of their advanced curriculum. Many times, I add a goal to their ILP of finding an expert in their topic of interest to interview. One student who was interested in food preservation, spent time with a local farm-to-table chef and learned all about pickling vegetables. Two eighth-graders who loved performing and cooking shows chose to create a weekly "Bake Off" show as their independent project. Working from separate homes, they took their humor and love of baking to a new level by learning how to tape and edit each edition. They created five, thirty-minute episodes and went on to a local high school for the arts, where they are both involved in theater.

Kristen McGinness
Gifted & Talented Coordinator

BTT Learning Units in Speech-Language Pathology Practice

In the Brain-Targeted Teaching® Model, learning activities should foster deep learning and long-term retention of content. However, it is not uncommon to have a student with an Individualized Education Plan (IEP) who experiences difficulties with some aspect of memory as associated with or attributed to their neurology or other internal factors. I've found that employing creativity in activity design has been beneficial in mitigating any potentially deleterious effects associated with memory difficulties. Such forms of creativity have included incorporating physical movement associated with the target content or skill, using culturally relevant and relatable content to activate prior knowledge, using diverse forms of visual supports, and engaging in highly motivating tasks as the context for instruction or learning. I've been asked if support service providers should use curriculum content rather than highly motivating content in their learning activities. I've found that it depends on numerous factors and is most often dependent upon the

(Continued)

(Continued)

individual learner, as well as the learning targets and desired outcomes. If a learner has a skill deficit and is generally unmotivated, hesitant, or resistant, it may be beneficial to start with highly motivating activities and contexts to promote engagement. Curriculum content can be incorporated into activities at the discretion of the service provider. Efficacy of instruction and activities can be determined through evaluation.

A support service provider's evaluations and assessments most often are different from evaluations administered in the classroom by general education teachers. Evaluation can be analysis of data tracked over a certain period of time. It can also be a single instance of questioning. When asking questions, service providers should determine if the purpose is evaluative or to facilitate deeper learning. Questions can be used for both simultaneously. However, to effectively serve both purposes, I've found it most beneficial to pre-plan how the data collection and question scaffolding were going to take place simultaneously. Additionally, I've commonly had to assess a student's ability to perform a skill before they integrated curriculum content, as well as assess their comprehension of specific content and concepts outside of their connection to categorically- or curriculum-related content. Assessment of skill or knowledge application may take place at some point, but these are assessed and evaluated as different components. As such, evaluations for support service providers can look vastly different, depending upon what aspects of comprehension, performance, or application are being targeted.

Kyle Greene-Pendelton
Speech-Language Pathologist

Integrating the BBT Model in Educational Therapy and Professional Development in Puerto Rico

In Puerto Rico, Brain Connections Corp. has integrated Mariale Hardiman's Brain-Targeted Teaching® Model into our professional development activities and educational therapy courses in a significant and structured manner. This model, based on neuroscientific research, has provided us with a comprehensive

framework for effectively planning, implementing, and evaluating instruction.

Professional Development

In our professional development activities, we have adopted Hardiman's six brain targets to guide educators in creating more effective, brain-centered learning environments:

- *Positive Emotional Climate (Brain-Target One): We foster a positive emotional environment that promotes high levels of learning. This is achieved through the deliberate planning of positive emotional connections within study units, using strategies such as integrating visual and performing arts to activate students' emotional responses and enhance long-term retention.*
- *Physical Environment (Brain-Target Two): We design physical learning environments that optimize attention and provide a safe and supportive learning experience. Factors such as novelty in the environment, lighting, sound, and scents are considered to enhance the learning experience.*
- *Learning Design (Brain-Target Three): We help educators use content standards and curriculum guides to design overarching objectives and concepts, presenting them in visual representations like concept maps and graphic organizers. This facilitates a comprehensive understanding of the content and connection with students' prior knowledge.*
- *Teaching for Mastery (Brain-Target Four): We promote knowledge acquisition through diverse and creative lessons that frequently integrate the arts. This helps to "wire" important content into students' long-term memory.*
- *Teaching for Application (Brain-Target Five): We encourage deep thinking and learning by applying skills and content in real-world problem-solving tasks, such as investigations, experiments, and creative projects.*
- *Assessing Learning (Brain-Target Six): We implement relevant and timely assessments as an ongoing, bidirectional process from the beginning of the learning unit. We use written assessments, rubrics, and student self-reflections.*

(Continued)

(Continued)

Educational Therapy Courses

In our certification courses in Educational Therapy, we have incorporated the Brain-Targeted Teaching® Model to provide a neuroeducational and multisensory approach. This approach is designed to benefit both children and adults in their academic performance. The courses include interactive modules, videos, assignments, live lectures, and forums, all aligned with Hardiman's model principles.

Participants in these courses learn the following skills:

- *Implement neuroeducational activities in their work environments and at home.*
- *Apply the latest knowledge from neuroeducation research.*
- *Design and evaluate instructional programs based on Hardiman's six brain targets.*

In summary, Brain Connections Corp. has adopted the Brain-Targeted Teaching® Model as a cornerstone in our professional development activities and educational therapy courses, ensuring that our programs are grounded in the latest neuroscientific research and effective pedagogical practices.

Suzette Mirabal
Education Coordinator, Entrepreneur

BTT Meets Early Childhood Education Professional Development

While in the EdD program at Johns Hopkins University I became aware of research showing that teacher professional development (PD) using the Brain-Targeted Teaching® Model can increase teacher self-efficacy. In my own experience working with early years teachers, I observed that when teachers actively engage students in the learning process and then witness an increase in student learning, it, in turn, alters their own teacher mastery experiences and, thus, their self-efficacy.

After leading and teaching PD in the United Arab Emirates for many years, I came to recognize that some of my more successful PD courses were aligned with many elements of the Brain-Targeted Teaching® (BTT) framework. I have used BTT to deliver PD to show teachers how to take a more holistic approach in their teaching and to create a more student-centered classroom. What I love about the individual brain targets is that they work together, somewhat analogous to how different parts of a human brain interact, not necessarily in sequence but as an interconnected system. When teachers come to this realization, it shifts their view of what good teaching looks like.

After implementing PD using BTT, I was inspired to replace the standard 5E's of learning with the BTT Model because teachers were able to see the relationship between what current research says about how the brain learns and their students' learning. I also realized that while teachers knew the importance of the emotional climate and arts-integration in early childhood, teachers were not balanced in how they implemented the targets. At the end of the study, one teacher in my study reflected by saying, "I knew the importance of application of learning and assessment, but I didn't realize how interconnected these targets are and how important it is to cover all targets in measuring student success. Sometimes I just stopped at mastery through arts-integration assuming I have given students time to master [a concept] and therefore I have taught well. I now know that learning has taken place only when a student is able to transfer the learning to a new situation."

The BTT Model works in the context of early childhood education. I now format PD sessions using the BTT framework and see a positive shift in teachers' confidence. I have always presented PD on topics that allow teachers to expand their understanding of inquiry-based learning or project-based learning. Although the teachers enjoyed the sessions, sustainability was difficult. Now, I see that supporting their understanding of solid pedagogy starts with the structure of the Brain-Target Teaching® Model. Starting a PD with the knowledge of the brain, for example, always fascinates them. It helps engage the teachers and motivates them to ask questions and elaborate on their own learning. Teachers seem more willing to engage in the process of showing their understanding and applying their newly acquired knowledge.

(Continued)

(Continued)

In my dissertation study, I found that teachers who transformed their teaching by applying BTT in their classrooms demonstrated an increase in teacher efficacy. Such a change can sustain a teacher in their practice and motivate them to try new approaches in their classrooms. These efforts may ultimately be reflected in better student outcomes. I feel rewarded every time I see teachers plan lessons using the BTT pedagogical framework. I absolutely love it!

Hiea Mizyed
Education Practitioner

BTT in Online MBA Higher Education

I was introduced to Dr. Hardiman's Brain-Targeted Teaching® Model while attending Northeastern University. My professor at that time was a former student of Dr. Hardiman and assigned reading in The Brain-Targeted Teaching® Model for 21st Century Schools (2012). I wanted to learn more and enrolled at Johns Hopkins University. I was more than intrigued and knew this material had great potential for Master of Business Administration (MBA) faculty and adult learners in my full-time work as a Senior Associate Dean of Business.

When our MBA program was due for a redevelopment for both the on-ground and online versions, I was able to apply what I learned to the redesign. We consulted with Dr. Hardiman on the program redesign with curriculum and instructional designers and subject matter experts. We also asked her to teach faculty about the new design and the BTT Model. While we implemented all six brain targets into the design, a major success in the program was Brain-Target Four: Mastery of Concepts, Skills, and Concepts.

Every course in the core program was designed around a "real-life" business problem, taught with scenario-based learning (SBL) that scaffolded over three weeks, or three modules. Business subject matter experts wrote original scenarios that contained current business content. The SBL design helped the learners to enhance short-term and working memory of new material, novelty, and allowed them to "chunk" the learning of concepts and content over the three-week period, followed by an assessment, that supported Brain-Target Six: Evaluating Learning. The design helped adult learners to connect new material with previously learned content.

In the first module week, learners were introduced to the business scenario and completed assignments with "no one right answer" to promote divergent thinking. Learners used first-week content in discussion boards, and/or short paper assignments, and/or preparing spreadsheets and graphs, to elaborate on what they learned about the new content and apply the material to various aspects of the scenario.

In the second module week, learners were introduced to new aspects of the scenario, such as customer satisfaction and marketing or sales information, and used material from module one to address new content. The learners were challenged to build on previously learned content with new material and propose solutions. As in module one, learners used short assignments to display their learning.

In the third module, the scenario completely unfolded for the learners as they were presented with all aspects of the business problem to be solved. In this module, aspects of Brain-Target Five: Teaching for the Extension of Knowledge were utilized as novelty was blended with previous learning. Student learning was assessed with a more extensive assignment like a multiple page PowerPoint presentation where the learners recorded their presentation for the instructor. The presentations helped foster creative thinking as they used material across various business disciplines, preparing a narrative to explain concepts, to solve business problems. The use of presentations also integrated a semblance of art integration as learners were encouraged to use design thinking in their work products.

Throughout the rest of the semester, learners continued the three-week learning process that fostered long-term memory potentiation (LTP) for use in their professional lives. Both students and faculty enjoyed the SBL design evidenced in course evaluations and real-time surveys built into the course. The success of the program design was also evidenced by enrollment growth of more than five hundred learners, term over term, for more than two years. When I retired from my position, the program was nearing nine thousand learners. The Brain-Targeted Teaching® Model was a huge success for this nationally known MBA program.

Mark I. Hobson
Former Senior Associate Dean of Business, Education Consultant

11

Culturally Relevant Pedagogy Meets Brain-Targeted Teaching® in Online and Hybrid Learning Environments

by Ranjini JohnBull and Mariale Hardiman

The essence of the Brain-Targeted Teaching® (BTT) Model aligns with the major tenets of Culturally Relevant Pedagogy (CRP) (Gay, 2018; Hammond, 2014; Ladson-Billings, 2021, 2022). Ladson-Billings (2021) describes culturally responsive teaching core principles as 1) an emphasis on high expectations for student learning, 2) supporting students' cultural competence, and 3) facilitating students' sociopolitical and critical consciousness. These tenets are woven throughout the fabric of the brain targets in numerous ways. These two frameworks are not prescriptive methods, rather they both represent what teachers say are *just good teaching* (Ladson-Billings, 2021). These frameworks intersect in the following ways:

1. ***Brain-Targets One and Two and cultural competence.*** Supporting students' growth and awareness of their own cultural competences. This means that educators support students in their awareness of and the affirmation of their intersectional identities (i.e., female, African American, mid-westerner, artist, step-sister, Minecraft-gamer, athlete, etc.). Both models describe how to *build relationships and rapport* with students by getting to know who they are. These models provide examples and strategies for how to

help students discover their identities in *safe and inclusive spaces.* This allows students to become more fluent in their identified cultures and identities so that, in turn, they can navigate and better understand the perspective of people with different intersectional identities. By creating these safe spaces, students feel ready to learn because their basic needs for safety are regulated.

2. ***Brain-Targets Three and Four and an emphasis on student-centered teaching and learning.*** Both models demonstrate how providing the big picture for students helps them not only learn discreet knowledge but also understand *why* this knowledge is important and connected to larger concepts and real-life connections. Further, both models describe how learning through multiple modalities and connecting the learning to students' interests drive long-term memory. They both remind us about the *joy* of teaching and learning through the integration of the arts (i.e., dance, hip-hop, poetry, visual art) into non-arts content, and how to leverage joy through novelty and fun.
3. ***Brain-Targets Five and Six and sociopolitical and critical consciousness.*** Both frameworks emphasize how students need more than memorization to live full lives. They need to understand how to creatively solve problems, ask important questions, and learn how to engage in their learning by addressing issues and problems that are important to their lives. The examples and strategies provide educators with ways to help students *ask critical questions about problems* they see in their lives and help them engage in ways to address those questions and solve those problems through research, creative problem-solving, collaboration, and critical thinking. Both frameworks emphasize multiple types of data to assess learning and to help students use those types of assessments for their work in solving problems in their worlds. These final components of both models are helping us prepare *caring, committed, and creative citizens* for our school communities now and for our nation in the future.

My teaching and leadership are infused with what I have learned from both of these frameworks: to bring a sense love, kindness, humanity, and joy to the learning process. In this chapter, I describe examples from my practice of implementing the integration of the BTT Model and CRP principles in my instructional practices in the online and hybrid contexts. I also include summaries from students' anonymous course evaluations, in which they have shared how course elements have supported their learning. I also have used each of these strategies in my face-to-face work with teachers, and I encourage all practitioners to consider how any of these activities can be adapted to one's own contexts from PK–12 teaching to college instruction to organizational leadership and adult learning spaces.

Brain-Targets One and Two: The Culturally Relevant Emotional and Physical Environments

All students enter my courses with complex lives, identities, stressors, and intense personal and professional goals. To set their fears and worries aside, I use several culturally relevant neuroeducation strategies to create a warm and inclusive emotional and physical learning environment in my online and hybrid classrooms.

1. Welcome announcement and Meet and Greet forum: As referred to in Chapter 4 on Brain-Target One, I welcome my students by describing some of my identities and welcoming them to also share their identities in a meet and greet post on the video platform. This is designed to create a foundation of trust between the students and me. By sharing my intersectional identities, I provide them with a map and a way forward for how I think and approach the coursework. I work with my students as both professionals and individuals with personal lives. Because I share with them about my personal life, I encourage them to let me know if they need support in their academic work in relation to whatever is happening in their personal lives. This is especially important when teaching in asynchronous learning platforms as students are working in their own space and time. Personal connection with the instructor goes a long way to mitigate students' concerns and stress.

2. Announcements are used to provide information about upcoming deadlines, comment on their discussions, and provide thoughts for further reflections. I include the following in my announcements:

    a. Comics or relevant images, pictures, or artwork to try to capture attention and promote joy in the classroom.

    b. Affirmations of students' responses within the discussion forum to encourage building their knowledge, extending their thought processes, and bringing new information to the discussion. The regular act of affirming and building upon students' knowledge and strengths is a hallmark of culturally relevant neuroeducation.

    c. Video announcements: Throughout the semester, I provide short announcements about the content and about assignments so that students feel more connected to me in an asynchronous context.

In online, hybrid, and face-to-face learning environments, we can create emotionally safe spaces that allow our students to thrive. Simple adjustments to our practices from BTT and CRP allow us to affirm all identities, create warm climates, and provide interest through the novelty of creative *meet and greet spaces*. By creating these initial experiences with students, an instructor can build trust and learn more about students to better support their learning journeys and their goals. These interactions build rapport and relationships with students which leads to growth and learning, not only for the students but for the instructor as well.

Brain-Targets Three and Four: Culturally Relevant Learning Design and Teaching for Mastery

Two contexts for learning define effective online and hybrid learning spaces (and any learning environment). First, create time together in person with students through live synchronous sessions, and second, support their time apart in which they engage in individual learning on their own. I purposefully design learning experiences in both conditions so that students feel that their time was well-spent, that they were engaged within the community of learners, and know that the learning experience was meaningful and supportive.

During our time together in online synchronous sessions, live face-to-face video meetings, I use a variety of strategies to keep my students engaged. I use both whole group and small group activities, *workshopping* of example assignments in collaboration with students, and collaborative online notetaking spaces (i.e., Padlet or Google Docs) to help make students' thinking visible.

In live video meetings (online synchronous sessions) or in face-to-face in-person meetings, I adhere to a particular format that includes the following:

1. Mindfulness breathing activity—By engaging in this, everyone takes a moment to transition into the learning environment. They calm their bodies through deep breathing that supports attention to refocus on the time together.

2. An agenda—By providing this, my students know what to expect and it alleviates concerns about how their time will be used.

3. A concept map—Through a visual representation such as a concept map, I share how the content and activities of the meeting are related to the big picture of what we are working on.

4. Breakout group discussions—Time is provided to engage with peers without me in the conversation. In online meetings, I assign

> them to breakout groups with specific topics to discuss. This time allows students to build critical social connections related to the content. The students discuss graded assignments from previous cohorts in which they identify strengths of former students' work together and look at comments and feedback I've provided to previous students. Engaging in this type of *workshopping* activity allows them to see the individualized choices previous students have made to create meaningful projects. It also communicates my high expectations for student work, demonstrates how I provide feedback, and begins to build connections with their peers through their discussions.

What I have found over the years with providing *examples* of former student work to discuss in a live collaborative setting, is that students aim higher than what my rubrics provide for them. They see the creativity and passion in previous students' examples, and their excitement for their own projects is ignited.

For asynchronous time apart and individual learning, I developed an interactive lecture on teacher self-efficacy beliefs using Articulate software, which was one of the first of its kind in our online courses. This interactive illustrated digital learning experience takes students through several sequenced activities, short videos, quizzes, clickable content to explore new concepts, drag-and-drop activities on the content, and authentic teaching scenarios. This activity provides a game-like atmosphere with avatar characters in richly illustrated environments to engage in the interactive digital lesson.

Students explore the content in a more fun setting than listening to me flip through slides with my voice-over recording. Integrating what we know from both arts-integrated strategies and from digital media creation, students' attention can be captured through the novelty and fun, and their memory for the content can be enhanced through the variety of learning activities built into the content. This type of activity also allows us to build in characters who look like our students so that they can see representations of their identities in the learning activities.

Brain-Targets Five and Six: Culturally Relevant Application of Knowledge and Assessment *for* Learning in the Real World

"So how does this help me?" This is the question that I try to answer with my assignments. The major assignments are designed to allow students to reflect on their current practices, acquire new knowledge from the course and their own research, and adapt that new knowledge to improve their professional practice. The two assignments or projects from two different courses are a policy briefing paper and a research conference proposal and research poster. Both of these assignments provide students with the opportunity to choose what they want to focus on from the course material and additional outside content, and to produce a usable product for their real life outside the course.

The policy briefing paper development includes two drafts and a final draft. They write this paper to either a leader from their organization or a local elected leader about a problem in their context and the need for a new policy or a set of practices to address the problem. They provide real data to support their claim about the problem, and then they research and describe three viable solutions to this problem. They then argue for one or a combination of the solutions to move forward based upon their balanced discussion of the pros and cons of each solution.

Many students have taken these policy briefing papers and shared them with their educational leaders while they were developing them. In some cases, students have reported that new district policies were designed based on the students' course-based policy briefing paper solutions. Real change happens when we give students assignments that they can use in the real world. These real-world projects can help them be more effective community members and professionals.

In a different online course, the final assignment is a professional conference research poster where students communicate their research findings. The intention of this assignment is to help scaffold ways for practitioners to take research and share their insights in a condensed and accessible format to practitioners. Major projects should be usable and shared rather than collecting dust on a shelf at the end of a course. As a class, they create a shared conference list on an online platform (i.e., Google Sheets), and each student finds and contributes three conferences and their information to the group list. From this list, students choose a conference to apply to and build their research paper proposal and research poster for their chosen conference. Students receive feedback on drafts from me, my teaching assistant, and from their peers on each draft of the project. The purpose of this project and the policy briefing paper is to help them grow their nuanced understanding through integrating multiple perspectives from the community of learners in the course rather than developing their course projects in isolation.

This collaborative molding and shaping of their course assignments and research projects helps build their self-efficacy as they receive affirmations from their peers, and it helps to continue to build their identities as competent research consumers and equity-oriented neuroeducation educators and leaders.

It is gratifying to read students' feedback at the conclusion of the course. Many students share that they plan to use some of the strategies described above in their own practice. For example, even though the course is designed to be asynchronous, students appreciate the opportunity to come together as a group, to get to know classmates, share ideas and ultimately feel that they are part of community of learners. Students also comment on how they feel more connected to the instructor after learning about my own personal and professional interests and identity. Applying content into real-world assignments is frequently highlighted in students' evaluations of the course. They feel that rather than merely learning content, they are experiencing the content through practical applications within their own context. And finally, I share some comments from students that exemplify how an online or hybrid course can impact learning: *"It was really motivating and inspiring to get to talk with our instructor about ways to apply our studies to the real world and seek solutions to societal ills and work toward social justice and equity!"* Here I share another example of how this approach is recognized by students: *"A rare instructor who empowers students and bonds in ways that challenge but also encourage rather than threaten."*

The student comments indicate how their level of engagement in my online and hybrid courses has enriched their knowledge. Further, their learning has helped them to grow in their professional competence, their personal identities, and their awareness of how to utilize their knowledge to create more just and equitable communities.

Igniting Equitable Online and Hybrid Learning Through the Brain-Targeted Teaching® Model and Culturally Relevant Pedagogy

As our world moves further into the digital age, and our learning environments become more integrated with technology in online and hybrid learning platforms, we need to critically consider how we design these spaces. I affirm that integrating the tenets of the Brain-Targeted Teaching® Model and Culturally Relevant Pedagogy will help foster the meaningful growth of critically conscious citizens for our small and large communities in digital and in-person learning environments. This chapter brings forward examples to help educators and leaders think about how to facilitate warm and inclusive learning environments for students of any age, even if the online learning environment is only asynchronous engagement. These spaces and the activities that we build in these online and hybrid learning can attend to students' emotions, foster deep learning, and provide catalysts for deeply creative work (JohnBull & Hardiman, 2022).

By integrating the tenets of the Brain-Targeted Teaching® Model and Culturally Relevant Pedagogy, our highest hopes for our students can be realized in online, hybrid, and face-to-face learning environments. Before my eyes, I have seen students become people who create more beautiful and equitable communities where everyone is welcomed. My world becomes brighter because of their brilliant beams of hope. Let us carry these frameworks with us into *all* education environments to help ignite this joy and light together.

Implementing the Brain-Targeted Teaching® Model at Home and Out-of-School Learning

12

by Clare O' Malley Grizzard, Jacqueline Renfrow, and Mariale Hardiman

There is no denying the critical role that parents and caregivers play in a child's education. The often-used phrase, "Parents are the child's first teacher" should be adapted to add that parents are the child's "continual teacher" (even when the wisdom of a parent is offered to children as they become adults). Parents, as they know their child best, play a critical role in bridging the home to school environment.

We believe that the tenets of the Brain-Targeted Teaching® (BTT) Model can assist parents and caregivers in multiple ways. First, most parents and caregivers are involved in some way with supporting their child with assignments from school. Additionally, this work is intended to assist those involved in home-schooling, micro-schooling, hybrid schools, athletics, and other out-of-school learning activities. There are many ways that parents, caregivers, and coaches can use BTT tenets to guide learners in flourishing in their academic world, social life, and in spirit as they become competent, heartful individuals.

This section of the chapter contains strategies associated with each of the components of the BTT Model that can be used in the home and multiple other settings. In particular, educators who use the model might find this information useful in supporting the home-school connection that is so necessary for success at every level of education.

Earlier chapters of this book describe the BTT Model as an instructional framework informed by the learning sciences. The model focuses on positive and effective emotional and physical learning environments; the development of *big-picture* concepts; mastery of content, skills, and concepts; real-world, creative application of learning; and evaluation *for* learning, as well as *of* learning. The model supports meaningful integration of the arts and technology as sound instructional tools. The model has successfully informed teaching and learning from early childhood learning environments to adult learning classrooms, training programs, and online learning experiences.

We now describe briefly each of the six brain targets and provide ways that parents, caregivers, and other professionals can adopt the practices as they guide and support learning and leading.

Brain-Target One—The Emotional Climate for Learning

In this target, we focus on creating a positive learning climate and reducing stress. Research tells us that learning best occurs during positive emotional states. On the other hand, negative or stressful emotional states impede learning. Most of us as parents might have felt the stress of helping with homework or making sure the school project is done on time. It is obviously impossible to remove all stressful situations from our lives or in our children's experiences. However, we offer below some general research-supported strategies that could help to create a positive emotional mindset.

- *Behavior specific praise:* Praising a child for their work or actions is something we all engage in, using various approaches. One important strategy is to praise for specific behaviors. For example, rather than praising a child for *being smart*, research shows that praising for effort is much more potent in establishing a mindset of accomplishment. So rather than saying "good job" you might add "you worked hard on the project, and I know you learned a lot."
- *Direct versus veiled language:* Some children may need direct language rather than what we refer to as indirect or veiled language. Here is an example–you want your child to clean their bedroom. A direct expectation for accomplishing that task might be more effective than saying "Your room is a mess" and expecting that the child understands that statement is not just an observation but a directive to clean it up.
- *Rewards:* We all like to receive some type of acknowledgement of our accomplishments. Rewards can take on many forms. Tangible rewards such as awarding a favorite activity, object, or star on a

chart can boost confidence and encourage continuing the desired behavior. Rewards can also be more intangible such as behavior specific praise described above. Consistent, clear reward systems seem to work the best in helping to develop self-confidence. Ultimately, the goal should be to instill in the child the feeling of satisfaction in the accomplishment itself as the reward. Fostering internal rather than external rewards can lead to more personal satisfaction, motivation, and sense of purpose.

- *Choice:* Giving children choices in activities or anything tangible (e.g., meals, clothing, rewards, etc.) can promote a sense of empowerment and confidence. Be aware, however, that based on a child's age and maturity, offering too many choices at once can be confusing and produce unwelcomed stress. Limiting the number of choices may be helpful for some children.

- *Mistakes:* We are not perfect creatures, and we all make mistakes. Research shows that focusing on what a mistake can teach us is better than taking on shame or discouragement. So a poor grade on a test can be met with a plan for improvement.

- *Behavior:* One strategy that we suggest for correcting a negative behavior is a three-step process that begins with asking the child to describe the behavior, *"What did you do?"* The next step is for the child to judge the behavior, "*Was that the right thing to do?*" The third step is to ask the child to name the expected behavior, "*What will you do the next time in this situation?*" This strategy is only one of many that a parent or caregiver can use. Typically, once a situation calms down, productive conversation can help with children at any age.

- *Moods: Affect naming* is a term used to describe the process of identifying one's mood. Being able to name how you feel helps to mitigate the effects of negative feelings. There are multiple *mood charts* online to help children to identify how they feel (happy, sad, depressed, scared, excited, bored, etc.). Research shows that when children can name how they feel, especially if they are in a negative state, they are more successful in moving beyond the emotion than if the mood is not addressed or ignored.

- *Feedback:* True emotional stability is a two-way street that requires responsiveness and communication between the child and adult. Parents and caregivers should give frequent feedback and soon after an event. For example, don't wait a week to discuss an argument between siblings. Wait until all parties have calmed down and then bring them together to talk. Discuss how they feel and what they could've done differently. And remember not to ask questions that can be answered with only a "yes" or a "no." Encourage everyone to share their feelings with emotionally charged questions. Once you have built this solid emotional foundation, your child will be mentally set up for academic success.

Brain-Target Two—The Physical Learning Environment

The second brain target focuses on how the physical space in which a child works helps to promote attending behaviors and is another tool for ensuring optimal learning. Below are some ideas for how to think about learning space at home. Knowing that every suggestion might not be possible, attention to at least some of the ideas below may make learning at home more effective and enjoyable.

- *Environmental factors—Sound:* To help with attention in learning, certain environmental factors are important to consider. Noise in the environment can be distracting to anyone, especially for those who tend to frequently lose attention to the task at hand. Soft background music can be relaxing when doing routine tasks, but when we need to focus on learning or practicing a new skill, a quiet environment is important. It may be difficult to control sounds coming from outside such as the noise from traffic, construction, or other outdoor sounds, but within one's control might be the sound in the room or house such as televisions or other media devices that could easily cause distractions.
- *Environmental factors—Light:* Research strongly supports the use of well-lit natural lighting as an important factor in a learning environment. If natural light from windows is not available, adding soft lamps can mitigate the effects of harsh florescent lighting.
- *Environmental factors—Scent:* The enjoyment of pleasant scents can also add to a positive learning environment. Research supports the use of scents such as peppermint, orange, vanilla, lavender, and other scents to support both focus and relaxation. While the use of soy scented candles is one way to bring scent into a room, the danger of fire might be a reason to avoid that for children unless an adult is attending to the space. Other ways to bring scent into a room might be to use natural or commercial scented products. Be aware of any allergies that a child may have to either of those suggestions.

- *Workspace:* A home learning environment requires a workspace that is comfortable, uncluttered, clear of distractions, and organized. Materials such as computers, paper, and writing utensils should be readily available.
- *Novelty:* A large body of research supports the fact that novel items in the environment are stimulating and help to avoid boredom. The trick is to strike the balance of consistency in the environment with a dose of novelty. This can be achieved by hanging up a bulletin board above the child's desk where they can swap out artwork, notes from friends, schedule, photos, etc.
- *Creativity space* is a personal laboratory for generating ideas. Think about organizing dedicated space with a variety of tools and materials based on the child's age. Consider artistic expression including art supplies and musical instruments. Explore some exhibition options—whether it is a clothesline or a bulletin board for inspiring charts, diagrams, illustrations, etc. that support creative investigation.
- *Movement:* Recent research has shown how movement is important for thinking and learning. Think of ways to use gestures, body poses, or just plain walking while learning math skills, remembering words, or understanding a story line. And frequent spacing of learning episodes also supports learning, so make time for breaks to take a walk outside or do some exercise to *clear the brain*!

Brain-Target Three—Big-Picture Concepts: Understanding the *Why*

This target focuses on helping learners to obtain *big-picture* understanding of content, skills, and concepts. The intent is to help children understand how the learning task fits into an overarching picture of the learning goal. A visual representation is an important way to wholistically see the *bigger picture* and also helps to retain what has been learned. Here are some ideas:

- *Concept Maps:* A visual representation of a child's assignment can be easily mapped out using a concept map or mind map. A way to do this might be to take a blank piece of paper and draw bubbles that connect. A large bubble in the middle of the paper represents the learning goal. Smaller bubbles connect to the larger one and contain individual tasks that must be accomplished to arrive at the goal. This is a way for the child to see how individual tasks are connected to the larger goal of learning. For example, to understand a writing assignment, determine what the final product might look like, then outline the steps that need to be taken to get to the final product.

- *Visual Frameworks:* Graphic organizers help organize information into cohesive concepts. Venn diagrams, prioritization charts, and fishbone diagrams are discussed more fully in Brain-Target Three.
- *Chunking:* Chunking is taking a large amount of information and breaking it down into organized smaller amounts. See Brain-Target Four for more information and strategies on chunking.
- *Back mapping:* A good way to plan component parts of instruction is to start with the end in mind. Related to the suggestion above, write or draw the goal for the assignment. Start with the goal, think in reverse order, and plan what activities need to be accomplished to find the starting point.
- *Visualization:* Making learning visible can be done through drawing, doodles, stickers, avatars, etc. The idea is to break down learning tasks into components that can be seen and understood wholistically.
- *Organize around core concepts:* Related to the suggestions above, research points to the idea that knowledge is not a list of facts but organized around core concepts or big ideas that shape thinking. Be sure that your child understands *why* the task is important.

Brain-Target Four—Teaching for Mastery of Content, Skills, and Concepts

Brain-Target Four focuses on activities to learn and retain information—the content, skills, and concepts needed for school and general life endeavors. Learning involves the ability to acquire and remember information and apply it meaningfully. This typically requires repeated rehearsals. Just as we would not expect to hit that perfect tennis serve after being taught once, learning skills requires practice. Memory can also be dependent on certain elaborations. We often recall content that has some meaning or personal connection. Below are a few ideas for helping the learner recall and make meaning from learning tasks.

- *Active Retrieval:* As learners approach academic work, don't forget the importance of *active retrieval* versus passive studying. Suppose a child is learning basic skills in reading or math, studying for a test or quiz, or trying to recall the lines for a play. Rather than rereading and highlighting a passage, it is much more productive to make flashcards, draw a concept map from memory, or design a quiz of the materials from memory. To achieve long-term memory, actively remembering information is far superior to passively studying.

- *Coaching:* At home, the parent may be a collaborating partner who coaches rather than leads, allowing for mistakes and independent growth. As a coach, first model the activity while thinking through the process out loud. Then let the learner take over.
- *Brainstorming:* Invite children to brainstorm and generate ideas for family activities. What field trips or activities can extend school experiences? Online resources at museums of science, history, industry, and art are better than they have ever been and are mostly free. In person and virtual field trips make school subjects come alive. Create extension field journals that hold notes, recipes, artifacts, anything that makes the connection to other aspects of learning.
- *Draw. Draw. Draw.* Sketchbooks are a safe place to explore ideas, record adventures, collect ideas, and watch growth. Take them everywhere and treat them as part journal, part diary, part scrapbook. Museums like The Tate Gallery and The National Gallery of Art are just a few online treasure troves to be explored. The Museum of Modern Art (MoMA) offers great drawing prompts and fun interactions with art that require no advanced skill. https://www.moma.org/magazine/articles/254

Brain-Target Five—Teaching for Extension and Application of Knowledge

Brain-Target Five promotes applying learning in ways that extend knowledge in real-world tasks. It includes creativity and innovative problem-solving. Creativity can and should be taught so that students are able to think in ways that go beyond merely acquiring knowledge. Below are some ideas for how to promote creative thinking:

- *Creative Modalities:* Identify the big ideas behind schoolwork and reinterpret them in unexpected modalities. For example, place a literature study in a contemporary setting–Hollywood loves doing this: We all know *West Side Story* is based on *Romeo and Juliet*. Consider the chemistry in art, in gardening, in cosmetics, cleaning, or baking. Use the essential questions behind the unit to extend ideas into other disciplines. Ask how this idea applies to the real world; is there an artist/scientist who deals with this issue or concept? Let's look at their work. How do I use this idea in a 3D construction? In metaphor? In a drama game such as a role-play.

- *Mistakes are OK:* We want students to be persistent in effort and resilient in the face of failure. To encourage risk-taking, a parent has to model it. Share tales of a mistake that was ultimately a benefit, stories about failure and resilience; celebrate experimentation and *not knowing*.
- *The ARTS:* Together with your child, generate a memory aid that represents the concepts of a school unit *within an artform*. Memorizing the phases of the moon is much more fun and effective when written as a song with accompanying gestures. Explore *cause and effect* by building a Rube Goldberg-like sculpture from found objects.
- *Creative Thinking:* Brain-Target Five is about creativity, and creativity loves company. Social, active, and collaborative work helps to generate new ideas and to build curiosity and inquiry. Encourage children to become creative problem-solvers by applying open-ended thinking to real-world issues. Where do you want to go with this new knowledge? How can we use it? How does this idea apply to your interests? Those problems to solve may be found in your supermarket, local government, favorite science museum, or in your neighborhood park.
- *Motivation:* Intrinsic motivation will be the best way to keep learners involved with their own learning. If the child feels passionately about a pursuit—if its anime, cooking, skateboarding, or dinosaurs—first nurture that passion, then find a way to tie it into the concepts and skills in school subjects.

Brain-Target Six—Teaching for Evaluation

Evaluation is a process that involves knowing what you know. In other words, how well have you mastered the information you wanted to learn? How well have you applied your knowledge in creative ways? So this target is not about grades or scores or winning or losing. It is meant to measure our learning, and by doing so, we support learning. Our motto is that evaluation is not just *of* learning, it is *for* learning.

- *Role Reversal:* Offer a situation that empowers students. Let the student lead in an inspiring transition of roles—the learner becomes the teacher who brings home classroom experiences and presents/ instructs the parent who is now the learner.

- *Feedback:* Feedback was described earlier within the various components of the BTT Model. It is important enough to mention again. Students don't want parents to just hang their work on the refrigerator and love it unconditionally. They want feedback that indicates the viewer's interest in the work. Rather than "Good job" or "I like it," ask your child to talk about their drawing or the project they completed. How did you think of the work you created? How would you describe it to a friend or family member?
- *Evaluation for Learning:* Don't focus simply on *academic achievement*. Did you finish your homework? What grade did you get? Sometimes these are the only ways parents start a conversation. Instead, think about open-ended, generative questions that will build a relationship of trust and support between growing students and parents. Questions that reflect interest in the learning process, intent, and growth rather than the end product will be less judgmental. Ask questions that avoid shallow responses, that will help them review their thinking and effort and thereby, extend their learning: How did you make or do this work? What was the goal? When did you feel you were finished? What was challenging? What are you surprised by? Satisfied with? What would you do differently if you could do it again?
- *Goals:* Set goals that are measurable and that the child has some choice in. Celebrate their incremental accomplishments.
- *Family Meeting Time:* Families have told us about the importance of having a set meeting time to share *little joys* or *worries* that allows for sharing emotions and keeping communication open. Each member of the family shares something from their day or week. This can be made into a fun ritual. For example, pass a talking cube or stick, and whoever holds the object gets to speak. If words are hard to find, have emotion emojis available, and each member can choose one to describe how they feel. Other games can do the same trick. The important thing is to build a spirit of open communication that supports resilience and connection.
- *Home to School Communication:* Open the door with school and teachers if it is not already happening to a satisfactory degree. Successful communication invites parents to give reactions and comments to teachers about the schoolwork including whether their child understood the homework, whether they enjoyed the activity, whether they learned about what the child is learning in class, and if they have any questions.

Below are a few websites that may be helpful in navigating the world of parenting:

https://americanspcc.org/about/#mission

https://childmind.org/guides/

https://explainingbrains.com/parents/

https://drdansiegel.com/

Podcast:

https://podcasts.apple.com/us/podcast/wonder-of-parenting-a-brain-science-approach-to-parenting/id1436262138

From the Expert Practitioner

Using the BTT Model at Home

I've learned from the Brain-Targeted Teaching® (BTT) Model how crucial it is to reduce learners' stress levels to enhance their learning abilities. As a proponent of the BTT Model, I apply these principles not only in my Business School classrooms but also at home as the mother of an eight-year-old son with ADHD.

To create a stress-free environment at home, I've implemented structured approaches that help my son feel emotionally safe. For instance, we follow a predictable routine starting at eight o'clock in the morning daily. Our schedule, always visible on the fridge, outlines his day from waking up and having breakfast to completing various activities. This consistency significantly reduces his stress and anxiety about what to expect.

Another key strategy I employ is the use of positive language, including specific praises and clear directions, to boost his confidence and foster an emotionally supportive home environment. As Dr. Hardiman emphasizes, I avoid general praise in favor of detailed recognition. For example, instead of a generic "good job," I might say, "I noticed how patiently you helped your brother with his puzzle. Your kindness made a real difference." This approach of acknowledging specific positive behaviors has led to remarkable improvements in his conduct at home and in his interactions with siblings and friends.

I've observed significant progress in my son's overall demeanor and social interactions since I focused on positive reinforcement. This implementation of BTT principles has not only enhanced his learning environment but also contributed to his personal growth and social skills development.

Clara Fangfang Ma
Mom & Entrepreneur, Researcher, Educator

Technology Supporting the Implementation of the Brain-Targeted Teaching® Model

13

by David Toia, Katherine Fu, and Mariale Hardiman

Part 1: Virtual Reality and the Brain-Targeted Teaching® Model

Author: David Toia, MAH

Manager of Immersive Media, Adjunct Faculty

One of the most dismaying 21st century terms is "a failure of imagination." The term can be found in a host of news articles describing various tragedies, disappointments, and shortcomings of individuals or groups, who lack the will or ability to anticipate problems before they happen. McKinney (2022) observed that our society is plagued by the lack of imagination to craft alternatives to the way things are currently.

These types of failures begin to take on an increased importance when we consider the role that innovation, which relies on our active imaginations to thrive, plays in promoting a modern knowledge-based economy. In the previous edition of the Brain Targeted Teaching® (BTT) Model (Hardiman, 2012), we were reminded in the chapter on Brain-Target Five—Teaching for the Extension and Application of Knowledge—that our economy has become one built on innovation and the creation of knowledge. This kind of economy requires cognitive capabilities more than on physical inputs or natural resources (Powell & Snellman, 2004). As educators, we need to provide learning experiences that propagate *successes of imagination* by providing tools and teaching modalities that promote creative, divergent thinking.

Divergent and Convergent Thinking

As described in Chapter 8 focused on Brain-Target Five, divergent thinking encourages learners to find multiple solutions to problems rather than a single, convergent, one. In his seminal lecture, "Changing Education Paradigms," author and educator Sir Ken Robinson (2010) reminded us that the current education system was designed for the industrial age and not the intellectual culture of our current times. The educational paradigm of the time emphasized a didactic teacher-centered instructional model. Instruction was transmitted from the front of the room to the students sitting in rows, who were expected to take notes on the presented lectures. Assessments were designed to focus on students learning the *correct* answers instead of being given the opportunity to explore multiple pathways to find their own unique solutions. For decades this style of convergent-based education was passed generationally from teachers to students and became the norm in our education system.

The benefits of a convergent thinking model include speed, accuracy, and logic; common assessments include multiple choice tests, standardized tests, and quizzes, which emphasize that only one answer can be correct (Shrestha, 2017). Some of us may recognize these kinds of assessments and thinking styles as being common in education, perhaps even from our own academic experience. The reality is that convergent thinking deserves its place in our classrooms, especially when it comes to skill building and acquiring foundational knowledge. It allows students to obtain mastery of content and learn to apply that knowledge effectively and quickly.

This style of learning is also pedagogically aligned with an economy focused on standardized manufacturing where convergent thinking is rewarded. However, there is growing evidence that the global knowledge economy is transforming the demands of the labor market throughout the world (The World Bank, 2003).

We regularly celebrate and uphold leaders who demonstrate divergent and radical thinking in their work and life as champions of the knowledge economy. One example of this can be found in the *Forbes* list of America's Most Innovative Leaders which provides a quantified Company Innovation Premium score for industry leaders such as Jeff Bezos, Elon Musk, Mark Zukerberg, Marc Benioff, and Reed Hastings

(Forbes, 2024). The number one consideration in generating this score is Media Reputation for Innovation. The power of visible, transformative, divergent thinking related to products, processes, and services from business leaders is translated into moving our nation's companies and global economy forward. For our students to thrive in this reality, we need to reach for learning tools that encourage imaginative, creative thinking.

Virtual Reality Pedagogy

Since the introduction of the Oculus Rift virtual reality (VR) headset to the consumer market in 2016, marketers and educators have dreamt of how this tool could transform the classroom just as the Apple IIe computer did in 1980s. The educational IT infrastructure has changed significantly since the 1980s, becoming far more complex, which has led to a variety of challenges implementing VR at scale. Xiao et al. (2024) highlight the challenges of incorporating technology into schools and classrooms, including keeping up with technology developments such as VR, increased demands on students' digital literacy, and the need to educate a teaching workforce to be proficient in effectively using VR. Other issues educators have identified include equity, application licensing, maintenance, product availability, and accessibility.

The reality of VR is that it's a technology that is still maturing but has not reached the ease of use and interoperability that we have come to expect from our devices. In spite of these challenges, the immersive nature of VR cannot be denied, and we should not quickly dismiss this tool simply because it is evolving. There are a vast number of pedagogical benefits to this technology, including the way application developers are harnessing it to promote divergent thinking skills. In fact, virtual reality contains several unique features and tools that, by design, both align to multiple targets in the BTT Model and promote higher order thinking skills.

Bloom's Taxonomy and VR

One of the pillars of education theory is Bloom's taxonomy of learning which is often represented as a list of ascending skills (Armstrong, 2010). The stages include a hierarchy of cognitive skills from simple recall to creating original work. From the bottom of the learning pyramid to the top, Bloom's Taxonomy includes remembering, understanding, applying, analyzing, evaluating, and creating.

In my classroom, I often challenge my students to describe why "create" is at the top of the model. When they reflect on the lessons of Brain-Target Four, they recall that to create something in response to a stated academic learning outcome, a learner needs to move the idea through Bloom's preceding stages. For learners, the act of moving an idea from merely remembering a piece of information, to understanding it, requires that the learner contextualize the information for themselves by adding onto their existing body of knowledge. This process can be described as constructivist learning theory. Moving knowledge from the understanding phase to the application phase means that they can use that information in new environments or situations. When learners analyze this information, they need to create their own unique associations to generate their personal inferences and ideas. Once this has been accomplished, they are ready to evaluate this information because they have a clear picture of where the information came from, its different parts, and how they are connected. Finally, armed with this knowledge, they are ready to create new content or media scaffolded by the preceding stages that came before. This taxonomy has been applied by educators to a variety of classroom activities, assessments, learning tools, and instructional best practices.

Examining Bloom's Taxonomy Through Virtual Reality

As Delage (2021) points out, virtual reality is more than passing on information for consumption of content, which is at the lower level of Bloom's taxonomy. Rather, VR supports higher cognitive skills of creative and higher order thinking.

Virtual reality is a spatial computing technology that can be used as a multimodal teaching platform. It incorporates visual and auditory stimuli with kinesthetic movement as key parts of its interface systems. Haptic feedback increases the sense of touch, thus heightening the sense of presence or *being there* and creating a sense of embodiment through the creation and agency of avatars (McAnally et al., 2021). All of these factors combine to give the user an increased sense of emotional connection to the content due to the programmed kinesthesia in the experience. Brain-Target One reminds us of the connections between emotions and memory.

Experiences in VR can be designed to place the user as the protagonist of the story. Once described as an *empathy generating machine*, virtual reality replicates the kinds of emotional experiences we find in the real world, creating analogous experiences in virtual space (Satpathy, 2015). The link between this *machine induced* memory and emotion are further heightened when combined with a compelling narrative, to provide the user with a sense of agency, or the ability to affect change within the confines of the program. Complex VR applications allow the user to respond verbally and kinesthetically as if they are facing the experience in the real world. Virtual reality researchers often describe this sensation as "embodiment" or "the sensations of being inside, having, and controlling a body" (Guy et al., 2023). In the midst of one of these experiences, the learner is not passive—as if they were simply watching a video online—the headsets and controllers contain tracking technology which maps the movement of the user's motions to the world being projected inside the headset. This interplay between user, device, and software creates a complex feedback system whereby sophisticated concepts can be explored using visual, auditory, tactile, haptic, and kinesthetic stimuli.

It is important to mention that most virtual reality experiences tend to fall into one of two categories, which are used to qualify the level of agency the user has. The first is described as three degrees of freedom (3 DOF). This modality is the more passive of the two, allowing the user to primarily turn their head on three axis and from side to side. Additionally, the user can manipulate the experience to some degree using the controllers. This interaction method is contrasted with the more robust six degrees of freedom (6 DOF) which allows the user to not only interact with the experience by turning their heads and using their controllers but to move their whole bodies in space—forward, backward, and side to side. Some of these more complex experiences allow for hand and finger tracking. Thinking about agency and whole-body immersion in this way leads us to reconsider the lessons of Brain-Target Two—the physical learning environment.

Virtual Reality Simulation

One of VR's primary functions is to allow users to simulate performing a wide variety of jobs or gain skills outside their normal experience. "Walking a mile in someone else's shoes" is a powerful teaching tool, as students have the opportunity to become a virtual cognitive apprentice—performing tasks and roles they are unpracticed in, by role-playing as a more experienced professional.

When considering the physical learning environment in terms of virtual reality, we quickly realize that the physical learning environment can be anywhere, and we can role-play as anyone within that experience. Consider the Emmy-Nominated "Mission ISS" VR application. One part of the experience allows the user to practice operating the robotic arm on the International Space Station to dock a spacecraft—a job that many of us are completely unqualified for. When the user looks down, they see control screens in front of them, below them is the earth imperceptibly turning, above them are the windows that show the stars and other portions of the station. As they sit in front of the controls, the intercom crackles with commands instructing them that the task is to use the robotic arm to capture and dock an approaching spacecraft. Using the controllers, they tentatively extend the arm, immersed in the virtual environment around them. The immediacy of the experience makes it memorable and palpable.

Brain-Target Two states that "teachers can take advantage of the brain's natural propensity to seek novelty by providing stimulating environments that support learning objectives" (Hardiman, 2012, p.61). This experience provides a compelling example of how engagement can work by combining a novel location, multiple means of interactivity, and a unique task. The moment feels real and transports the learner from their normal environment to one far outside their realm of experience. While the "Mission ISS" VR experience may have limited practical applications for training real astronauts, it does provide inexpert learners with an in-depth and simulating environment that can be paired with predefined learning objectives. The engagement a student feels in the moment comes from the simulation designer's adherence to the core tenants of simulation fidelity. Simulation, as a sub-specialization of virtual reality content, should be understood as a unique learning activity with its own set of governing concepts and pedagogical design. Sauvé et al. (2007) clearly explain how simulations differ from games. A game is considered competitive and not necessarily related to real-world applications. A simulation is not a conflict or competition that one is looking to win; it is designed to develop real-world skills that could be used in any environment.

Increasingly, simulations are being designed to comply with an accrediting body's standards so that learners who complete the exercise and gain a passing score would be able to operate certain kinds of equipment, apply for jobs, or justify promotions. In this way, simulations tend to fall under Brain-Target Five—Teaching for the Extension and Application of Knowledge whereby students must apply acquired skills and content in, real-world creative problem-solving tasks (Hardiman, 2012).

Virtual reality simulations continue to gain traction as a useful tool to train students in a variety of fields especially within the health professions. Evidence of divergent thinking can be found in a variety of these kinds of experiences including at the George Mason College of Public Health which created a VR application to allow students to build skill competencies in working with substance-engaged clients. The experience allows students to practice basic client engagement, assessment, and intervention skills in which they need to find novel applications, which require creative problem-solving for many of the student learners (Matto et al., 2023).

The act of practicing creative problem-solving and divergent thinking in virtual reality provides users with a set of transferrable skills they can use once the simulation has ended. Part of what makes these trainings effective skill-building experiences is that they provide meaningful learning scenarios imbued with simulation fidelity, which delivers an immersive activity for the user.

Simulation Fidelity

Simulation fidelity is typically defined as exactness with which something is reproduced. Carey and Rossler (2020) identify three domains of fidelity that define the realism or authenticity found within an experience:

Psychological Fidelity: Psychological fidelity refers to how real the experience feels to the participant. In other words, did the individual participating in the simulation feel transported by the sights, sounds, and things they touched during their experience? Did they forget that they were wearing a headset and holding controllers? Did they feel that they were part of the narrative of the simulation? Did the experience feel like a credible facsimile of the real world? When users of VR describe the *wow* factor of the format, they are usually describing the psychological fidelity. Makers of virtual reality headsets often tout the quality of the graphics as the leading technology necessary to generate this kind of experience.

Psychomotor Fidelity: Psychomotor fidelity is found when the physical/kinesthetic actions that a participant engages in translate to real-world gestures or movements as if they are performing the simulated activity in real life. This domain does not require high-quality graphics or realistic sounds. The intent is to provide users with the opportunity to gain muscle memory skills by performing movements that they could replicate in different environments. Instrumentation and the operation of instrumentation become the primary source of focus for designers who want users to operate a piece of surgical equipment, fly a plane, or wire an electrical panel. In some cases, simple interactive geometric shapes may sufficiently impart the key kinesthetic skills, as reproducibility of muscle memory outside the simulation is more important than the believability of the presented visuals or audio.

Conceptual Fidelity: Simulation designers often endeavor to imbue their work with conceptual fidelity, which is intended to ensure that the experience is true-to-life. The experience should provide the participant with the same kinds of situations they may face in the real world. This domain is often understood as the area most associated with skill development. Maintaining conceptual fidelity allows users to practice real-world decision-making in a carefully constructed simulation. This area most directly ties with the user's ability to practice divergent thinking. Learners are presented with fictional scenarios, which require them to respond using problem-solving strategies that they learned outside the simulation.

Not every educational simulation employs these modalities in equal measure. For educators employing simulations in their classrooms, it is recommended that they begin by examining the stated learning objectives of a section and then research different applications to see which ones would help the learners understand the core principles.

At Johns Hopkins University's Bloomberg School of Public Health, my team and I were tasked to create a virtual reality experience that demonstrated a specific series of laboratory experiments that needed to be taught to incoming student workers every year. We learned that the experiments involved taking detailed measurements, examining organs, and using specific laboratory instrumentation. It was decided that the most important part of the experience was to focus on the psychological fidelity, or the sensation that the viewer was actually in the lab. We recorded the experience using high resolution 8K 360-degree spherical cameras and mapped a feed on top of the primary image, a high resolution 4K bench camera so the learners could see the trainers' hands.

We also produced the content in digestible sections so the trainee could put on a VR headset, orient themselves in space, and watch a few steps of the procedure before removing the headset and attempting the procedure themselves. Producing a 360-degree video in this way allows the learner to turn their head in any direction while wearing the headset. The high-resolution videos allow the user to zoom in on different parts of a complex procedure, pause the video, and see in detail what the trainer is doing, which would be impossible in a real-life demonstration. This method of capturing the training had the additional benefit of avoiding the need to generate, or find, scientific grade images of the specific instrumentation that was used in the lab, which would have been costly and time consuming.

Understanding the most critical parts of a lesson is essential in curating meaningful virtual reality content for academic use. This becomes even more important when attempting to generate content from scratch. Clearly defined lesson-based learning objectives—derived from the curriculum—can provide criteria for the selection of meaningful content, which in turn provides a roadmap for choosing the appropriate type of simulation fidelity.

Assessment and Virtual Reality

In Brain-Target Six, the author shares that, " . . . evaluation in various forms should be happening during every phase of the teaching and learning process in order to provide guideposts for both teachers and students to help assess progress and continually improve instruction" (Hardiman, 2012, p. 145). Assessment usually takes one of three forms:

Diagnostic assessment: Diagnostic assessment is conducted before formal instruction begins. Its purpose is to assess student knowledge so that the teacher can identify any content gaps the class might have. Armed with this information, the teacher may decide to emphasize certain concepts or change their approach to covering a particular topic.

Formative assessment: This kind of assessment is given when the instructor has begun to determine whether students are meeting prescribed learning objectives. This kind of assessment can take a variety of approaches from informal daily check-ins to large mid-term projects, or papers. Like diagnostic assessment, this information can provide the instructor with useful feedback on student knowledge so lessons can be amended as necessary to ensure that the learners meet their targeted goals.

Summative assessment: Summative assessment is provided at the end of a module or after a significant period of time and encapsulates all of the primary learning objectives covered. Preparation for this assessment often requires analysis of content, application of knowledge, or the creation of new work as evidence of the student's learning.

These methods are classroom-tested and effective ways to track student progress along their learning journey. The growth of educational virtual reality applications offers another means of measuring student knowledge, one that can provide moment-by-moment assessment and can be done without a learner even knowing they are being evaluated.

Stealth Assessment: Stealth assessment is a powerful tool for teachers to evaluate a student's knowledge by examining data collected by simulation or game systems, which can track the performance of a user in real time. First coined in 2005 by researcher Valerie Shute at the AERA symposium on diagnostic assessments, the term describes how " . . . we can support learning by using automated scoring and machine-based reasoning techniques to infer things that would be too hard for humans (e.g., estimating competency levels across a network of skills, addressing what a person knows they can do, and to what degree)" (Tobias & Fletcher, 2011, p. 83).

Let's imagine you sit down to play a video game. You move your joystick to the right, and as you do, the character on the screen moves accordingly. Suddenly, you see a rock blocking your path and you deftly depress the "jump" button neatly clearing the obstacle. Every action described in this scenario is tracked and logged within the programming of the game system. This information needs to be rigorously monitored by the system to ensure that the game is responding in accordance with user input.

Pushing the "jump" button too early would result in the character landing in front of the obstacle instead of on the other side of it, just as pushing the "jump" button too late would result in the character potentially landing on top of the obstacle.

Once an educator identifies goals and objectives of a learning episode, a competency or evidence model can be applied to observable behaviors in gameplay, which demonstrate mastery, or lack thereof, of either knowledge or skill. While stealth assessment has been used as a tool to connect video games to real-world learning, modern virtual reality simulations have begun using similar assessment techniques to evaluate a learner's performance.

Virtual Reality in the Workplace

For leaders and anyone who gives professional development presentations, an example to help individuals practice public speaking is a virtual reality application called "Ovation" which blends artificial intelligence (AI) feedback and data collection with virtual reality. The simulation offers two methods for participants to interact. It can be run from a Window's computer or on a Meta Quest VR headset. I recommend that anyone using this application to practice their presentation skills use the VR device as it greatly increases the sense of presence and agency. The application provides a wide variety of ways to tailor the presentation experience to the needs of the participants. This customization includes features like the following:

- Choosing the location: a stage in a large conference hall, an office, a conference room, a university lecture hall, or a school classroom.
- Selecting the audience: students, policymakers, law enforcement, lawyers, teachers, parents, etc.

"Additional Context" instructions further allow for even greater control of the experience by including a text box where detailed directions can be given. Some examples might include a description of the hostility of the audience, whether they should respond in a specific language, the question difficulty, and so forth.

These settings functionally describe how the system—in conjunction with ChatGPT—should respond to the presenters. Once a response or comment is made by the user, the remarks are examined by ChatGPT for analysis, which then provides a response driven by the initial context, as well as what was last said. The application *responds* to the user by having the avatars or characters engage with them on the topic. Users can also choose if they would like to use PowerPoint slides, note cards, lecterns, a microphone, or a laser pointer to aid in the realism of the experience. Finally, the system uses stealth assessment methods to provide real-time feedback to the presenter letting them know if they are using too many *filler words*, speaking in a monotone, or speaking too fast by occasionally showing warnings on the screen if one of these errors is made. At the end of the session, the user is provided with a customized summative assessment, which includes a complete transcription, an analysis of the speaker's presentation style, a detailed breakdown of the most commonly used words, speaking rate, and a customized list of tips on how to improve.

The application provides realistic experiences for learners looking to improve their presentation skills and is an excellent example of successfully applying all three domains of simulation fidelity.

- Psychomotor activities: holding a microphone, using a laser pointer, advancing slides, and making eye contact with the avatars.
- Psychological realism: using responsive avatars and locations, having the avatars applaud, cough, or sneeze during a presentation, the positioning of the participant in the front of the room, and the option to include a timing clock.
- Conceptual authenticity: having the avatar audience ask questions, engage in thoughtful debate or discussion, and challenge presented ideas.

The imbued realism of the VR experience, when combined with the responsiveness of the AI system and the detailed assessment tools, allows users to actively practice divergent thinking skills while receiving frequent and timely feedback from the system using the stealth assessment model. Using this model, "Feedback can be effectively 'scaffolded' by providing hints incrementally rather than just giving students the correct answer" (Hardiman, 2012, p. 148). Learners who are interested in improving their public speaking skills can use tools like this one to practice their craft and make improvements before addressing a live audience.

From Failure of Imagination to Success of Imagination

Ovation is evidence of the maturation of virtual reality as a learning tool. It seamlessly connects public speaking training, high-quality simulation fidelity, and assessment into one package that is useful for the development of higher order thinking skills. According to a 2023 report by the World Economic Forum, cognitive skills are critical to complex problem-solving in the workplace. By fostering divergent thinking, we create pathways for successes in imagination. VR, by its nature, is a unique tool that can prepare students for a modern workplace that prioritizes creative thinking in the face of complex global issues. Educators should take every opportunity to harness the divergent power of virtual reality to prepare students for the needs of actual reality.

Part 2: Technology in Education: Artificial Intelligence (AI), Virtual Reality (VR), and Beyond

Author: Katherine Fu, Educational Consultant

Quality education to ensure inclusive and equitable education for all is one of the fundamental components of the United Nations's sustainable development 2023 agenda (Haleem et al., 2022). In the past decade, advances in digital technology have emerged and created a paradigm shift within the education system, thus becoming an essential tool to achieve this goal. The digital age has also generated a generational shift where children are increasingly likely to have access to technology (Neumann et al., 2019). This phenomenon paired with the accelerated usage of digital technologies in education will continue to challenge the traditional pedagogy and design of education systems and encourage adaptation in accordance to current technological trends.

The recent COVID-19 pandemic has further institutionalized the role of technology within education. The need for digitalization, technological preparedness, and integrated online platforms were highlighted during this time for conducting classes, knowledge sharing, conducting assessments, and providing learning tools to supplement curriculum learning objectives and day-to-day activities and assignments. Schools that demonstrated a lack of preparedness, training, and digital resources experienced widening gaps in learning retention, engagement, and inequities (Timotheou et al., 2023).

The global crisis in education for access to education and connectivity highlighted the necessity for digital transformation within the education system and the continued investment for developing digital technologies to assist in upskilling for students, including problem-solving. Increased investment post-COVID has reinforced the focus to develop technology in the classroom. For the $190B investment in education from the COVID relief package in 2021, an Associated Press analysis of public records found many of the largest school systems spent tens of millions of dollars in pandemic money on edtech software and services from tech companies, including licenses for apps, games and tutoring websites (Binkley, 2023). Still, the integration of digital technologies is complex and a continuous process that involves a multitude of factors starting from the classroom. For the long-term digital transformation of schools, this chapter section will cover the role of technology in the classroom, how it supports the Brain-Targeted Teaching® (BTT) Model, the impact of technology tools such as virtual reality (VR), and more broadly, how technology improvements in education will continue to impact the classroom experience to create an inclusive and equitable learning environment.

Role of Technology in the Classroom & BTT Model

Educational resources and digital tools help improve the classroom climate and make the teaching-learning process more customized for each student. Reinforcing the focus of Brain- Target One on the importance of a positive emotional climate in the classroom, a study of 305 entrepreneurship program students from five different universities in China revealed that the school's innovation climate has a positive impact on students' attitudes toward technology and improving motivational outcomes for students (Yuan et al., 2022). Educational technology has also become an integral component from language education to STEM classrooms, with a wide range of computer-assisted instruction (CAI) and usage of web4.0, including artificial intelligence tools, machine learning, virtual and augmented reality, and Internet of Things (IoT) (Haleem et al., 2022). It is important to use these tools as a supplement rather than substitute instruction to enhance student learning, and the benefits include positive increase in attention engagement, motivation, communication, and cognitive processing skills.

Studies have shown positive effects of computer technology on student self-efficacy for independent and personalized learning, leading to a positive emotional climate among students in classroom settings using integrated technology. Usage of learning platforms (LPs), including virtual learning environments, communication technology, management information systems, and resource-shared technologies, provide opportunities for teacher assessment and feedback; they also allow students to access a wider variety of quality learning resources and conducting self and peer reviews (Timotheou et al., 2023). Access to digital information facilitates learning aligned with Brain-Target Four by providing opportunities for retention of information and improvements in content areas such as language and literacy (Neumann et al., 2019).

With Brain-Target Five focusing on creative problem-solving and divergent thinking, classroom tactics such as gamification and integrating mixed media can be used to improve creative thinking and problem-solving skills. Solutions for increasing accessibility in education is the use of touch screens for young children, especially those with disabilities who may lack fine motor skills to effectively use a standard keyboard and mouse (Lu et al., 2017). Early literacy skills studies support the observation that children as young as two to three years can use a tablet to provide a valid assessment of cognitive skills.

For Brain-Target Six, with the focus on demonstrating learning and the importance of evaluation, technology offers different avenues to enhance test administration, scoring, and reporting to develop a customized curriculum. The development of teacher efficacy to collect student assessments using digital technology in the classroom is critical. Rigorous testing of reliability of test scores produced by digital assessment tools in the classroom will allow classroom knowledge to be collected in a cost effective and accurate method (Neumann et al., 2019).

This approach will increase knowledge of how technologies are used in assessment, how data can be linked across curriculum areas and across students, and how to represent data for education purposes to achieve individual learning goals and student success. Furthermore, touch screen tablets, computers, and virtual modalities have features to give students opportunities to strengthen learning, motivation, collaboration, and productivity that can be used for multiple formats in assessment (Woloshyn et al., 2017). The two categories of online tools, those that support increasing student contributions in the classroom and those focused on peer feedback and the peer grading process, also support the goal of Brain-Target One for creating a positive emotional climate in the classroom.

Digital technologies have the potential to be a powerful assessment tool for teachers and students (Woloshyn et al., 2017). Ultimately, both educators and administrators have a role in effectively integrating new technologies into the classroom. Technology can be a tool for learning, and assessments lead to evaluation, but it is not the evaluation of learning. The development of technology is continuously evolving, and additional technology tools such as augmented reality and virtual reality (VR), AI integrated platforms, and other upcoming platforms will continue to challenge educators and education systems to find the balance between innovation, cost, and efficiency in the classroom and beyond for culturally relevant teaching and integration of the arts and technology (Lin et al., 2024).

14 Review of Research on the Brain-Targeted Teaching® Model

Evidence From National and International Studies

by Katherine Fu and Mariale Hardiman

Previous chapters have explored research and practices of the six components of the Brain-Targeted Teaching® (BTT) Model. In this chapter, we share how the BTT Model has been studied in multiple contexts in the United States and worldwide. Over the last twenty years, many educators and other professionals have offered anecdotal information about how the BTT Model influenced and enhanced their practice. While their stories have been inspiring, we are pleased to present evidence of its effectiveness in studies conducted by researchers and doctoral students. Research studies using the BTT Model that are included in this review were conducted across the United States, United Kingdom, United Arab Emirates, Indonesia, Thailand, India, Chile, Puerto Rico, and China. The review includes research studies in which the BTT Model served as an intervention to measure the impact of professional development on teaching practices with educators in multiple settings, including K–12, early childhood, and higher education. Other studies focus on the use of the BTT Model in curriculum development, second-language acquisition, and online learning. Research continues to show how the student-centered approach rooted in the BTT Model has the potential to transform a system of traditional teaching environments, helping to eliminate bias and delivering long-term positive impact for all learners.

The Brain-Targeted Teaching® Model in Professional Learning Studies

Dedicated professionals in all occupations seek to continuously improve their practice, staying updated on new and current trends that would enhance outcomes for their organizations and constituents. Professional development is one tool that supports practitioners in upskilling and improving practices within a collaborative environment. Effective professional development is characterized by its focus on both content and pedagogy, aligned with goals and standards of the institution, and addressing the complexities in teaching, leading, and learning environments.

Furthermore, professional development should embody what we know about how the learner receives, interprets, and applies new knowledge. Embedding the BTT Model into professional learning experiences aims to provide practitioners with information from the learning sciences to improve their practice, first by experiencing the BTT Model as learners, and then applying the BTT framework in the classroom and workplace.

Research in the BTT Model is showing promising results in enhancing an understanding of how the learning sciences inform effective teaching, leading, and learning. For example, in a study conducted by Parr (2016), forty-four K–12 public school educators enrolled in a six-hour professional development session on the implementation of the BTT Model. Parr used a mixed-methods approach with pre- and post-session surveys and semi-structured interviews to examine the impact of the professional development on teaching practices. The analysis of data yielded three major findings: an increase in participants' awareness and knowledge of neuroeducation and BTT concepts, an increase in the application of BTT strategies in the classroom, and an ongoing need for deeper understanding of the learning sciences to inform practical experiences in the classroom (Parr, 2017).

Other studies addressed the integration of the BTT pedagogy into professional development to increase teacher self-efficacy beliefs. Teachers' preconceived bias of students, the school environment, and student characteristics influence teacher self-efficacy, which ultimately affects student learning. Therefore, there is a pressing need for professional development that focuses on teacher efficacy in relation to student achievement as a key component of learning and classroom management. Jackson-Butler (2017) addresses teacher efficacy and the impact on student achievement in a study involving low socioeconomic status (SES) minority students in independent schools. Five teachers from a school in a northwest American state formed the focus group for the intervention. Jackson-Butler employed a mixed-method approach using a teacher efficacy scale, classroom observations, and interviews to assess teachers' perceptions of academic, socioemotional, and cultural barriers to student learning. After implementing the BTT Model, findings indicated a difference in teachers' feelings and beliefs in their ability to teach students from different cultures and various socioeconomic backgrounds. Key themes emerging from the research included the importance of cultural awareness, understanding environmental influences that affect student learning, and the association between teacher efficacy and how students are engaged and motivated in their learning. Overall, results yielded an increase in teachers' ability to adjust lessons, manage classroom behavior, and use effective teaching approaches to increase student attention.

In a similar study in the United Kingdom (UK), Torrance Jenkins (2018) conducted a one- to two-year case study using the BTT Model (along with a different neuroeducation framework) to deliver professional learning to a group of science teachers. Through observation of teaching practices, interviews, and focus groups with students, she documents ways in which the use of the BTT Model and neuroeducation principles generally enhanced teachers' practices with new techniques as well as boosting their confidence in their own established practices. The study provides specific examples of how each of the six brain targets was used by teachers in science instruction.

JohnBull and Hardiman (2023) conducted research on the use of the BTT Model to determine if the tenets of neuroeducation might influence teachers' efficacy beliefs. Over the course of two years, a neuroeducation professional development (PD) program using the BTT Model was delivered to three cohorts of in-service PK–12 teachers (N=80) from a mid-Atlantic urban school district to explore the impact of the professional learning experiences on teacher self-efficacy beliefs. The sessions for Cohorts 1 and 3 were conducted in ten, three-hour sessions, while Cohort 2 received the same training over a condensed timeline of two weeks during the summer. A sample of nonparticipating teachers was also included to represent a business-as-usual comparison-matched sample. Pre-and post-efficacy scores showed statistically higher personal and general teaching self-efficacy among participating teachers for each cohort. The positive link between integrating the BTT Model and teacher self-efficacy beliefs highlights the potential benefits of the BTT framework for teacher professional development, further igniting the belief in the power of education to reach all learners.

The Brain-Targeted Teaching® Model in Early Childhood Studies

Professional development as a significant aspect in curriculum implementation has further focused on researching how to apply the learning sciences to early childhood-centered instructional design and practice, while also building a stronger sense of teacher self-efficacy. Walker (2016) addresses the importance of integrating the principles of neuroeducation within early childhood education, recognizing the crucial developmental stage in a child's life in the early years. She conducted a three-year study focused on the implementation of the BTT Model at early childhood centers in India, where staff and teachers received extensive training in the BTT Model and then developed curriculum based on the framework. The research examines the implementation of BTT training, reflects on the curriculum implementation, and identifies factors influencing the adoption of the BTT Model and its adaptation within an early-childhood setting in India. Findings highlight how the participants used the BTT Model to refine their curriculum and instructional practices for their early-childhood centers and suggest that the BTT Model can be a valuable resource for early-childhood educational institutions interested in integrating learning sciences into daily practice. Walker's research begins to fill a gap between research and practice in early childhood education and, in particular, for early-years in-service teachers.

Mizyed and Eccles (2023) also highlight the ongoing urgency and relevance of professional development in the context of implementing the learning sciences and child-centered pedagogy for early-years teachers to enhance practices and self-efficacy. Their research aimed to understand the challenges faced by Emirati teachers in fostering problem-solving skills development in early education in the United Arab Emirates (UAE). Challenges include combatting the gap between UAE's goal of moving to a more knowledge-based economy, the multiple factors influencing Emirati teachers' attitudes toward implementing change, and the urgency of additional educator training. They interviewed ten teachers over a two-week period and used a mixed-method approach that combined quantitative survey data with qualitative interview answers to probe for low teacher self-efficacy and a lack of proper exposure to professional training to develop problem-solving skills.

To address the need for effective in-service training, Mizyed and Eccles (2024) implemented a thirteen-week professional development program using the BTT Model that featured collaboration, observation, and self-reflection aimed at improving teaching practices and strengthening teacher self-efficacy. Results indicated a shift toward child-centered strategies, greater collaboration, and improvement in teachers' self-efficacy scores. The researchers found that applying the BTT Model increased understanding of how to implement problem-solving instructional methods across grade levels. They recommend building early-years teachers' knowledge in the BTT framework and child-centered pedagogy to advance their teaching skills. The study concludes that developing a contextual, collaborative professional development model grounded in reflection has the potential to positively change teacher self-efficacy and have a long-term impact on teacher training pathways in the UAE and beyond.

Araya Crisóstomo (2022) provides another example of the use of the BTT Model to develop collaborative professional development across the span of early-childhood to adult learning. In the Bío-and Maule regions of Chile, the goal of professional development was to equip teachers with the knowledge and skills necessary to implement innovative and evidence-based teaching practices in the classroom using knowledge from the field of neuroeducation. Twenty teachers across primary, secondary, and higher education received training on the BTT Model. After the training, participants' classroom sessions were recorded. The videos were used for ethnographic observation to understand the application of the BTT Model on the stages of the neuroeducation didactic cycle for the participating teachers. Elements of the physical classroom such as the physical space, conditions of the classroom, and dynamics of the students were recorded and proved to be essential for understanding the current state and evolution of teaching practices. While there were varying levels of efficacy, the most common themes for positive growth for students were authentic exploration, interactive groups, and experimentation. These themes align with the core of the BTT Model. This research recognizes the ongoing plasticity of the brain and highlights the significance of enriched learning environments in shaping cognitive development. The researcher concludes that there is a need for a paradigm shift in educational practices, integrating elements of cognitive neuroscience and constructivist approaches to enhance the quality of teaching and learning.

The Brain-Targeted Teaching® Model in Higher Education Studies

Beyond the PK–12 landscape, integrating the BTT Model into professional development has also been applied to higher education. Seegers (2020) conducted a study with community college faculty to examine the use of the BTT Model as a tool to integrate the learning sciences into their pedagogy. Faculty at a California community college were invited to participate in the Brain-Targeted Teaching® Lab (TL). Twelve participants received a minimum of six, one-hour meetings and engaged in outside reading and writing. The BTT Model was used to present effective strategies during the TL sessions. The sessions covered the six brain targets, including emotional climate, physical environment, learning design, teaching for mastery, teaching for application, and evaluating learning. Seegers reports that participants changed their pedagogy after participation in the TL. The results showed the ways in which participants implemented changes after the sessions, with varying percentages of participants implementing changes related to each of the brain targets. Seegers concludes that fusing the BTT Model into higher education pedagogy has the potential to impact student success, inform education leaders and politicians, and assist faculty seeking to refine their pedagogy.

Focusing on higher education in the STEM fields, Stassinopoulos (2023) examined socioeconomic barriers related to gender bias in the classroom and workplace, particularly the gender gap for women of color in higher education STEM fields. According to study findings, there is a significant difference in how STEM faculty and students perceived student engagement based on gender, as well as a predominant instructor-centered instructional practice rather than student-centered. The researcher noted that non-STEM faculty displayed more student-centered, supportive, and accessible teaching practices than STEM faculty. To address this issue, Stassinpoloulos created a professional learning community (PLC) for STEM faculty, focusing on increasing teaching self-efficacy and implementing student-centered practices. The BTT Model was customized for the higher education STEM environment and used as part of the intervention over the course of a nine-week program with four in-person meetings and six online content modules. After the PLC intervention, the STEM faculty treatment group demonstrated positive changes in teacher self-efficacy, improvements in instructional strategies, and stronger student engagement. The research showcases how enhancing faculty teaching self-efficacy and implementing student-centered instructional practices in STEM education can foster greater student engagement and an equitable environment for both educators and students. This study shows a need to address a more deeply rooted call for action for a cultural shift for educators in higher education to be able to provide more inclusive and equitable learning environments for students. In particular, by shedding light on the complexities and challenges faced by women, especially those from underrepresented groups in higher education STEM, it is important for educators and institutions to continue creating professional learning experiences that result in inclusive and supportive learning environments for their adult learners.

The work of Cai (2020) at the Nanchang Institute of Technology in China provides additional application of the BTT Model in higher education, focusing on developing and refining curriculum and instruction in English language courses. Cai provides examples of how faculty can employ each of the six brain targets to enhance students' achievement in college courses. Similarly, at the University of Puerto Rico, Ferrer López (2016) reported that the use of the BTT Model for course development increased the quality of the content and instructional strategies.

The Brain-Targeted Teaching® Model in Second Language Studies

Several international studies sought to improve instruction for students learning a second language by embedding the BTT Model into pedagogical practices. At a university in Thailand, Kasempi and Yoonisil (2023) developed a supplementary curriculum for foreign students by infusing the tenets of the BTT Model to advance listening and speaking competency. A sample group of twenty undergraduate students received twenty-four hours of training in an eight-step model that included problem identification, needs evaluation, assumption formulation, action-plan development, implementation, performance evaluation, reflection, and decision-making. They were given an enrichment curriculum, language achievement tests, and a reflection form. After the training concluded, results indicated a significant improvement in both listening and speaking skills. The research provides insights for educators and curriculum developers who seek to enhance language skills for students coming from different lived experiences and varying language proficiency levels by using the components of the BTT Model to build a comprehensive curriculum development process and implementation.

Chowdhury (2020) also employed the BTT Model in teaching English to tenth graders in the United Arab Emirates (UAE). In an action research study, results show overall improvement in language achievement as well as gains in interpersonal and social-emotional skills. The researcher provides a detailed BTT learning unit that demonstrates how each of the six brain targets were developed for a unit focused on the topic of the country's transit system. It is interesting to note Chowdhury's observation about the model's focus on the arts. The author states, "It was evident that this method helped the shy students to participate as individuals in artwork, group discussions, and role-plays" (p. 101).

Another example of the use of the BTT Model in the context of second-language learning focused on Japanese students who underperformed in English language acquisition. The research focused on how the BTT Model could create a classroom atmosphere that fosters student participation and development (Wastila, 2015). The author states that education in Japan traditionally uses a more teacher-centered approach. Moreover, Wastila suggests that there has been a historical tendency in the classroom to discourage student interaction, leading to delayed development of communication skills. The research proposes the need to shift toward a student-centered and team-based approach, in which students take on a more active role in their education. This work provides another example in which the BTT Model was used to improve language proficiency among students in second-language courses. The author encouraged English as a Foreign Language teachers to increase English language proficiency through embracing the BTT Model's team-based learning and alternative assessment methods, fostering a more collaborative and interactive learning environment. Moreover, the researcher encourages the use of the BTT Model to recognize cultural inclusivity, classroom culture, deeply rooted teacher pedagogy, and to offer opportunities for teachers to develop a student-based curriculum and the classroom environment.

Kumar and Amin (2023) also found that using the BTT Model significantly improved students' acquisition of English as a second language. They conducted a rigorous study in which eighty senior secondary school students were randomized into two groups–one group receiving the BTT Model to learn English prose and poetry and the second group to receive a program focused on content-based language teaching. Each group received forty sessions of instruction over twenty days in each condition. Achievement data were collected using four validated testing measures for pre-tests and post-tests at the start and the end of the intervention. Results showed "substantial evidence that the Brain-Targeted Teaching® Model is more effective than content-based language teaching for enhancing academic achievement and language proficiency among students" (p.18). They further state that they believe their research findings have "significant implications for educators and policymakers who seek to improve the equational quality for all pupils" (p. 18).

The Brain-Targeted Teaching® Model in Online Teaching

Practitioners' beliefs and practices can be influenced by a multitude of factors—from resources, organizational climate and culture, physical environment, and biases—to socioeconomic conditions. The unprecedented disruption caused by the COVID-19 pandemic significantly impacted teachers and teaching practices, leading to a need for rapid adaptation in response to school closures and reopening, the shift to online teaching, and a new emotional climate in the classroom. The ongoing nature of the pandemic demands that teachers rapidly develop skills for a wide array of teaching scenarios, including in-person, hybrid, and online.

According to TeVault (2022), teachers subsequently had to develop general pedagogical knowledge (GPK) of online teaching practically overnight, highlighting the importance of teacher self-efficacy (TSE), collective teacher efficacy (CTE), and general pedagogical knowledge in teacher adaptations and practices. She aimed to explore the relationships between teacher beliefs and pedagogy before and during the COVID pandemic to understand how TSE, CTE, and GPK interrelate and what practices and beliefs were and were not adapted in response to the pandemic. The study spanned three explored time periods: teachers' classroom activities and experiences before COVID-19, during Emergency Response Online Teaching, and return to in-person teaching. TeVault combined quantitative and qualitative methods by pulling from pre-existing surveys and referencing a fall 2015 BTT Introductory overview workshop series for eighty educators, a book study of the BTT Model, and a series of "Brain Bytes" (email messages sharing evidence-based practices aligned with BTT). She also conducted a semi-structured interview process for the end of the 2020–2021 school year with teachers in a school on the east coast of the United States.

Teachers who had prior experiences with BTT through workshops or book studies readily applied these tools during the pandemic, indicating the adaptability of the BTT framework to support teaching in challenging circumstances. The researcher claims that this shows how the BTT Model had a positive impact on educators, providing them with the necessary tools to translate research into practice, address the emotional climate for learning, and redesign learning opportunities to best meet the needs of their students during the disrupted time in their education.

Also motivated by online instruction due to the COVID pandemic, Rukminingsih et al. (2021) conducted quasi-experimental research to determine the effects of teaching English using the Brain-Targeted Teaching® Model versus a program focused on *content schemata*. The study was conducted in a private higher education institution in Indonesia with undergraduate students majoring in English and taking an online course in Critical Reading. The study design consisted of an experimental group of thirty students who learned English using the BTT Model and thirty students in a control group using a content schemata approach. Both groups consisted of fifteen students who were assessed to have high motivation for learning and fifteen with low motivation. Data analysis using a two-way ANOVA showed that "the brain targeted teaching model with online instruction had a statistically significant influence on the students' reading achievement and motivation" (p. 516). While both types of instruction were effective to teach reading comprehension, the researchers state that the "BTT Model gave better effect than activating students' content schema with high and low motivation level" (p. 511). The researchers attributed the academic gains to the focus of BTT on stimulating positive emotions; introducing multiple modalities; employing critical thinking; and giving frequent, relevant feedback.

In the post-COVID-19 landscape, the nuances of interacting virtually bring to light the importance of emotional and physical learning environments in schools that moved from in-person instruction to online and hybrid learning formats. However, even before the pandemic, online learning has been an increasing mode for teaching courses in higher education. In similar research conducted at a university in Puerto Rico, the BTT Model was used for the design and administration of online continuing education courses (Ferrer López, 2016). Ten best practices for course design and twenty best practices for course administration in a Learning Management System were identified and implemented with participants enrolled in the courses. The practices ranged from developing discussion activities and forums for student interaction to rubric development. It underscored the importance of the six brain targets: emotional and physical learning environments, the design of learning experiences, teaching for mastery, knowledge extension, and evaluation in the online context. In addition, the research highlighted the need to enhance the quality of instructional materials, instructional dynamics, and participant feedback in the online continuing education courses. The findings further highlight the importance of comprehensive guidelines for educators, emphasize the significance of student engagement and clear communication, and advocate for the use of the latest technology to enhance the online learning experience. Similar to the other studies, this research underscores the use of the BTT Model's tenets to positively enhance the quality of online education in order to create a well-prepared educator workforce equipped with BTT implementation techniques.

Applications of Brain-Targeted Teaching®

Building a more inclusive, creative, and technologically savvy workforce requires a sustained investment in professional learning experiences, pedagogical enhancements, and curriculum adjustments. The evidence provided in this review suggests that the BTT Model can contribute to this work by guiding a system of evidence-based, effective instruction. Whether in the classroom, corporate trainings, or corporate onboarding, the model has the potential to provide a framework for the acquisition and creative application of knowledge within a positive and inclusive environment.

In summary, as neuroeducation research continues to expand, it provides unique global opportunities for cross-cultural collaboration to make learning rigorous, joyful, and relevant for all learners at any age and in any classroom, workplace, or learning experience. Anywhere.

Last Words

Written in Honor of the Late Gordon Porterfield

15

The Brain-Targeted Teaching® Model in Teacher Preparation Programs: A Story From a Teacher Educator

Throughout this book, I have focused on implementing the BTT Model in elementary and secondary schools, higher education, corporate settings, and at home. Knowing that the model could be incorporated into higher education teacher preparation programs, I became intrigued with a story that a former colleague at Johns Hopkins University School of Education, the late Gordon Porterfield, shared with me about using the model with his class. And I will now share it with you:

Gordon Porterfield was there at the inception of the BTT Model when he taught theater to middle school students. As a faculty associate at Johns Hopkins, Gordon developed an innovative graduate-level course for first- and second-year teachers, all of whom teach in urban school districts. The course at the time, "Teacher as Thinker and Writer," applied a variety of BTT approaches to promote creative teaching and learning. He used his own classroom to model arts-based activities and application of knowledge so teachers could see relevance of these techniques at every grade level and in any subject area. Gordon was an especially strong advocate for the use of theater in urban classrooms. He believed that theater is accessible to *all* students and can be used by *any* teacher, whether experienced in theater or not, to engage students in meaningful learning. According to Gordon, teachers often know their content but beg for concrete suggestions to motivate their students, many of whom seem impervious to conventional instructional techniques and strategies. He contended that theater, much like play, can be a powerful motivational tool to foster student engagement. In thinking about ways to use the tenets of BTT in his graduate level class, he had a dream one night about a new class activity and implemented it as shown below:

"Boys and girls," he said, addressing his class of early career teachers as if they were middle schoolers, "I'm giving you a choice of assignments for this week. You may either write a summary of an article from an educational journal (assigned by me) or memorize and verbatim recite to the class an eight-line poem (also assigned by me). Which do you prefer?"

His graduate students, having done more than their share of journal article reviews, opted unanimously to memorize and recite the poem. Gordon then gave each student a different eight-line poem, all by the notoriously dense and difficult Emily Dickinson, and directed them to memorize the poem and be prepared to recite it for the next class.

Gordon was amazed when, having had seven days to learn the poem, many of the students were unprepared for the recitation. He knew, had he given the journal article assignment, every member of the class—without exception—would have turned it in. The students who claimed to be prepared to recite were clearly ill at ease and struggled just to get the words out, giving scant attention to the meaning of the poem. Those not ready to recite offered myriad excuses: "It was too hard," "I couldn't figure out what some of the words meant," "I was exhausted," and "I had too much else to do." Gordon was shocked by their excuses as he knew that they would have spent hours on the journal article and turned it in on time but found themselves paralyzed by having to memorize and recite an eight-line poem.

The activity occasioned a lively, productive discussion as to the workings of the brain while memorizing, the value of memorization in itself (knowing something *by heart*), the value of spacing study times, the deep thinking that the poems required, and the challenge of performing in front of their peers a poem that stretched their minds and imaginations. At the end of the next class, when everyone had finally done the recitation, Gordon asked each student to evaluate the activity (anonymously) in terms of its value and application in a teacher education class. Gordon expected the worst and was surprised and delighted by the positive response. Every teacher felt the experience was a unique and valuable way to move them beyond traditional teaching methods and to better understand the needs of the learners in their own classrooms. Many said that being pushed beyond their comfort zone gave them perspective of how some of their own students felt in the learning environment. They gave examples of how they might be able to use the arts, especially theater, to promote their own students' deeper engagement with the content.

When Gordon and I discussed the significance of this activity in relation to the tenets of the BTT Model, his closing comment was, "Well, the students certainly learned much about pedagogy with this assignment, and

Emily would've been pleased." I was pleased too. That simple activity and the students' responses to it reinforced my conviction that applying relevant research from the learning sciences can have an enormous impact on how educators *at any level* should approach the teaching and learning process. Successful schools must reflect the growing evidence from the learning sciences about how students think and learn.

It is my hope that the research and practical applications presented throughout this book and through the framework of the Brain-Targeted Teaching® Model will enlighten practitioners to consider *how* learning best occurs so that all instructional activities—from those offered to young children to adults—result in deep, engaging, joyful, and lasting learning.

Let's give the last word to Ms. Dickinson:

The Brain—is wider than the Sky—
For—put them side by side—
The one the other will contain
With ease—and You—beside—

The Brain is deeper than the sea
For—hold them—Blue to Blue—
The one the other will absorb—
As Sponges—Buckets—do—

The brain is just the weight of God—
For—Heft them—Pound for Pound—
And they will differ—if they do—
As Syllable from Sound—

Appendix I

The Brain-Targeted Teaching® Model Implementation Checklist

The Brain-Targeted Teaching® Model Implementation Checklist is a tool designed to help practitioners successfully put into practice the Brain-Targeted Teaching® Model. It is intended to serve as a guidepost for self-assessment and coaching rather than a rigid system of evaluation. The checklist provides a snapshot of each of the six brain targets by offering indicators that should be considered in effective instruction or in a work environment. Naturally, not every indicator will be observed during every lesson or every work encounter, and some indicators are relevant to more than one brain target. The checklist should be viewed as a communication tool for peer-to-peer and peer-to-leader guidance and support.

Practitioners working in other contexts are encouraged to adapt the indicators below to meet their own professional standards and needs.

BRAIN-TARGET ONE: *SETTING THE EMOTIONAL CLIMATE FOR LEARNING*	
POSITIVE LANGUAGE	
Strategy	**Noted**
Activities promote a sense of belonging within the school or workplace	
Praise for expected performance is regularly offered within the school or workplace	
Behavior-specific rather than general praise is offered within the school or workplace	
Direct communications are preferred over veiled (or indirect) language	
Language acknowledges cultural identities and differences	
Notes:	
PREDICTABILITY	
Strategy	**Noted**
Classroom and work routines are evident with clear communication for expectations	
Special events, goals, and/or successes are celebrated	
Notes:	
EMOTION AND CONNECTEDNESS IN SCHOOL OR WORK ENVIRONMENT	
Strategy	**Noted**
Students' or workers' emotions are gauged and acknowledged	
Positive teacher/leader connection reaches every member of the community	
Consistent classroom and work expectations are provided	
All participants are involved in the lesson or work task	
Instructional and work activities are content-based, rigorous, engaging, differentiated, and meaningful	
Multicultural themes are evident in instructional activities and valued in all settings	
Opportunities are available for cooperative work with peers	

Positive messages are given to students and family members; workers receive positive feedback through badges, certificates, public announcements, etc.	
Emotional temperature is gauged through varied activities	
Practitioner demonstrates warmth and kindness	
Humor (not sarcasm) helps promote relaxation and reduces stress	
Notes:	

STUDENT CONTROL AND CHOICE	
Strategy	**Noted**
Activity centers are used in the classroom or workspace	
When appropriate, choice is offered in learning tasks	
Students are given the opportunity to demonstrate their understanding of content via multiple assessments	
Traditional, standardized assessment methods are supplemented with authentic assessments, engagement in the arts, and/or critical thinking	
Notes:	

REFLECTION AND MINDFULNESS	
Strategy	**Noted**
Breaks are offered for social/rest time/brain breaks and to encourage movement focusing on positive interactions	
Students are given opportunities for quiet reflection or mindfulness activities	
Notes:	

BRAIN-TARGET TWO: *CREATING THE PHYSICAL LEARNING ENVIRONMENT*

ATTENTION AND NOVELTY

Strategy	Noted
Rooms and workspaces are free of clutter and organized to benefit flow of traffic and time management	
Posters and work visuals reflect current content; displays reflect multicultural themes	
Displays featuring racially, ethically, and neurodiverse individuals from the present and from history are rotated regularly and demonstrate students' work	
Desks and seating arrangements are flexible (e.g., small clusters, large circle, theater style, etc.) and alternative seating options are available to regulate attention (e.g., wobble chairs, seating balls, etc.)	
Window coverings optimize natural light; alternative lighting provides for optimal visual environment (e.g., the use of lamps or other lighting options)	
Students and workers are encouraged to add items into the physical environment that represent their home, favorite art, or sense of identity	
Notes:	

SOUND/SCENT

Strategy	Noted
A relaxing atmosphere is created using background sounds when appropriate (e.g., relaxing music, wind chimes, or nature sounds)	
Time for quiet reflection is built into the lesson or work environment; noise-cancelling headphones are available when appropriate	
Classrooms and workspaces emit suitable scents such as orange, vanilla, and lavender to help establish a warm, inviting environment (be aware of allergies to some products)	
Notes:	

MOVEMENT

Strategy	Noted
Meaningful movement is encouraged and integrated into learning episodes as appropriate	
Various workstations (e.g., reading center, math center; art/creativity center) are set up throughout the classroom or workspace	
Yoga-like stretching, and/or creative movement breaks are taken	
Notes:	

BRAIN-TARGET THREE: *DESIGNING THE LEARNING EXPERIENCE—CREATING THE BIG PICTURE*	
Strategy	**Noted**
Visual representations such as graphic organizers are used to give the *big-picture* framework for an instructional unit or work plan	
Essential concepts, content, and skills are evident in the lesson or work plan and communicated in accessible ways	
Learning or work goals are identified and communicated through various mapping techniques (e.g., concept map, conceptual framework, strategic plan, etc.)	
Relationships among work activities and major learning or work goals are clearly identified	
Learning or work activities are purposeful and relate to learning goals or strategic plan	
Required evaluations (benchmarks, end-of unit test, mid-work feedback, etc.) are communicated in advance	
Encourage students to create their own concept maps to demonstrate understanding of learning or work goals or for visual note-taking	
Notes:	

BRAIN-TARGET FOUR: *TEACHING FOR MASTERY OF CONTENT, SKILLS, AND CONCEPTS*	
Strategy	**Noted**
Emotional connections are incorporated into learning episodes that reflect culturally relevant pedagogy and student agency	
Learning and work activities call upon prior knowledge	
Lessons begin by giving context through visual representations such as concept maps	
Repeated rehearsals of information using multiple modalities are incorporated into units or work plans (e.g., arts-based activities)	
Learning episodes are spaced to allow time between rehearsals to promote consolidation of information into long-term memory	
Learning tasks are varied in order to provide novelty and sustain attention	
Information is *chunked* into smaller cohesive segments	
Mnemonics are used to help students retain patterns, rules, or word lists	

(Continued)

(Continued)

Students are encouraged to summarize/paraphrase information that is presented through text or lecture	
Creativity is fostered through the use of visual arts, music, and movement	
Visual note-taking during learning or work tasks is encouraged through concept maps or visual images	
Appropriate technology informs the teaching and learning process	
Notes:	

BRAIN-TARGET FIVE: *TEACHING FOR THE EXTENSION AND APPLICATION OF KNOWLEDGE—CREATIVITY AND INNOVATION*	
Strategy	**Noted**
Students acquire knowledge and demonstrate mastery in traditional and nontraditional ways (see examples below)	
Learning is extended through activities that require application of information in new and creative ways that go beyond what was presented in text or by the instructor	
Open-ended divergent thinking questions are part of lessons, allowing for multiple and innovative responses	
Creative problem-solving includes real-world issues and fosters investigations, predictions, experiments, classifications, analysis, and synthesis	
Scaffold project-based learning activities allow for regular feedback through guided questions	
Notes:	
***The following are examples of activities associated with Brain-Target Five**	
Conducting investigations and surveys	
Engaging in problem-based learning by designing a task that requires thinking across disciplines	
Generating multiple solutions to a problem	
Designing experiments to test hypotheses in project-based learning models	
Analyzing perspectives of historical figures or literary characters	

Building projects that tap into multiple artistic domains (role-play, music, visual arts, dance, theater, improvisation, etc.)	
Connecting unusual elements of a question to produce an innovative answer	
Creating metaphors and analogies to explain a concept	
Discussing open-ended questions to probe for assumptions, clarifications, or consequences	
Restating a problem in multiple ways	
Diagramming a solution in visual representations	
Creating stories and narratives to explain concepts	
Collaborating in group learning activities within the classroom and within the broader learning environment	

BRAIN-TARGET SIX: *EVALUATING LEARNING*	
FEEDBACK	
Strategy	**Noted**
Students and workers receive immediate, frequent, and relevant feedback about their performance	
Feedback includes explanations of why responses are accurate or inaccurate	
Feedback is scaffolded (e.g., teacher provides hints so that students arrive at answers on their own)	
Students continue on tasks until they achieve success	
Models or examples of expected work or targeted performance are provided when appropriate	
Opportunities are provided for peer feedback	
Notes:	
ACTIVE-RETRIEVAL OF CONTENT	
Strategy	**Noted**
Retrieval of learned information is strongly encouraged through strategies such as self-quizzing, creating concept maps, flash cards, or other methods to retrieve information from memory	

(Continued)

(Continued)

All methods of visual representation or artistic activities such as sketching, hand/body movements, or role-playing is encouraged to assist with retention of information	
Content is studied, revisited, and assessed at appropriate intervals	
Notes:	
ASSESSMENT	
Strategy	**Noted**
Multiple types of assessments take into consideration students' learning goals, neurodiverse learners, and emerging bilingual learners	
Authentic performance assessments are a regular part of the evaluation process	
Rubrics or other type of scoring guides or performance expectations are given prior to completing activities	
Evaluation includes both oral and written responses	
Portfolios can be a regular part of the evaluation process in schools and the workplace	
Self-reflections and revisions are encouraged	
Notes:	

Appendix II

Sample Learning Unit—*Hatchet*

What Does a Brain-Targeted Teaching® Model Unit Look Like in the Classroom?

Learning Unit: Surviving Alone in the Wilderness: A study of the novel *Hatchet* by Gary Paulsen

Grade/Content: Fifth-Grade/Language Arts

Author: Clare O'Malley Grizzard

Overarching Goal of Unit: Students will increase language arts skills of reading for understanding through analysis of character, plot, main idea, and symbolic language.

Brain-Target One: Establishing the Emotional Climate for Learning

Reinforcing the positive emotional environment was a residual process throughout the teaching of this unit. Exploring *Hatchet,* an enticing action-packed adventure that also offers quiet, reflective moments, was rich in opportunities to do so. All activities and assessments throughout the learning unit were designed through the lens of the emotional climate.

To encourage a deeper connection through perspective taking, we retitled the unit "Surviving in the Wilderness"—in order to make the students *a part of the story* rather than just a passive audience. This journey was going to be *theirs* as well as Brian's (the main character in the book). Visualization and guided-imagery exercises furthered the connection with the novel. Tapping into children's natural ability to visualize vivid images and detailed action, the students followed the narrative of Brian's story more closely with their feelings leading the way. They began to recognize themselves in the book and identify with the action.

Our activities led students to ask, "What does the character think, believe, want, or feel? And how would I show it if it were me?" They made self-portraits of what they would look like if they found themselves in Brian's situation (stranded alone in the wilderness). This exercise required that they put themselves into the story rather than simply illustrate a scene from the book as an outside observer.

We used several drama exercises throughout the unit to study character, setting, and even vocabulary. We used tableau to describe a *frozen moment* in the story. To build empathy, we found role-playing allowed students to look at issues from another perspective—Brian's—and to build a deeper emotional bond with his fate.

In creating a nurturing emotional environment, Linda Bluth, my coteacher, and I constructed ongoing positive supports throughout the year, not just during this particular novel study. These activities ranged from greeting each student by name at the door to noncompetitive discussion and class critique using positive, supportive language.

Mrs. Bluth was a practitioner of yoga, and she used it daily to help students disengage from the outside into a new state of mind in the classroom and as a means to teach children to relax, encourage their creative imagination, and invoke their imagery skills. It also changed the rhythm of a typical school day routine, which often is rife with distraction. Criteria for excellence were clearly displayed and discussed to reduce anxiety. For artwork especially, we used exemplars to make expectations clear and to inspire so that all students could succeed.

Students make a personal connection with the main character by visualizing themselves stranded alone in the wilderness.

The Writing Process
South

Brain-Target Two: Creating the Physical Learning Environment

Brian's adventures in the Canadian wilderness and our journey through the novel gave us many opportunities to expand the boundaries of the typical classroom. Because the main setting of this novel is the natural environment, we pursued the question of how Brian used that to survive. Since the unit was taught both in the language arts room and the art studio, we were able to express the theme of the novel in both *environments*. We structured the students' encounter with the novel to be multisensory—engaging them through sight, sound, touch, and smell. Below are some of the activities that transformed our classroom during this unit:

- We brought the natural environment into the classroom and went outside for short field trips to encounter the school environment in broader terms. On walks around the campus, we focused on a new sensory awareness of our surroundings. We took field notes, drew maps, carried sketchbooks, and did observational drawings of plants and insects, which were displayed and used as points of references for other activities.
- We revamped bulletin boards and room displays to reflect the theme of our journey through the novel and displayed Canadian landscape paintings that became a focal point in dialogue and descriptive writing activities. Students decorated the room with observational drawings of natural specimens, personal visualizations of scenes from the novel and events from the plot, and their self-portraits.
- A guest artist created a mural of a wilderness scene that became the background for many activities, including theater strategy creating a sound poem.
- Students did field study drawings of what they encountered outside the building. They *observed* and *documented* their environment in a new way, which mirrored the main character's development as a more acute observer of his environment.
- Students collected items from our nature walks to create a naturalist station in the room. Plants (including edible ones) lined the windowsills throughout the year.

Brain-Target Three: Designing the Learning Experience

In approaching the design of the learning unit, we used graphic information displays from the beginning to the end of the planning process: teacher planning maps, discussion guides for students, and global unit concepts maps that were referred to by students as we proceeded through the lessons.

The first step was to identify the common core standards in standards in English and Language Arts that our unit would address (www.corestandards.org/the-standards/english-language-arts-standards/reading-literature/grade-5/). Those standards included the following:

- Determine a theme of a story, drama, or poem from details in the text, including how characters in a story or drama respond to challenges or how the speaker in a poem reflects upon a topic; summarize the text.
- Explain how a series of chapters, scenes, or stanzas fits together to provide the overall structure of a particular story, drama, or poem.
- Describe how a narrator's or speaker's point of view influences how events are described.

In order to create a map of the unit, we decided on the essential questions or big ideas derived from the standards that deconstructed the themes of the novel and guided our investigation into "Surviving Alone in the Wilderness." We identified three aspects of Brian's ability to survive were ingenuity, keen observation, and use of the materials at hand. We used these three aspects to organize the unit into three big ideas:

- Learning to use the environment
- Listening to one's inner voice
- Becoming a different kind of an observer

We mapped supporting activities and strategies, meeting our curriculum standards, according to the three different themes. We used relevant guiding questions to create a unit map with students:

- How would you use the environment?
- What would you be saying to yourself?
- How would this experience change the way you look at the world?

Study of *Hatchet* by Gary Paulsen
Surviving Alone in the Wilderness

Surviving Alone in the Wilderness

Learning to use the natural environment

Listening to one's inner voice

Becoming a different kind of observer

Nature walks Collection of natural objects

Journal entries, diary, essays, reflection statements

Field studies, observational drawings

Guidebook and box for survival unit materials

As they engaged in various activities of the unit, students used relevant graphic icons, which they designed, to identify which big idea they were pursuing and to track their progress on unit maps.

Brain-Target Four: Teaching for Mastery of Content, Skills, and Concepts

As we moved into Brain-Target Four and planning for instruction, we held onto the three essential questions or big ideas of our study: learning to use the natural environment, listening to your inner voice, and becoming a different kind of observer. Each aspect used multiple arts-based activities, including drawing, mural-making, role-play, and creative writing, which created a level of personal connection and added depth to our novel study.

Learning to Use the Natural Environment

It was important to relate to the physical setting of *Hatchet* to build the empathetic bond between reader and character. Investigating our school's campus environment led to a unique learning experience for the urban students of the fifth grade. With binoculars, sketchbooks, and collection buckets, they journeyed out, as if on an expedition, to discover the environment in a new way. We took nature walks with the mission of collecting natural objects to bring back to our classroom. We used them in creating nature centers and for drawing from observation. We used natural materials to create journal and handmade paper for sketchbook pages. Classroom discussions covered issues on environmentalism, conservation, and tales of survival. The related subjects made for very lively and engaged debate throughout the novel study.

One student shared how he enjoyed these activities: "I really liked going outside during class time. It made it easier for us to think about Brian and what he went through when his plane crashed. We could close our eyes, listen to the birds, feel the cool wind, and pretend we were there with him. When we opened our eyes, we saw the details of our environment in a new way."

Listening to Your Inner Voice

Drama provided many opportunities for evoking the lived-through experience. Using drama techniques seemed at first challenging for our teachers, but never for the students. Whether being prompted to put themselves in the shoes of young Brian the survivor, or to perform vocabulary in frozen tableau, or to act out the reaction of Brian's desperate parents at home, they reacted with enthusiasm and a natural ability to put themselves into new roles and explore their own responses. Beyond skills-based instruction, knowing just a few drama techniques was all we needed; role-play and tableau activities and variations on them gave students the chance to react to much more than just the immediate text at hand.

In addition to supporting traditional activities for reading and writing, our approach to writing took on a very personal voice when it was integrated with the arts. Assignments were approached as reflective statements, whether they were journal entries, diary posts, field notes, or letters to family. Students were introduced to the concept of an Artist's Statement. It reinforced classroom arts vocabulary and methodology and used students' writing to help them more effectively understand their own learning and the process of building of literacy skills. As my coteacher indicated, "The kind of writing that I want to encourage is that in which I hear the student's voice in their writing . . . their own voice."

Becoming a Different Kind of Observer

Developing keen focus and becoming aware of detail are the tools that Brian used to finally find his food source in the novel—a key learning experience. We translated that experience to the students by introducing observational drawing. This is not drawing from memory or from imagination. In this approach to drawing, students are taught to draw only what they observe. Students emerged from the task not only having read about someone who is a keen observer, but also having gained new vision themselves.

Compared with teaching this unit through traditional methods, students were more engaged, assessments demonstrated deeper understanding, and the sense of investigation and discovery made the classroom come alive.

Brain-Target Five: Teaching for the Extension and Application of Knowledge:

In Brain-Target Four, we saw a nontraditional journey through the novel *Hatchet.* The students' understanding of the story's plot, characters, and themes were enhanced through various art experiences. Students engaged in role-playing, explored drawing from observation, and used sensory, descriptive words from the story to create a tone poem. Other activities included investigating nature through walks during different times of the day to observe the changes of sounds and light in the environment.

Our next goal was to deepen students' engagement with the novel through Brain-Target Five activities that would encourage creative thinking and application of the learning unit themes. Students were charged with designing an original product structured on the three main story themes: *learning how to use the natural environment, listening to one's inner voice, and becoming a different kind of observer*. The product was to be a guidebook of survival tips. Students were told that they were to imagine they had survived a similar experience as the main character and were to leave behind a *how-to* guide for the next person who might be in the same circumstance—stranded in an unfamiliar space.

We led the students through guided visualization of being stranded in the wilderness. Students were then given the option of choosing the Canadian wilderness, which is the setting of the book, or creating their own space to display survival skills and develop a guidebook.

One student, for example, chose his inner city neighborhood as the subject of the survival guidebook. He explored the theme of *becoming a different kind of observer* by looking through the lens of a camera for the first time and creating a photo essay of his neighborhood. He used his *real-world* environment by interviewing neighbors to learn about what resources existed in the community and how those changed over time. He learned where the daycare centers were in the neighborhood; found a church-based youth group; and met the city employees such as sanitation workers, firefighters, and police who tended to the community. He created for his city block a *survival booklet* that included available services and contact information for those who could help in an emergency.

In the guidebook's reflective writing, he addressed the theme *listening to one's inner voice* by answering questions such as these: How can I feel safer at home? Who can I turn to in an emergency? What will make me feel stronger when I experience peer pressure from older boys in the neighborhood?

Teaching the novel in this way became an emotionally rich experience for the children. The active participation with the characters was much deeper for them than when it was taught through traditional methods such as choral reading, vocabulary development, and essay writing. They demonstrated heightened attention during all of the tasks throughout the learning unit. Moreover, the children's retention of the details of the novel was impressive. Their writing became alive with description and feeling in a way we had not seen before. Students clearly enjoyed the learning experience—they simply rediscovered the pure joy of reading.

Brain-Target Six: Evaluating Learning

As an arts specialist working with classroom teachers, evaluating learning in the BTT Model speaks to my way of teaching: promoting divergent thinking, open-ended problem-solving, and expression of a personal connection to the curriculum.

In collaborating with Linda Bluth in the design of the *Hatchet* unit, we used portfolios extensively to exhibit the students' efforts and progress. The portfolio contents were chosen by the students and the teacher and included reflective writing and self-assessment relative to the content students are learning. During the unit, students were able to review their portfolios, which provided them with continual feedback, enabled them to recognize growth, and allowed them to reset their own goals.

Although some traditional methods such as quizzes and tests were still part of our units, most of the evaluation of student learning was based on performance of real tasks, such as the creation of a guidebook/box, which documented performance as well as students' writing.

Performance assessments included rubrics, checklists, and observational charts to assess students' achievement in perceptual, language, and motor skills. We used rubrics that measured individual growth and customized them for learning differences among students. Students were given the rubric at the start of the task so they knew the goals and outcomes for learning.

We expanded the rubrics, checklists, and observational charts to demonstrate students' mastery of specific objectives using drama, which included collaborative work, understanding of vocabulary though drama, tableau, and role-playing.

Visual art assessments included the following:

- Reflective writings, including artist's statement
- Landscape criteria—background, middle ground, foreground
- Expressive portraits criteria
- Printing with natural materials checklist
- Handmade paper checklist
- Sketchbook checklist
- Natural materials survival kit checklist

Our goal was to encourage students to become more thoughtful judges of their own work and others' work through critical dialogues and critiques and artists' statements.

Prompts for Artist Statement:

- In this artwork, I became a different kind of observer by ______________________.
- I found it challenging when ______________________.
- I found it easier when I ______________________.
- I surprised myself when I ______________________.
- I think that this artwork helped me understand Brian better because ______________________.
- I can see that using materials from the environment has improved my art making because ______________________.
- Some of the details of my environment I see in a new way are ______________________.
- I was able to write about my feelings better because ______________________.
- My thoughts about art making were changed because ______________________.
- I like this artwork because ______________________.

ANALYTIC RUBRIC FOR GUIDEBOOK AND SURVIVAL BOX				
ANALYTIC RUBRIC FOR GUIDEBOOK/ SURVIVAL BOX	OBSERVATIONAL DRAWING	CONSTRUCTION OF THE SURVIVAL BOX	FIELD SKETCHES	JOURNAL CONSTRUCTION
3 Points	At least three drawings of natural objects with a strong realistic style, relative size agreement.	Completed box that is sized for books. Used natural-themed materials. Shows careful craftsmanship.	At least three sketches out of doors of natural objects or settings.	Journal construction shows excellent craftsmanship, using natural materials for cover, and four handmade papers for inside pages.
2 Points	At least two drawings of natural objects with some realism	Somewhat completed box that is sized for books. Used natural-themed materials. Shows somewhat careful craftsmanship.	At least two sketches of natural objects or settings.	Journal construction shows good craftsmanship, using some natural materials for cover. At least three handmade papers for inside pages.
1 Point	At least one drawing of natural objects with some realism.	Unfinished, sized poorly, not carefully done, little nature-themed materials.	One sketch done out of doors of natural objects or settings.	Journal construction shows poor to basic craftsmanship, using some natural materials for cover. At least one to two handmade papers for inside pages.

Appendix III

Sample Learning Unit—Genetics & Heredity

Learning Unit: Genetics and Heredity—Thinking Outside the Punnett Square

Grade/Content: Tenth-Grade/Biology

Author: Suzanne P. McNamara

Overarching Goal of Unit: Students will apply their understanding of genetics and heredity in discussions centered on current medical and social issues as well as an appreciation for human diversity.

Brain-Target One: Establishing the Emotional Climate for Learning

Biological Family Histories

Although often ignored, emotions play a vital role in the learning process. A *great lesson plan* can be completely useless if children do not feel comfortable in their classroom. For many of my students, safety is a central part of a positive emotional classroom environment. Every day, I see that before a child can learn, they need to be confident that my classroom culture is welcoming, engaging, and supportive. All students should feel a sense of belonging in their classroom. Most teachers would agree that it is impossible to separate a child's emotions from the learning process. A positive emotional climate sets the tone for high levels of learning and performance.

For a variety of reasons, I have seen many students becoming disenfranchised, feeling as if they are not connected to their school and perpetuating a cycle of failure. For some, life outside the classroom is so filled with hardship; stress; and, often, despair that it can be challenging to find purpose in their schooling. For others, school is not an exciting place that engages students, but rather a worn-out institution that fosters low expectations. Reconnecting these students to a meaningful and supportive school experience may require drastic measures to break this cycle of failure.

When creating a positive emotional classroom environment, I see how important it is to provide opportunities for *all* students to feel comfortable and confident. At the beginning of this unit, students were encouraged to bring in pictures of biological family members. (Students had the option to bring in pictures of their own biological family members, or nonbiological family members with whom they live.) At the beginning of each class period, a picture was projected. Students had to figure out the biological family member of the person in the picture. In order to offer a guess, a student had to identify three genetic similarities between the person in the picture and the suggested family member. When the class determined who supplied the picture, that student had an opportunity to share more information about their family with the rest of the class.

In high school, students are not often asked to share information about their families with their classmates. This ongoing activity provided an opportunity for all students to feel confident that they have background knowledge about genetics. It encouraged students to talk about and share information about genetics with family members and friends outside the classroom. Throughout the unit, students continued to bring in pictures and share them with their peers during the school day, which helped to strengthen positive friendships at school. It also helped to set the tone for mature conversations in a high school biology classroom. When learning about various genetic disorders later in the unit, for example, students were reminded of the personal information that classmates volunteered about their families.

Students developed a sense of tolerance and appreciation for diversity throughout the genetics unit. The family picture activity helped to establish a culture of respect and encouraged students to be confident in sharing their thoughts and ideas.

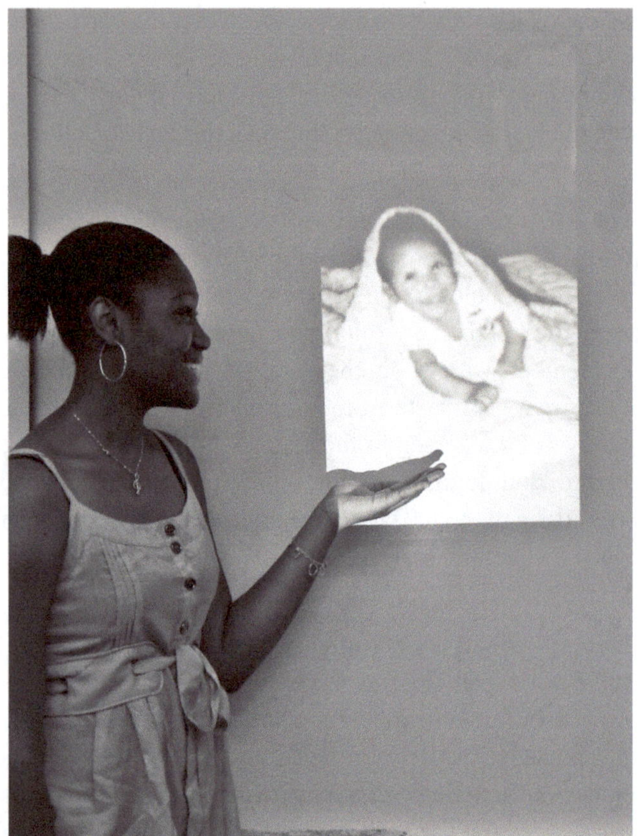

Brain-Target Two: Creating the Physical Learning Environment

Creating a Classroom Art Gallery

I used to think of decorating my classroom in the same way I thought about decorating my home. I would try to fill open walls with pictures, windowsills with plants, shelves with books, and bulletin boards with flyers. My classroom looked wonderful at the beginning of the year, but the environment remained static until I took everything down to pack up for the summer. Although it is helpful to keep consistency and order so that children know what to expect, it is also important to create a dynamic environment aligned with the curriculum. I was using the same posters, hung the same pictures, referenced the same signs, and showed the same images. Although my students knew what to expect each day, their environment did not impact their learning experience. I have come to recognize the importance of a visually appealing, novel classroom.

Teachers can take advantage of the brain's natural propensity to seek novelty by providing visually stimulating environments that support learning objectives. Capturing students' attention helps to keep them engaged and interested in what's next. There are not many other professions that allow (and encourage!) employees to occupy and decorate a fairly large space and call it their own. In some cases, however, there are strings attached to this privilege, including mandated word walls and posted standards. Furthermore, some teachers are not given their own room but are forced to travel. Although these obstacles present challenges, it is important to incorporate as many visually appealing learning aids as possible.

Keeping walls clear at the beginning of each new unit, I was able to create an atmosphere that marked a change in focus and invited student participation. Many of the work products from student groups would be hanging on the wall the very next day. Not only could students see their own work and that of their classmates, but they also could see the work from other class periods. Each time there was a change to the walls, students wanted time to walk around the classroom to see all of the work samples, almost as if they were viewing artwork in a gallery. As the unit progressed, student groups reflected on their work and wrote captions so that other students could learn more about each sample. This process helped me hold groups accountable for their work because they knew that other students would be learning from them. The captions helped often answer questions from observing students, similar to captions in a museum.

When learning about mitosis and meiosis, student groups were required to create models of a particular stage and answer questions about the stage. These models were collected at the end of the period, and by the next day, they were up in sequence in the classroom. Students were amazed to see how all the pieces fit together and were easily able to identify similarities and differences among the stages. The next day, students entered the classroom with some of the models removed and had to determine which ones were missing and sketch them.

Students gained ownership of their classroom and started bringing in relevant items to include. Newspaper articles, pictures of twins in a student's family, cartoons and sketches of a DNA molecule, and many more items were brought into class to be included among the work on the walls. I began to think of my classroom more like an art gallery and less like a living room. The walls displayed deliberate pieces of student work that reflected the learning objectives of a particular unit. I focused more on quality artifacts and less on filling blank walls with posters. When the students became a part of creating their physical classroom environment, they started to treat it like their own. Cleaning up after themselves and rehanging fallen student work became part of the classroom culture. The science classroom turned *art gallery* was a dynamic, visually appealing place of learning.

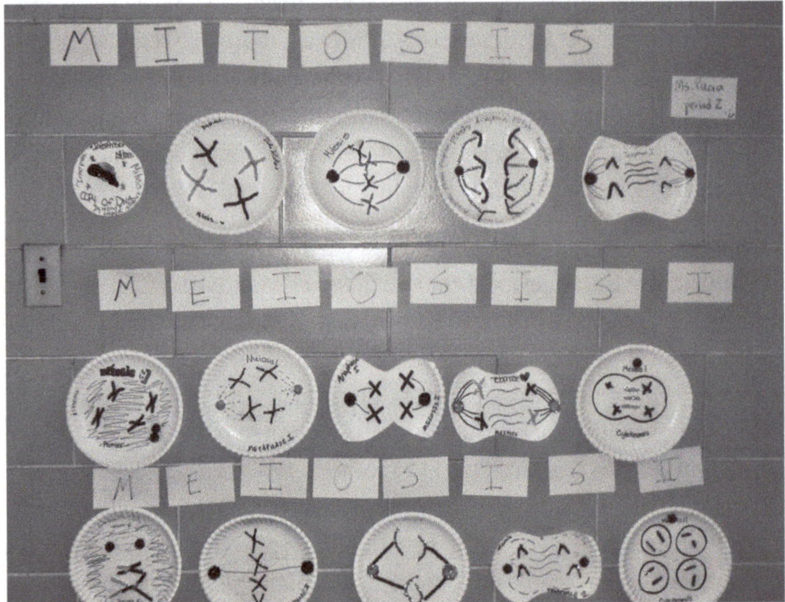

Brain-Target Three: Designing the Learning Experience

The Big Picture

Using the concepts from Brain-Target Three is extremely important for my students when they are presented with new information. I see everyday how students must be able to use prior knowledge as a filter to establish the meaning and relevance of new information.

I also have found that providing my students with *big-picture* ideas, including the corresponding supporting concepts, helps them to organize the new ideas that I am teaching and better enables them to process, integrate, apply, and retain the key elements of the unit. It is clear that when my students are taught skills and concepts taught in isolation, they are often meaningless or confusing to them. Concept maps are critical to visually displaying key concepts that students will learn throughout the unit and how these concepts relate to prior learning.

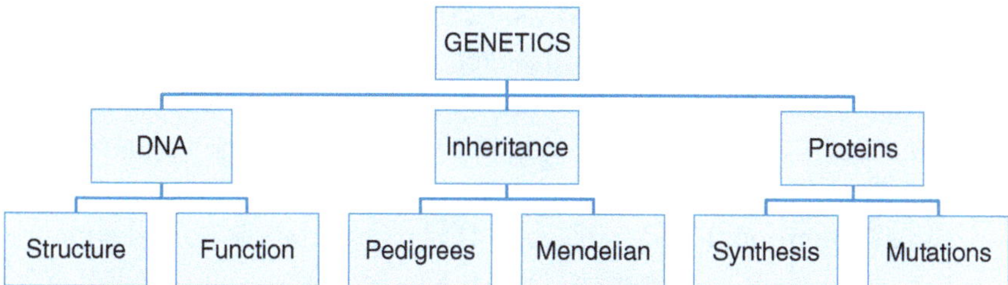

When first introducing this concept map, I encouraged students to start making connections with their prior knowledge. The students brainstormed any relevant words to add to the concept map in order to surface what they already knew about the various concepts. This activity helped to introduce the main concepts of the unit and provided a foundation upon which to build. This map was referenced constantly, and students were required to use it as a skeleton for adding new concepts. Manipulating this concept map to make it their own helped students to organize the new information learned throughout the unit.

Brain-Target Four: Teaching for Mastery of Content, Skills, and Concepts

As educators, it is our goal to help students acquire skills and knowledge that can be used meaningfully throughout their lives. Simply exposing students to new information in creative ways is not enough. Students need to be given the opportunity to allow their brains to process, store, and retrieve information. Teachers could be viewed as *brain developers*, and all classroom doors could hold signs: "Construction Zone: Brains in Progress." A well-planned and executed lesson does not necessarily translate to student learning.

Just because a child can memorize a chant "2 + 2 = 4," this does not mean that he or she actually understands the concept of addition. The material covered in a high school genetics class can be very conceptual, requiring students to visualize processes that they cannot actually see. Therefore, it can be difficult for some students to truly understand the information and not just memorize it. Teachers must use instructional practices that best target the brain's ability to acquire and store information.

A major concept in a high school genetics class for students to learn is the structure and function of deoxyribonucleic acid (DNA). Students were exposed to this information in a variety of ways so that they had time to reorganize, modify, and consolidate these new memories from the material covered during class. At the beginning of the genetics unit, students were asked to draw a sketch of a DNA molecule and describe its importance in the study of life. This short activity helped to determine and assess prior knowledge of the material. The students were first shown a BioFlix animation, created by a graphic-design artist, of a three-dimensional DNA molecule. This interpretation walked students through a visual representation of the molecule, specifically noting its structure, function, and location. After students were introduced to this molecule from the animation, they were given the opportunity to work in groups to make a model using candy. Binding together Twizzlers with toothpicks and marshmallows, the students identified the major molecules that make up DNA.

In the lab, students extracted DNA from strawberries. Although they could not see the individual molecules, they were able to distinguish a small sample of wound-up DNA. By following the various steps of this procedure, they were given a *hands-on,* inquiry-based approach to figuring out where the DNA is located in the cells. Outside of the classroom, students were given an assignment to create a cartoon about DNA's structure and function. Many students came up with clever ways to remember the various molecules that make up DNA and used other characters to help convey their message. Students were given the opportunity to read and view their classmates' cartoons in a *gallery walk* around the classroom, providing feedback on sticky notes.

As the exploration of the DNA molecule continued, students were placed into small groups and given the task of putting on a play about DNA replication, a major function of the molecule. Not only did this activity help foster creativity but it also helped to reinforce and consolidate this newly learned information. Finally, as an extension to this instruction, students watched a short video clip, read articles, and participated in a discussion about the Human Genome Project. By providing real-world references to this information, students could make connections between what they learn in their biology class and what they experience in the world around them.

Together, these instructional strategies fostered personal connections with the material, engaged students to keep their attention, assessed their prior knowledge, and provided a variety of ways for students to *rehearse* this new information. All of these influence how well students retain and store information.

Brain-Target Five: Teaching for the Extension and Application of Knowledge

Project Description: Students will prepare a medical history chart including proper diagnosis, a treatment plan, and prognosis of various human genetic disorders. They will use information that they have gathered from their research to diagnosis their *patient* and present their medical opinion to their classmates.

Genetics is one of my favorite units to explore with high school students. Engaged in the content, students often ask many questions concerning their genetic makeup. They want to know, for example, why they look more like one parent, why broad shoulders *run in the family*, or why their biological sister has green eyes when the rest of their family has shades of brown. These relevant and higher order thinking questions are often suppressed, however, by vocabulary-dense lessons about pea plants, monohybrid crosses, and Punnett squares. Students quickly realize that their genetic family tree is far too complex to discuss in class, and the majority of their time will be spent studying monogenetic traits like peapod shape and color.

When teaching for 21st century skills, students need to be given opportunities to think critically and apply these fundamental concepts of genetics to the world around them. Throughout this unit, students were challenged to hypothesize the answers to their complex questions by generating ideas concerning the role that DNA plays in their uniqueness. Challenged by applying genetic concepts to their own lives, students were required to make sense of this content. Working in teams, students were asked to assume the role of doctors assigned to a genetic disorder patient case. In order to solve the case, students needed to work together to properly diagnosis their assigned patient with an appropriate genetic disorder and provide an adequate treatment plan including an accurate prognosis. Students were provided with the basic medical history of their patient and were given resources rich in research about human genetic disorders.

At first, putting together the pieces of the puzzle was challenging for students. They would have felt much more comfortable if assigned a certain genetic disorder to research and present. Not only did this activity challenge them to solve a problem but it also required them to work together and think critically about the impact that DNA can play on gene expression. In teams, students collaborated to share their research and ideas with each other in order to solve the medical case of their patient.

I launched this activity with a video segment from the NOVA program titled "Cracking the Code of Life." Students watched parents Allison and Tim Lord interact with their oldest son, Hayden, who was diagnosed with the genetic disorder Tay-Sachs, an incurable degenerative brain disease. My students were shocked to learn that this one-letter mutation in Hayden's genome could result in creating a protein that is unable to dissolve fat in his brain. The video unfolds relevant genetic information that parallels other recessive traits discussed previously in class, which made the content more meaningful and allowed students to develop a personal connection with the content through Hayden. They could see, firsthand, the impact that a genetic mutation could have on a person. Students were then instructed to use Hayden's medical case as a model for their own patient.

Their task was to use the provided basic medical history of their patient to make an accurate diagnosis, develop a treatment plan, determine a prognosis, and present their medical opinion to their peers. Wearing white lab coats, teams prepared a presentation highlighting relevant information about their patient and the diagnosed genetic disorder. This project gave students an opportunity to engage in activities that promoted creativity, innovation, critical thinking, and problem-solving. In addition, students gained a deeper appreciation of human diversity and continued to ask challenging genetics questions.

This problem-based activity encouraged students to use their knowledge and skills learned from this unit and apply them in a real-world creative thinking exercise. After all, this is what medical professionals do every day!

Brain-Target Six: Authentic Assessment of Learning

In order to truly help students in the learning process, they must be given immediate, frequent, and relevant feedback about their performance. This type of constant evaluation supports the brain's natural learning systems. Too often, however, feedback is limited to the grades received on tests and quizzes, and maybe an occasional project or paper. Although more manageable for teachers, this traditional approach to assessment does little to inform instruction or enhance learning. Traditional forms of assessment provide students with information about how well they could answer questions about this new material but do not provide them detailed information about the progress of their learning. For many forms of traditional assessment, a 70% does not necessarily mean that the student really understands 70% of the information covered on the assessment. Furthermore, these numbers provide little guidance for students in understanding what they know and don't know.

In this unit, students were given several nontraditional assessments. Toward the middle of the unit, after learning about pedigrees, they were assigned a family pedigree project, which would continue throughout the remainder of the unit. Students were asked to pick a genetic trait that runs in their own biological family or in a famous biological family (i.e., Jacksons, Obamas, the British Royal Family, etc.). Then they were to construct a pedigree for this genetic trait, including at least three generations of family members, using accurate symbols and notations.

The students were to bring in a draft of this assignment so that their peers and the instructor could review it and provide helpful feedback. The final draft of the assignment was turned in one week later and was graded and returned so that students could use the feedback to continue with the second part of the assignment. The next part required students to use the information they learned about Mendelian inheritance to show the cross between two mating individuals of their family and report the possible outcomes; they did this for three sets of mating individuals. In addition to the feedback that they received about this portion of the project, each student was given a hypothetical statement about his or her family, "What would happen if . . . ?" This final portion of the project allowed the instructor to further differentiate the project to address the needs of each student and encouraged all students to think critically about the information covered in the assignment.

Another authentic assessment used in this unit was a lab practical in which students were required to work in their groups, applying the information they learned about inheritance, to figure out the lab scenario. Each lab group received information about a crime scene, where samples of human urine were found as evidence. Students had to work together to determine which individuals had the black urine disease, alkaptonuria, to solve the case. Using Punnett squares and lab testing techniques, the students were required to apply the information they learned throughout the unit. This assessment gave them the opportunity to think critically about genetics and solve complex problems.

Appendix IV

Concept Maps for the Sample Units *Hatchet* and Genetics and Heredity

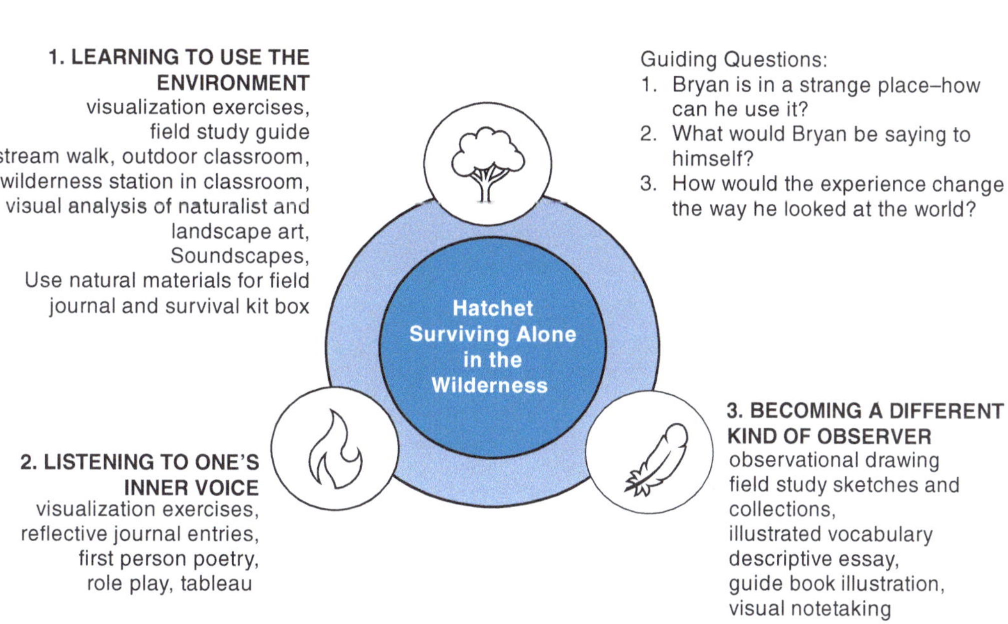

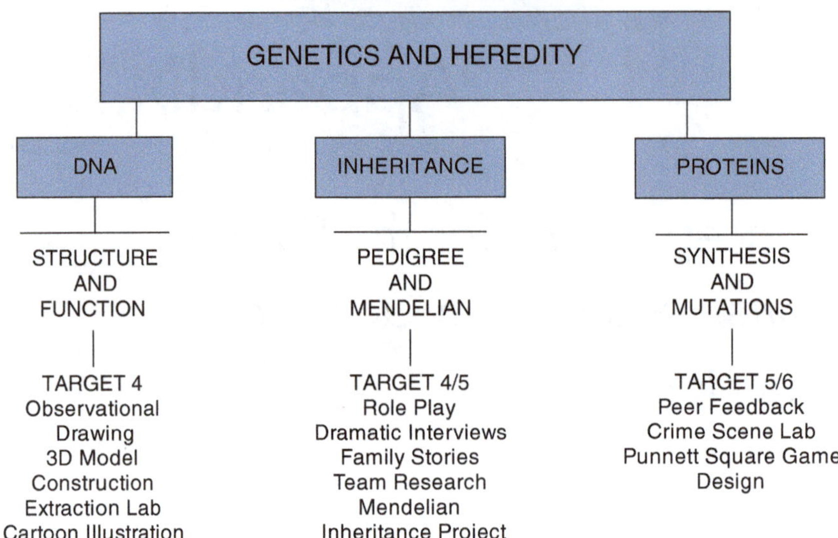
OUTSIDE THE PUNNETT SQUARE
10TH GRADE BIOLOGY
GENETICS AND HEREDITY
DNA
INHERITANCE
PROTEINS
STRUCTURE AND FUNCTION
PEDIGREE AND MENDELIAN
SYNTHESIS AND MUTATIONS
TARGET 4
Observational Drawing
3D Model Construction
Extraction Lab
Cartoon Illustration
Gallery Walk
TARGET 4/5
Role Play
Dramatic Interviews
Family Stories
Team Research
Mendelian Inheritance Project
TARGET 5/6
Peer Feedback
Crime Scene Lab
Punnett Square Game Design

References

Abdulla, A. M., & Cramond, B. (2017). After six decades of systematic study of creativity: What do teachers need to know about what it is and how it is measured? *Roper Review*, *39*(1), 9–23. https://doi.10.1080/02783193.2016.1247398

Akpan, J., Notar, C. E., & Beard, L. (2021). The impact of mnemonics as instructional tool. *Journal of Education and Human Development*, *10*(3), 20–28. https://doi.org/10.15640/jehd.v10n3a3

Alexander, R., Aragón, O. R., Bookwala, J., Cherbuin, N., Gatt, J. M., Kahrilas, I. J., Kästner, N., Lawrence, L., Lowe, L., Morrison, R. G., Mueller, S. C., Nusslock, R., Papadelis, C., Polnaszek, K. L., Richter, H., Silton, R. L., & Styliadis, C. (2021). The neuroscience of positive emotions and affect: Implications for cultivating happiness and wellbeing. *Neuroscience & Biobehavioral Reviews*, *121*, 220–249. htpps://doi.org/10/1016/j.neubiorev.2020.12.002

Alonso, M., Petit, A. C., & Lledo, P. M. (2024). The impact of adult neurogenesis on affective functions: of mice and men. *Molecular Psychology*, *29*, 2527–2542. https://doi.org/10.1038/s41380-024-02504-w

Amabile, T. M. (1996). *Creativity in context: Update to the social psychology of creativity*. Westview Press.

Amabile, T. M. (2012). Componential theory of creativity. *Encyclopedia of Management Theory*. SAGE.

Amsterlaw, J., Lagattuta, K. H., & Meltzoff, A. N. (2009). Young children's reasoning about the effects of emotional and physiological states on academic performance. *Child Development*, *80*(1), 115–133. https://doi.org/10.1111/j.1467-8624.2008.01249.x

Anastasiou, D., Wirngo, C. N., & Bagos, P. (2024). The effectiveness of concept maps on students' achievement in science: A meta-analysis. *Educational Psychology Review*, *36*(2), 39. https://doi.org/10.1007/s10648-024-09877-y

Araya Crisóstomo, S. P. (2022). Educational model based on empirical evidence from neuroscience and its implications for teaching practice [Modelo educativo basado en evidencia empírica de la neurociencia y sus implicancias en la práctica docente]. Revista de Pedagogía de la Universidad de Salamanca. https://revistas.usal.es/tres/index.php/0214-3402/index

Armstrong, P. (2010). Bloom's Taxonomy. *Vanderbilt University Center for Teaching*. https://cft.vanderbilt.edu/guides-sub-pages/blooms-taxonomy/

Ashkanasy, N. M., & Dirrusm, A. D. (2017). Emotions in the workplace. *Annual Review of Organizational Psychology and Organizational Behavior*, *4*, 67–90. https://doi.org/10.1146/annurev-orgpsych-032516-113231

Auble, P., & Franks, J. (1978). The effects of effort toward comprehension on recall. *Memory & Cognition*, *6*(1), 20–25. https://doi.org/10.3758/Bf03197424

Ausubel, D. P. (1960). The use of advance organizers in the learning and retention of meaningful verbal material. *Journal of Educational Psychology*, *51*(5), 267–272. https://doi.org/10.1037/h0046669

Baddeley, A. (2020). Working memory. In *Memory* (pp. 71–111). Routledge.

Baddeley, A., & Hitch, G. (1974). Working memory. In *The psychology of learning and motivation* (pp. 47–89). Academic Press. https://doi.org/10.1016/S0079-7421(08)60452-1

Ballarini, F., Martínez, M. C., Perez, M. D., Moncada, D., & Viola, H. (2013). Memory in elementary school children is improved by an unrelated novel experience. *PLOS One, 8*(6), e66875. https://doi.org/10.1371/journal.pone.0066875

Bartlett, F. C. (1932). *Remembering: A study in experimental and social psychology.* Cambridge University Press.

Bartoli, E., Devara, E., Dang, H. Q., Rabinovich, R., Mathura, R. K., Anand, A., Pascuzzi, B. R., Adkinson, J., Kenett, Y. N., Bijanki, K. R., Sheth, S. A., Shofty, B. (2024). Default mode network electrophysiological dynamics and causal role in creative thinking. *Brain, 147*(10), 3409–3425. https://doi.org/10.1093/brain/awae199

Baumann, V., Birnbaum, T., Breitling-Ziegler, C., Tegelbeckers, J., Dambacher, J., Edelmann, E., Bergado-Acosta, J. R., Flechtner, H. H., & Krauel, K. (2020). Exploration of a novel virtual environment improves memory consolidation in ADHD. *Scientific Reports, 10*(1), 21453. https://doi.org/10.1038/s41598-020-78222-4

Beaty, R. E., Cortes, R. A., Merseal, H. M., Hardiman, M. M., & Green, A. E. (2023). Brain networks supporting scientific creative thinking. *Psychology of Aesthetics, Creativity, and the Arts.* Advance online publication. https://dx.doi.org/10.1037/aca0000603

Beghetto, R. A. (2006). Creative justice? The relationship between prospective teachers' prior schooling experiences and perceived importance of promoting student creativity. *Journal of Creative Behavior, 40*(3), 149–162. https://doi.org/10.1002/j.2162-6057.2006.tb01270.x

Bethell, C. D., Newacheck, P., Hawes, E., & Halfon, N. (2014). Adverse Childhood Experiences: Assessing the impact on health and school engagement and the mitigating role of resilience. *Health Affairs, 33*(12), 2106–2115. https://doi.org/10.1377/hlthaff.2014.0914

Bi, H., Mi, S., Lu, S., & Hu, X. (2020). Meta-analysis of interventions and their effectiveness in students' scientific creativity. *Thinking Skills and Creativity, 38,* Article 100750. https://doi.org/10.1016/j.tsc.2020.100750

Binkley, C. (2023, October 9). *Schools' pandemic spending boosted tech companies. Did it help us students?* AP News. https://apnews.com/article/edtech-school-software-app-spending-pandemic-e2c803a30c5b6d34620956c228de7987

Blodgett, C., & Lanigan, J. D. (2018). The association between adverse childhood experience (ACE) and school success in elementary school children. *School Psychology Quarterly, 33*(1), 137–146. https://doi.org/10.1037/spq0000256

Bloom, B. S., & Krathwohl, D. R. (Eds.). (1956). *Taxonomy of educational objectives: The classification of educational goals. Handbook I: Cognitive domain.* Longman.

Bookheimer, S. (2002). Functional MRI of language: New approaches to understanding the cortical organization of semantic processing. *Annual Review of Neuroscience, 25*(1), 151.

Boucher, J., Mayes, A., & Bigham S. (2012). Memory in autistic spectrum disorder. *Psychology Bulletin. 138*(3), 458–496. https://doi.org/10.1037/a0026869

Bowen, D. H., & Kisida, B. (2019). Investigating causal effects of arts education experiences: Experimental evidence from Houston's Arts Access Initiative. *Research Report 7*(4).

Bransford, J. B. (2000). *How people learn: Brain, mind, experience and school.* National Academy Press.

Bronson, P., & Merryman, A. (2010, July 19). The creativity crisis. *Newsweek,* 44–50.

Brookhart, S. M. (2010). *How to assess higher-order thinking skills in your classroom.* Association for Supervision and Curriculum Development.

Brookings Institution. (2022). The pandemic has had devastating impacts on learning. What will it take to help students catch up? Brookings.edu

Brown, P. C., Roediger III, H. L., & McDaniel, M. A. (2014). Make it stick. The science of successful learning. *The Journal of Educational Research*, *108*(4), 346. https://doi.org/10.1080/00220671.2015.1053373

Brunmair, M., & Richter, T. (2019). Similarity matters: A meta-analysis of interleaved learning and its moderators. *Psychological Bulletin*, *145*(11), 1029. https://psycnet.apa.org/doi/10.1037/bul0000209

Brynjolfsson, E., Horton, J. J., Ozimek, A., Rock, D., Sharma, G., & TuYe, H. Y. (2020). COVID-19 and remote work: An early look at US data. *National Bureau of Economic Research*. https://doi.org/10.3386/w27344

Burklund, L. J., Davies, C. D., Niles, A., Torre, J. B., Brown, L., Vinograd, M., Lieberman, M.D., & Craske, M. G. (2024). Affect labeling: a promising new neuroscience-based approach to treating combat-related PTSD in veterans. *Frontiers in Psychology*, *7*(15), 1270424. https://doi.org/10.3389/fpsyg.2024.127042

Butavand, D. R., Hirsch, I., Tomaiuolo, M., Moncada, D., Viola, H., & Ballarini, F. (2020). Novelty improves the formation and persistence of memory in a naturalistic school scenario. *Frontiers in Psychology*, *11*, 48. https://doi.org/10.3389/fpsyg.2020.00048

Byers, T., Mahat, M., Liu, K., Knock, A., & Imms, W. (2018). A systematic review of the effects of learning environments on student learning outcomes. *Innovative Learning Environments & Teacher Change*. https://minervaaccess.unimelb.edu.au/bitstream/handle/11343/216293/iletc_Technical%20Report%204_2018.pdf?sequence=2&isAllowed=y

Byrne, C. L., Shipman, A. S., & Mumford, M. D. (2010). The effects of forecasting on creative problem-solving: An experimental study. *Creativity Research Journal*, *22*(2), 119–138. https://doi.org/10.1080/10400419.2010.481482

Byrne, J. H. (2017). *Learning and memory: A comprehensive reference*. Academic Press.

Byrnes, J. P. (2008). *Cognitive development and learning in instructional contexts*. Pearson.

Cahill, L., & McGaugh, J. L. (1995). A novel demonstration of enhanced memory associated with emotional arousal. *Consciousness and Cognition*, *4*(4), 410–421. https://doi.org/10.1006/ccog.1995.1048

Cai, Y. (2020). Application of the Brain-Targeted Teaching Model in college English teaching. International Conference on Educational Innovation and Teaching Methodology. Nanchang Institute of Technology. http://proceedings-online.com/

Campbell, D. (1997). *The Mozart effect: Tapping the power of music to heal the body, strengthen the mind, and unlock the creative spirit*. Avon books.

Carey, J. M., & Rossler, K. (2020). The how when why of high-fidelity simulation. *StatPearls Publishing*. https://www.ncbi.nlm.nih.gov/books/NBK559313/

Carnevale, J. B., & Hatak, I. (2020). Employee adjustment and well-being in the era of COVID-19: Implications for human resource management. *Journal of Business Research*, *116*, 183–187. https://doi.org/10.1016/j.jbusres.2020.05.037

Carpenter, S. K., Pan, S. C., & Butler, A. C. (2022). The science of effective learning with spacing and retrieval practice. *Nature Reviews Psychology*, *1*(9), 496–511. https://doi.org/10.1038/s44159-022-00089-1

Cast, K. (2011). *Universal design for learning guidelines version 2.0*. Author.

Castellanos, F. X., Lee, P. P., Sharp, W., Jeffries, N. O., Greenstein, D. K., Clasen, L. S., Blumenthal, J. D., James, R. S., Ebens, C. L., Walter, J. M., Zijdenbos, A., Evans, A. C., Giedd, J. N., & Rapoport, J. L. (2002). Developmental trajectories of brain volume abnormalities in children and adolescents with Attention-Deficit/Hyperactivity Disorder. *JAMA: The Journal of the American Medical Association*, *288*(14), 1740–1748. http://dx.doi.org/10.1001/jama.288.14.1740

Catterall, J. S. (2009). *Doing well and doing good by doing art*. Imagination Group.

Cepeda, N. J., Pashler, H., Vul, E., Wixted, J. T., & Rohrer, D. (2006). Distributed practice in verbal recall tasks: A review and quantitative synthesis. *Psychological*

Bulletin, 132(3), 354–380. https://doi.org/10.1037/0033-2909.132.354

Cepeda, N. J., Vul, E., Rohrer, D., Wixted, J. T., & Pashler, H. (2008). Spacing effects in learning: A temporal ridgeline of optimal retention. *Psychological Science, 19*(11), 1095–1102. https://doi.org/10.1111/j.1467-9280.2008.02209.x

Chase, W., & Ericsson, K. (1981). Skilled memory. In J. R. Anderson (Ed.), *Cognitive skills and their acquisition* (pp. 277–293). Lawrence Erlbaum.

Chen, O., & Kalyuga, S. (2020). Cognitive load theory, spacing effect, and working memory resources depletion: Implications for instructional design. In *Form, function, and style in instructional design: Emerging research and opportunities* (pp. 1–26). https://doi.org/10.4018/978-1-5225-9833-6.ch001

Cheng, X., Xie, H., Hong, J., Bao, G., & Liu, Z. (2022). Teacher's emotional display affects students' perceptions of teacher's competence, feelings, and productivity in online small-group discussions. *Frontiers in Psychology, 12*, 795708. https://doi.org.10.3389/fpsyg.2021.795708

Choi, N., Yamanaka, T., Takemura, A., Tomohiro, K., Eto, A., & Hirano, M. (2022). Impact of indoor aroma on students' mood and learning performance. *Building and Environment, 223*, 109490. https://doi.org/10.1016/j.buildenv.2022.109490

Chowdhury, B. R. (2020). Implementing brain-targeted teaching model to enhance English language teaching and learning process. *The English Teacher, 49*(3). http://meltajournals.com/

Chua, R. Y. J., Morris, M. W., & Mor, S. (2012). Collaborating across cultures: Cultural metacognition and affect-based trust in creative collaboration. *Organizational Behavior and Human Decision Processes, 118*(2), 116–131. https://doi.org/10.1016/j.obhdp.2012.03.00

Chudler, E. *Myths about the brain: 10% and counting*. http://brainconnection.positscience.com/topics/?main=fa/brain-myth

Cowan, N. (2001). The magical number 4 in short-term memory: A reconsideration of mental storage capacity. *Behavioral and Brain Sciences, 24*(01), 87. https://doi.org/10.1017/S0140525X01003922

Crawford, V. M., & Brophy, S. (2006). *Adaptive expertise: Theory, methods, findings, and emerging issues*. http://ctl.sri.com/publications/downloads/AESymposiumReportOct06.pdf

Csikszentmihalyi, M. (1996). *Creativity: Flow and the psychology of discovery and invention*. HarperCollins.

Dahl, R. E. (2004). Adolescent brain development: A period of vulnerabilities and opportunities. keynote address. *Annals of the New York Academy of Sciences, 1021*(1), 1–22. https://doi.org/10.1196/annals.1308.001

Danielson, C. (1996). *Enhancing professional practice: A framework of teaching*. Association for Supervision and Curriculum Development.

Darling-Hammond, L., Flook, L., Cook-Harvey, C., Barron, B., & Osher, D. (2020). Implications for educational practice of the science of learning and development. *Applied Developmental Science, (24)*2, 97–140. https://doi.org/10.1080/10888691.2018.1537791

Dekker. S., Lee., N. C., Howard-Jones, P., & Jolles. J. (2012). Neuromyths in education: Prevalence and predictors of misconceptions among teachers. *Frontiers in Psychology, 3*, 33784. https://doi.org/10.3389/fpsyg.2012.00429

Delage, M. (2021). *Mailis Delage posted on linkedIn*. Linkedin. https://www.linkedin.com/posts/mailis-delage-51756a222_vr-vr-p%C3%A9dagogie-activity-6880573947310616577-4QeK

Delpit, L. (1988). The silenced dialog: Power and pedagogy in educating other people's children. *Harvard Educational Review, 58*, 280–298.

Denoth-Lippuner, A., & Jessberger, S. (2021). Formation and integration of new neurons in the adult hippocampus. *Nature Reviews Neuroscience, 22*, 223–236. https://doi.org/10.1038/s41583-021-00433-z

Diamond, A., & Ling, D. S. (2016). Conclusions about interventions, programs, and approaches for improving executive functions that appear justified and those that, despite much hype, do not. *Developmental Cognitive Neuroscience, 18*, 34–48. https://doi.org/10.1016/j.dcn.2015.11.005

Diekelmann, S., & Born, J. (2010). The memory function of sleep. *Nature Reviews Neuroscience, 11*, 114–126. https://doi.org/10.1038/nrn2762

Diemand-Yauman, C., Oppenheimer, D. M., & Vaughan, E. B. (2011). Fortune favors the bold (and the italicized): Effects of disfluency on educational outcomes. *Cognition, 118*(1), 111–115. https://doi.org/10.1016/j.cognition.2010.09.012

Diener, E., Thapa, S., & Tay, L. (2020). Positive emotions at work. *Annual Review of Organizational Psychology and Organizational Behavior, 7*, 451–477. https://doi.org/10.1146/ annurev-orgpsych-012119-044908

Dole, S., Bloom, L., & Kowalske, K. (2016). Transforming pedagogy: Changing perspectives from teacher-centered to learner-centered. *Interdisciplinary Journal of Problem-Based Learning, 10*(1). https://doi.org/10.7771/1541-5015.1538

Donahue, D. M., & Marshall, J. (2014). *Art-centered learning across the curriculum: Integrating contemporary art in the secondary school classroom illustrated edition*. Columbia University, Teachers College.

Dow, G. T., & Kozlowski, K. (2020), The creative brain. *Educational Leadership, 77*(8), 44–49. https://www.ascd.org/el/articles/the-creative-brain

Duckworth, A. (2016). *Grit: The power of passion and perseverance*. Simon & Schuster.

Dunning, D. L., Griffiths, K., Kuyken, W., Crane, C., Foulkes, l., Parjer, J., & Dalgleish, T. (2019). The effects of mindfulness-based interventions on cognition and mental health in children and adolescents – a meta-analysis of randomized controlled trials. *Journal of Child Psychology and Psychiatry, 60*(3), 244–258. https://doi.org/ 10.1111/jcpp.12980

Dweck, C. S., & Yeager, D. S. (2019). Mindsets: A view from two eras. *Perspectives on Psychological Science, 14*(3), 481–496. https://doi.org/10.1177/1745691618804166

Dyment, J. E., & O'Connell T. S. (2010). The quality of reflection in student journals: A review of limiting and enabling factors. *Innovations in Higher Education, 35*, 233–244. https://doi.org/10.1080/13562517.2010.507308

Elsayed, N. M., Vogel, A. C., Luby, J. L., & Barch, D. M. (2021). Labeling emotional stimuli in early childhood predicts neural and behavioral indicators of emotion regulation in late adolescence. *Biological Psychiatry: Cognitive Neuroscience and Neuroimaging, 6*(1), 89–98. https://doi.org/10.1016/j.bpsc.2020.08.018

Erdoğdu, F., & Çakıroğlu, Ü. (2021). The educational power of humor on student engagement in online learning environments. *Research and Practice in Technology Enhanced Learning, 16*(1), 9. https://doi.org/10.1186/s41039-021-00158-8

Erduran Tekin, Ö. (2024). Coping through humor predicts life satisfaction of teachers working in special education institutions: A quantitative and qualitative study. *Current Psychology, 43*, 16210–16227. https://doi.org/10.1007/s12144-023-05555-4

Esping, A. (2017). Are creativity and intelligence related? In J. A. Plucker (Ed.), *Creativity & innovation theory, research and practice* (pp. 223–234). Prufrock Press Inc.

Farah, M. J., Betancourt, L., Shera, D. M., Savage, J. H., Giannetta, J. M., Brodsky, N. L., ... Hurt, H. (2008). Environmental stimulation, parental nurturance and cognitive development in humans. *Developmental Science, 11*(5), 793–801.

Fazio, L. K., Huelser, B. J., Johnson, A., & Marsh, E. J. (2010). Receiving right/wrong feedback: Consequences of learning. *Memory, 18*(3), 335–350. https://doi.org/10.1080/09658211003652491

Fernandes, M. A., Wammes, J. D., & Meade, M. E. (2018). The surprisingly powerful influence of drawing on memory. *Current Directions in Psychological Science, 27*(5), 302308. https://doi.org/10.1177/0963721418755385

Ferrer López, J. R. (2016). *Adaptation of BTT for design and administration of online continuing education courses* [Adaptación del Modelo de Enseñanza Orientado al Cerebro de la Dra. Mariale Hardiman, para el diseño y administración de cursos en línea de educación continua]. https://drjoseferrer.blogspot.com/

Finn, B., & Metcalfe, J. (2010). Scaffolding feedback to maximize long-term error correction. *Memory & Cognition, 38*(7), 951–961. https://doi.org/10.3758/MC.38.7.951

Firth, J., Rivers, I., & Boyle, J. (2021). A systematic review of interleaving as a concept learning strategy. *Review of Education, 9*(2), 642–684. https://doi.org/10.1002/rev3.3266

Forbes. (2024). *America's most innovative leaders.* https://www.forbes.com/lists/innovative-leaders/#57b9805d26aa.

Fu, M., & Zuo, Y. (2011). Experience-dependent structural plasticity in the cortex. *Trends in Neurosciences, 34*(4), 177–187. https://doi.org/10.1016/j.tins.2011.02.001

Garbe, A., Ogurlu, U., Logan, N., & Cook, P. (2020). COVID-19 and remote learning: Experiences of parents with children during the pandemic. *American Journal of Qualitative Research, 4*(3), 45–65. https://doi.org/10.29333/ajqr/8471

Gardner, H. (1983). *Frames of mind: The theory of multiple intelligences.* BasicBooks.

Gardner, H. (1993). *Multiple intelligences: The theory in practice.* BasicBooks.

Gay, G. (2018). *Culturally responsive teaching: Theory, research, and practice.* Teachers College Press.

Gazzaniga, M. (2008). *Learning, arts, and the brain: The Dana consortium report on arts and cognition.* Dana Press.

Gazzaniga, M. S., Ivry, R. B., & Mangun, G. R. (2009). *Cognitive neuroscience: The biology of the mind* (3rd ed.). Norton.

Giedd, J. (2010). The teen brain: Primed to learn, primed to take risks. In *Cerebrum* (pp. 62–70). Dana Press.

Giedd, J. N. (2009). Linking adolescent sleep, brain maturation, and behavior. *Journal of Adolescent Health, 45*(4), 319–320. https://doi.org/10.1016/j.adohealth.2009.07.007

Gilchrist, J., Gohari, M. R., Benson, L., Patte, K. A., & Leatherdale, S. T. (2022). Reciprocal relationships between positive emotions and resilience predict flourishing among adolescents. *OSF Preprint.* https://doi.org/10.31234/osf.io/dwbhpa

Gobet, F. (2022). Memory for the meaningless: How chunks help. In *Proceedings of the Twentieth Annual Conference of the Cognitive Science Society* (pp. 398–403). Routledge.

Goodrich, J. M., Hebert, M., & Namkung, J. M. (2022). Impacts of the COVID-19 pandemic on elementary school teachers' practices and perceptions across the spring and fall 2020 semesters. *Frontiers in Education, 6*, 793285. https://doi.org/10.3389/feduc.2021.793285

Goswami, U. (2006). Neuroscience and education: From research to practice? *Nature Reviews Neuroscience, 7*(5), 406–413.

Graesser, A. C. (2020). Emotions are the experiential glue of learning environments in the 21st century. *Learning and Instruction, 70*, 101212.https.doi.org/10.1026/j.learninstruc.2019.05.009

Green, A. E., Beaty, R. E., Kenett, Y. N., & Kaufman, J. C. (2023). The process definition of creativity. *Creativity Research Journal, 36*(3), 544–572. https://doi.org/10.1080/10400419.2023.2254573

Gregory, E., Hardiman, M., Yarmolinskaya, J., Rinne, L., & Limb, C. (2013). Building creative thinking in the classroom: From research to practice. *International Journal of Educational Research, 62*, 43–50. https://doi.org/10.1016/j.ijer.2013.06.003

Grimshaw, G. M., Adelstein, A., Bryden, M. P., & MacKinnon, G. E. (1998). First-language acquisition in adolescence: Evidence for a critical period for verbal language development, *Brain and Language, 63*(2), 237–255. https//doi.org/10.1006/brin.1997.1943

Grohman, M. G., & Snyder, H. T. (2017). Why do we create? In J. A. Plucker (Ed.), *Creativity & innovation theory, research and practice* (pp. 165–179). Prufrock Press Inc.

Grospietsch, F., & Lins, I. (2021). Review of the prevalence and persistence of neuromyths in education – where we stand and what is still needed. *Frontiers in Education, 6*, 1–13. https://doi.org/10.3389/feduc.2021.665752

Guerriero, S. (Ed.). (2017). *Pedagogical knowledge and the changing nature of the teaching profession*. Educational Research and Innovation. OECD Publishing. https://doi.org/10.1787/9789264270695-en

Guggino, P. C., & Brint, S. (2010). Does the no child left behind act help or hinder K–12 education? *Policy Matters*, *3*(3), 1–8.

Guilford, J. P. (1959). *Personality*. McGraw-Hill.

Gunnar, M. R. (2021). Forty years of research on stress and development: What have we learned and future directions. *American Psychologist*, *76*(9), 1372–1384. https://doi.org/10.1037/amp0000893

Guy, M., Normand, J., Jeunet-Kelway, C., & Moreau, G. (2023). The sense of embodiment in virtual reality and its assessment methods. *Frontiers in Virtual Reality*, *4*. https://doi.org/10.3389/frvir.2023.1141683

Hajovsky, D. B., Chesnut, S. R., & Jensen, K. M. (2020). The role of teachers' self-efficacy beliefs in the development of teacher-student relationships. *Journal of School Psychology*, *82*, 141–158. https://doi.org/10.1016/j.jsp.2020.09.001

Haleem, A., Javaid, M., Qadri, M. A., & Suman, R. (2022). Understanding the role of digital technologies in education: A review. *Sustainable operations and computers*, *3*, 275–285. https://doi.org/10.1016/j.susoc.2022.05.004

Hammond, Z. (2014). *Culturally responsive teaching and the brain: Promoting authentic engagement and rigor among culturally and linguistically diverse students*. Corwin.

Hardiman, M. M. (2003). *Connecting brain research with effective teaching: The brain-targeted teaching model*. Rowman & Littlefield Education.

Hardiman, M. M. (2012). *The Brain-Targeted Teaching Model for 21st century schools*. Corwin.

Hardiman, M. M. (2017). Education and the arts: Educating every child in the spirit of inquiry and joy. In A.S. Canestrari & B. A. Marlowe (Eds.), *The Wiley handbook of educational foundation* (pp. 207–227). John Wiley & Sons.

Hardiman, M. M. (2019). The arts and creativity: From research to practice. In J. L. Contreras-Vidal (Ed.), *Mobile brain-body imaging and the neuroscience of art, innovation and creativity*. Springer.

Hardiman, M., & Denckla, M. (2010). The science of education: Informing teaching and learning through the brain sciences. In D. Gordon (Ed.) *Cerebrum* (pp. 3–11). Dana Press.

Hardiman, M. M., JohnBull, R. M., Carran, D. T., & Shelton, A. (2019). The effects of arts-integrated instruction on memory for science content. *Trends in Neuroscience and Education*, *14*, 25–32. https://doi.org/10.1016/j.tine.2019.02.002

Hardiman, M., Rinne, L., Gregory, E., & Yarmolinskaya, J. (2012). Neuroethics, neuroeducation, and classroom teaching: Where the brain sciences meet pedagogy. *Neuroethics*, *5*, 135–143. https://doi.org/10.1007/s12152-011-9116-6

Hardiman, M., Rinne, L., & Yarmolinskaya, J. (2014). The effects of arts integration on long-term retention of academic content. *Mind, Brain, and Education*, *8*(3), 144–148. https://doi.org/10.1111/mbe.12053

Hart, W., & Albarracín, D. (2009). The effects of chronic achievement motivation and achievement primes on the activation of achievement and fun goals. *Journal of Personality and Social Psychology*, *97*(6), 1129–1141. https://doi.org/10.1037/a0017146

Haverkamp, B. F., Wiersma, R., Vertessen, K., van Ewijk, H., Oosterlaan, J., & Hartman, E. (2020). Effects of physical activity interventions on cognitive outcomes and academic performance in adolescents and young adults: A meta-analysis. *Journal of Sports Sciences*, *38*(23), 2637–2660. https://doi.org/10.1080/02640414.2020.1794763

Hebb, D. (1949). *The organization of behavior: A neuropsychological theory*. Wiley.

Heilman, K. M., Nadeau, S. E., & Beversdorf, D. O. (2003). Creative innovation: Possible brain mechanisms. *Neurocase*, *9*(5), 369–379. https://doi.org/10.1076/neur.9.5.369.16553

Henriksen, D., Creely, E., & Henderson, M. (2019). Failing in creativity: The problem of policy and practice in Australia and the United States. *Kappa Delta Pi Record*, *55*(1), 4–10. https://doi.org/10.1080/00228958.2019.1549429

Heschong, L. (1999). *Daylighting in schools: An investigation into the relationship between daylighting and human performance*. Pacific Gas and Electric Company.

Hillman, C. H., Buck, S. M., Themanson, J. R., Pontifex, M. B., & Castelli, D. M. (2009). Aerobic fitness and cognitive development: Event-related brain potential and task performance indices of executive control in preadolescent children. *Developmental Psychology*, *45*(1), 114–129. https://doi.org/10.1037/a0014437

Howard-Jones, P. A. (2014). Neuroscience and education: Myths and messages. *National Review Neuroscience*, *15*(12), 817–824. https://doi.org/10.1038/nrn3817

Howard-Jones, P. A., Pickering, S., & Diack, A. (2007). *Perceptions of the role of neuroscience in education*. The Innovation Unit.

Hsu, W., & Yeh, Y. (2024). Investigating the neural substrate variation between easy and challenging creative association tasks during product design within and fMRI scanner. *IBRO Neuroscience Reports*, *16*, 550–559. https://doi.org/10.1016/j.ibneur.2024.03.006

Hubel, D. H., & Wiesel, T. N. (1970). The period of susceptibility to the physiological effects of unilateral eye closure in kittens. *The Journal of Physiology*, *206*(2), 419–436. https://doi.org/10.1113/jphysiol.1970.sp009022

Hussain, G., Akram, R., Anwar, H., Sajid, F., Iman, T., Han, H.S., Raza, C., & De Aguilar, J. L. G. (2024). Adult neurogenesis: A real hope or a delusion? *Neural Regeneration Research*, *19*(1), 6–15. https://doi.org/10.4103/1673-5374.375317

Hyde, K. L., Lerch, J., Norton, A., Forgeard, M., Winner, E., Evans, A. C., & Schlaug, G. (2009). Musical training shapes structural brain development. *The Journal of Neuroscience*, *29*(10), 3019–3025. https://doi.org/10.1523/JNEUROSCI.5118-08.2009

Hyerle, D. N, & Alper, L. (2011). *Student successes with thinking maps*. Corwin.

Immordino-Yang, M. H., & Damasio, A. (2007). We feel, therefore we learn: The relevance of affective and social neuroscience to education. *Mind, Brain, and Education*, *1*, 3–10. https://doi.org/10.1111/j.1751-228X.2007.00004.x

Immordino-Yang, M. H., Darling-Hammond, L., & Krone, C. (2018). *The brain basis for integrated social, emotional, and academic development: How emotions and social relationships drive learning*. The Aspen Institute.

Jackson-Butler, K. (2017). *Supporting low socio-economic status minority students in independent schools through a professional development learning community on The Brain Targeted Teaching Model* [Doctoral dissertation, Johns Hopkins University]. https://jscholarship.library.jhu.edu/items/189b1ac4-9ce7-42f8-8fa0-6f4600e3cc70

James, W. (1890). *Principles of psychology*. Holt.

Jenkins, J. (2001). The Mozart effect. *Journal of the Royal Society of Medicine*, *94*(4), 170–172. https://doi.org/10.1177/014107680109400404

Jimenez, M. E., Wade, R., Lin, Y., Morrow, L. M., & Reichman, N. E. (2016). Adverse experiences in early childhood and kindergarten outcomes. *Pediatrics*, *137*(2), e20151839. https://doi.org/10.1542/peds.2015-1839

JohnBull R. M., & Hardiman, M. (2022, April). *NeuroEducation for social justice: Integrating culturally relevant pedagogy and neuroeducation instructional practices*. [Paper presentation]. Annual meeting of the American Educational Research Association, San Diego, CA. https://doi.org/10.3102/1894084

JohnBull, R. M., & Hardiman, M. (2023). Exploring changes in teacher self-efficacy: Promising outcomes of neuroeducation professional development. *The Teacher Educator*. https://doi.org/10.1080/08878730.2023.2214555

Kampylis, P., Berki, E., & Saariluoma, P. (2009). In-service and prospective teachers' conceptions of creativity. *Thinking Skills and Creativity*, *4*(1), 15–29.

Kandel, E. (2006). *In search of memory: The emergence of a new science of mind.* W.W. Norton & Company.

Karpicke, J. D., & Blunt, J. R. (2011). Retrieval practice produces more learning than elaborative studying with concept mapping. *Science.* https://doi.org/10.1126.science.1199327

Karpicke, J. D., & Roediger, H. L., III. (2008). The critical importance of retrieval for learning. *Science, 319*(5865), 966–968. https://doi.org/10.1126/science.1152408

Kasempiti, S., & Yoonisil, W. (2023). *Development of an enrichment curriculum on communicating in Thai in daily life for foreign students using the brain-targeted teaching model* [Doctoral dissertation, Srinakharinwirot University]. http://ir-ithesis.swu.ac.th/dspace/

Kasirer, A., Adi-Japha, E., & Mashal, N. (2020). Verbal and figural creativity in children with autism spectrum disorder and typical development. *Sec. Psychology of Language.* (11). https://doi.org/10.3389/fpsyg.2020.559238

Kaufman, J. C., & Beghetto, R. A. (2009). Beyond big and little: The Four C model of creativity. *Review of General Psychology, 13*(1), 1–12. https://doi.org/10.1037/a0013688

Kempermann, G., Wiskott, L., & Gage, F. H. (2004). Functional significance of adult neurogenesis. *Current Opinion in Neurobiology, 14*(2), 186–191. https://doi.org/10.1016/j.conb.2004.03.001

Kennedy, T. J., & Sundberg, C. W. (2020). 21st century skills. In B. Akpan & T. J. Kennedy (Eds.), *Science education in theory and practice: An introductory guide to learning theory* (pp. 479–496). Springer International Publishing. https://doi.org/10.1007/978-3-030-43620-9_32

Kettle, K. L., & Häubl, G. (2010). Motivation by anticipation: Expecting rapid feedback enhances performance. *Psychological Science, 21*(4), 545–547. https://doi.org/10.1177/0956797610363541

Kim, S. K., & Webb, S. (2022). The effects of spaced practice on second language learning: A meta-analysis. *Language Learning, 72*(1), 269–319. https://doi.org/10.1111/lang.12479

Kirschner, H., Hilbert, K., Hoyer, J., Lueken, U., & Beesdo-Baum, K. (2016). Psychophsyiological reactivity during uncertainty and ambiguity processing in high and low worriers. *Journal of Behavior Therapy and Experimental Psychiatry, 50,* 97–105. https://doi.org/10.1016/j.jbtep.2015.06.001

Knabe, M. L., & Vlach, H. A. (2020). When are difficulties desirable for children? First steps toward a developmental and individual differences account of the spacing effect. *Journal of Applied Research in Memory and Cognition, 9*(4), 447–454. https://doi.org/10.1016/j.jarmac.2020.07.007

Kniffin, K. M., Narayanan, J., Anseel, F., Antonakis, J., Ashford, S. P., Bakker, A. B., Bamberger, P., Bapuji, H., Bhave, D. P., Choi, V. K., Creary, S. J., Demerouti, E., Flynn, F. J., Gelfand, M. J., Greer, L. L., Johns, G., Kesebir, S., Klein, P. G., Lee, S. Y., . . . Vugt, M. V. (2021). COVID-19 and the workplace: Implications, issues, and insights for future research and action. *American Psychologist, 76*(1), 63–77. https://doi.org/10.1037/amp0000716

Kornell, N., & Bjork, R. A. (2008). Optimising self-regulated study: The benefits—and costs—of dropping flashcards. *Memory, 16*(2), 125–136. https://doi.org/10.1080/09658210701763899

Kornell, N., Castel, A. D., Eich, T. S., & Bjork, R. A. (2010). Spacing as the friend of both memory and induction in young and older adults. *Psychology and Aging, 25*(2), 498–503.

Kornell, N., & Son, L. (2009). Learners' choices and beliefs about self-testing. *Memory, 17*(5), 493–501. https://doi.org/10.1080/09658210902832915

Korsavi, S. S., Montazami, A., & Mumovic, D. (2020). The impact of indoor environment quality (IEQ) on school children's overall comfort in the UK; A regression approach. *Building and Environment, 185,* 107309.https://doi.org/10.1016/j.buildenv.2020.107309

Kraft, U. (2007). Unleashing creativity. In F. Bloom (Ed.), *Best of the brain from Scientific American: Mind, matter, and tomorrow's brain* (pp. 9–19). Dana Press.

Kumar, A., & Amin, J. N. (2023). Assessing the efficacy of Brain Targeted Teaching and Content Based Language Teaching in enhancing language teaching among senior secondary school students. *International Journal of Indian Psychology, 11*(4), 011–020. DIP:18.01.002.20231104. https://doi.org/10.25215/1104.002

Ladson-Billings, G. (2021). *Culturally relevant pedagogy: Asking a different question.* Teachers College Press.

Ladson-Billings, G. (2022). *The dreamkeepers: Successful teachers of African American children.* John Wiley & Sons.

Lamotte, A. S., Essadek, A., Shadili, G., Perez, J. M., & Raft, J. (2021). The impact of classroom chatter noise on comprehension: A systematic review. *Perceptual and Motor Skills, 128*(3), 1275–1291. https://doi.org/10.1177/ 00315125211005935

LeDoux, J. E. (1996). *The emotional brain: The mysterious underpinnings of emotional life.* Simon & Schuster.

Lehmann, J. A. M., & Seufert, T. (2017). The influence of background music on learning in the light of different theoretical perspectives and the role of working memory capacity. *Frontiers in Psychology, 8*, 1902. https://doi.org/10.3389/fpsyg.2017.01902

Lei, H., Cui, Y., Chiu, M. M. (2018). The relationship between teacher support and students' academic emotions: A meta-analysis. *Frontiers in Psychology, 8*, 2288. https// doi.10.3389/fpsyg.2017.02288

Lekan-Kehinde, M., & Asojo, A. (2021). Impact of lighting on children's learning environment: A literature review. *WIT Transactions on Ecology and the Environment, 253*. https://doi.org/10.2495/SC210311

Li, L., Gow, A. D. I., & Zhou, J. (2020). The role of positive emotions in education: A neuroscience perspective. *Mind, Brain, and Education, 14*(3), 220–234. https://doi.org/10.1111/mbe.12244

Lillard, A. S. (2005). *Montessori: The science behind the genius.* Oxford University Press.

Limb, C. J., & Braun, A. R. (2008). Neural substrates of spontaneous musical performance: An fMRI study of jazz improvisation. *PLoS ONE, 3*(2), 1–9. https://doi.org/10.1371/journal.pone.0001679

Lin, X. P., Li, B. B., Yao, Z. N., Yang, Z., & Zhang, M. (2024). The impact of virtual reality on student engagement in the classroom–a critical review of the literature. *Frontiers in Psychology, 15*, 1360574. https://doi.org/10.3389/fpsyg.2024.1360574

Lopata, J. A., Barr, N., Slayton, M., & Seli, P. (2022). Dual modes of creative thought in the classroom: Implications of network neuroscience for creativity education. *Translational Issues in Psychological Science*, 8(1), 79–89. https://doi.org/10.1037/tps0000317

Lu, Y., Ottenbreit-Leftwich, A. T., Ding, A., and Glazewski, K. (2017). Experienced iPad-using early childhood teachers: Practices in the one-to-one iPad classroom. *Computers in the Schools, 34*, 9–23. https://doi.org/10.1080/07380569.2017.1287543

Luan, J., Yang, M., Zhao, Y., Zang, Y., Zhang, Z., & Chen, H. (2023). Aromatherapy with inhalation effectively alleviates the test anxiety of college students: A meta-analysis. *Frontiers in Psychology, 13*, 1042553. https://doi.org/10.3389/fpsyg.2022.1042553

Luiten, J., Ames, W., & Ackerson, G. (1980). A meta-analysis of the effects of advance organizers on learning and retention. *American Educational Research Journal, 17*(2), 211–218. https://doi.org/10.2307/1162483

Lupien, S. J., McEwen, B. S., Gunnar, M. R., & Heim, C. (2009). Effects of stress throughout the lifespan on the brain, behaviour and cognition. *Nature Reviews Neuroscience, 10*(6), 434–445. https://doi.org/10.1038/nrn2639

Lyle, K. B., Bego, C. R., Hopkins, R. F., Hieb, J. L., & Ralston, P. A. (2020). How the amount and spacing of retrieval practice affect the short-and long-term retention of mathematics knowledge. *Educational Psychology Review, 32*, 277–295. https://doi.org/10.1007/s10648-019-09489-x

Ma, Y. (2022). The influence of ambient aroma on middle school students' academic emotions. *International Journal of*

Psychology, 57, 387–392. https://doi.org/10.1002/ijop.12827

MacLeod, C. M., & Bodner, G. E. (2017). The production effect in memory. *Current Directions in Psychological Science, 26*(4), 390–395. https://doi.org/10.1177/0963721417691356

Mahoney, J. L., Weissberg, R. P., Greenberg, M. T., Dusenbury, L., Jagers, R. J., Niemi, K., Schlinger, M., Schlund, J., Shriver, T. P., VanAusdal, K., & Yoder, N. (2021). Systemic social and emotional learning: Promoting educational success for all preschool to high school students. *American Psychologist, 76*(7), 1128–1142. https://doi.org/10.1037/amp0000701

Makri, A., & Jarrold, C. (2021). Investigating the underlying mechanisms of the enactment effect: The role of action–object bindings in aiding immediate memory performance. *Quarterly Journal of Experimental Psychology, 74*(12), 2084–2096. https://doi.org/10.1177/17470218211019026

Marshall, J. (2019). *Integrating the visual arts across the curriculum: An elementary and middle school guide*. Teachers College Press.

Marzano, R. (1992). *A different kind of classroom: Teaching with dimensions of learning*. Association for Supervision and Curriculum Development.

Marzano, R., Pickering, D., & Pollock, J. (2001). *Classroom instruction that works: Research-based strategies for increasing student achievement*. Association for Supervision and Curriculum Development.

Massonnié, J., Rogers, C. J., Mareschal, D., Kirkham, N. Z. (2019). Is classroom noise always bad for children? The contribution of age and selective attention to creative performance in noise. *Frontiers in Psychology, 10*, 381. https://doi.org/10.3389/fpsyg.2019.00381

Matto, H. C., Ihara, E. S., Cieslowski, B., Hines, S. A., & Booth, J. (2023). Virtual reality case simulation to build skill competencies in working with substance-engaged clients. *Social Work Education*, 1–13. https://doi.org/10.1080/02615479.2023.2289452

May, K. E., & Elder, A. D. (2018). Efficient, helpful, or distracting? A literature review of media multitasking in relation to academic performance. *International Journal of Educational Technology in Higher Education, 15*(1), 1–17. https://doi.org/10.1186/s41239-018-0096-z

McAnally, K., & Wallis, G. (2021). Visual–haptic integration, action and embodiment in virtual reality. *Psychological Research, 86*, 1847–1857. https://doi.org/10.1007/s00426-021-01613-3

McBride, D. M., & Dosher, A. B. (2002). A comparison of conscious and automatic memory processes for picture and word stimuli: A process dissociation analysis. *Consciousness and Cognition, 11*(3), 423–460. https://doi.org/10.1016/S1053-8100(02)00007-7

McCraty, R. (2015). *Science of the heart, volume 2: Exploring the role of the heart in human performance* (2nd ed.). HeartMath Institute.

McCurdy, M. P., Leach, R. C., & Leshikar, E. D. (2017). The generation effect revisited: Fewer generation constraints enhances item and context memory. *Journal of Memory and Language, 92*, 202–216. https://doi.org/10.1016/j.jml.2016.06.007

McCurdy, M. P., Viechtbauer, W., Sklenar, A. M., Frankenstein, A. N., & Leshikar, E. D. (2020). Theories of the generation effect and the impact of generation constraint: A meta-analytic review. *Psychonomic Bulletin & Review, 27*, 1139–1165. https://doi.org/10.3758/s13423-020-01762-3

McKinney, P. (2022). Preparing for a failure of imagination. https://www.philmckinney.com/preparing-for-a-failure-of-imagination/

McLean, L., Espinoza, P., Janssen, J., Jimenez, M., & Lindstrom Johnson, S. (2024). Relationships between elementary teachers' enjoyment and students' engagement across content areas and among student groups. *School Psychology*. Advance online publication. https://doi.org/10.1037/spq0000633

Mealings, K., & Buchholz, J. M. (2024). The effect of classroom acoustics and noise on high school students' listening, learning and well-being: A scoping review. *Facilities, 42*(5/6), 485–503. https://doi.org/10.1108/F-06-2023-0049

Mendelson, T., Greenberg, M. T., Dariotis, J. K., Gould, L. F., Rhoades, B. L., & Leaf, P. J. (2010). Feasibility and preliminary outcomes of a school-based mindfulness intervention for urban youth. *Journal of Abnormal Child Psychology: An Official Publication of the International Society for Research in Child and Adolescent Psychopathology, 38*(7), 985–994. https://doi.org/10.1007/s10802-010-9418-x

Meng, X., Zhang, M., & Wang, M. (2023). Effects of school indoor visual environment on children's health outcomes: A systematic review. *Health & Place, 83*, 103021. https://doi.org/10.1016/j.healthplace.2023.103021

Miller, G. A. (1956). The magical number seven, plus or minus two: Some limits on our capacity for processing information. *Psychological Review, 63*(2), 81–97. https://doi.org/10.1037/h0043158

Mineo, R. (2023). The role of the environment and of space in the Reggio Emilia Approach. In *Book of Abstracts*, 9-9. https://hdl.handle.net/11380/1313947

Mirabal, S. C., Reed, D. A., Steinert, Y., Whitehead, C. R., Wright, S. M., & Tackett, S. (2024). Group concept mapping for health professions education scholarship. *Advances in Health Sciences Education*, 1–15. https://doi.org/10.1007/s10459-024-10331-5

Mizyed, H. A., & Eccles, C. U. (2023). Understanding Emirati teachers' challenges in fostering problem-solving skills development in early years – A preliminary study. *Social Sciences & Humanities Open, 8*(1), 100561. https://doi.org/10.1016/j.ssaho.2023.100561

Mizyed, H. A., & Eccles, C. U. (2024). *Improving early year teachers content knowledge and self-efficacy through peer coaching and reflection: A professional development model.* Manuscript in preparation.

Montessori, M. (1967). *The absorbent mind.* Henry Holt.

Morrow, B. L., & & Kanakri, S. (2018). The impact of fluorescent and LED lighting on students attitudes and behavior in the classroom. *Advances in Pediatric Research, 5*, 15. https://www.researchgate.net/publication/329637078_

Munro, J. K. (2019). Creativity in education: What educators need to know. *Education for a Changing World.* http://www.education.nsw.gov.au

Nadel, L., & Hardt, O. (2011). Update on memory systems and processes. *Neuropsychopharmacology, 36*(1), 251–273. https://doi.org/10.1038/npp.2010.169

National Academy of Sciences Engineering and Medicine. (2018). *How People Learn: Learners, contexts, and cultures.* National Academies Press.

National Center for Education Statistics. (2022). Drop out rate. www.nces.ed.gov

National Endowment for the Arts. (n.d.). https://www.arts.gov/impact/research

Neumann, M. M., Anthony, J. L., Erazo, N. A., & Neumann, D. L. (2019, October). Assessment and technology: Mapping future directions in the early childhood classroom. *In Frontiers in Education, 4*, 116. https://doi.org/10.3389/feduc.2019.00116

Norris, D., & Kalm, K. (2021). Chunking and data compression in verbal short-term memory. *Cognition, 208*, 104534. https://doi.org/10.1016/j.cognition.2020.104534

Okamoto, T., Endo, S., Shirao, T., & Nagao, S. (2011). Role of cerebellar cortical protein synthesis in transfer of memory trace of cerebellum-dependent motor learning. *The Journal of Neuroscience, 31*(24), 8958–8966. https://doi.org/10.1523/JNEUROSCI.1151-11.2011

Osher, D., Cantor, P., Berg, J., Steyer, L., Rose, T. (2021). Malleability, Plasticity, and Individuality. In P. Cantor & D. Osher Eds., *The science of learning and development* (pp. 3–54). Routledge.

Ozernov-Palchik, O., Pollack, C., Bonawitz, E., Christodoulou1, J. A., Gaab, N., Gabrieli, J. D. E., Kievlan, P. M., Kirby, C., Lin, G., Luk, G., & Nelson, C. A. (2024). Reflections on the past two decades of Mind, Brain, and Education. *Mind, Brain, and Education, 18*(1), 1–16. https://doi.org/10.1111/mbe.12407

Ozubko, J. D., & MacLeod, C. M. (2010). The production effect in memory: Evidence that distinctiveness underlies the benefit. *Journal of Experimental Psychology: Learning, Memory, and Cognition, 36*(6), 1543–1547. https://doi.org/10.1037/a0020604

Parr, T. L. (2016). A brain-targeted teaching framework: Modeling the intended change in professional development to increase knowledge of learning sciences research and influence pedagogical change in K-12 public classrooms [Drexel University]. https://drexel.edu/soe/research/student-research/

Parr, T. L. (2017). Modeling the intended change: Using concepts of brain-based teaching and learning in professional development. *Pennsylvania Educational Leadership*, 47.

Pashler, H., Cepeda, N. J., Wixted, J. T., & Rohrer, D. (2005). When does feedback facilitate learning of words? *Journal of Experimental Psychology, Learning, Memory & Cognition, 31*(1), 3–8. https://doi.org/10.1037/0278-7393.31.1.3

Pashler, H., McDaniel, M., Rohrer, D., & Bjork, R. (2008). Learning styles: Concepts and evidence. *Psychological Science in the Public Interest, 9*(3), 105–119. https://doi.org/10.1111/j.1539-6053.2009.01038.x

Payton, J. W., Weissberg, R. P., Durlak, J. A., Dymnicki, A. B., Taylor, R. D., Schellinger, K. B., & Pachan, M. (2008). *The positive impact of social and emotional learning for kindergarten to eighth-grade students: Findings from three scientific reviews.* Chicago, IL: Collaborative for Academic, Social, and Emotional Learning.

Pekrun, R., Goetz, T., Titz, W., & Perry, R. P. (2002). Academic emotions in students' self-regulated learning and achievement: A program of qualitative and quantitative research. *Educational Psychologist, 37*(2), 91–105. https://doi.org/10.1207/S15326985EP3702_4

Pekrun, R., & Linnenbrink-Garcia, L. (2014). *International handbook of emotions in education.* Routledge.

Phung, L., Nakamura, S., Reinders, H., Hiver, P., Mercer, S., & Al-Hoorie, A. H. (2021). The effect of choice on affective engagement: Implications for task design. *Student Engagement in the Language Classroom*, 163–181. https://doi.org/10.21832/9781788923613-012

Pinel, J. P. J. (2000). *Biopsychology* (4th ed.). Allyn and Bacon.

Plucker, J. A. (1999). Is the proof in the pudding? Reanalyses of Torrance's (1958 to present) longitudinal data. *Creativity Research Journal, 12*(2), 103–114. https://doi.org/10.1207/s15326934crj1202_3

Plucker, J. A. (2017). Creative articulation. In J. A. Plucker (Ed.), *Creativity & innovation theory, research and practice* (pp. 223–234). Prufrock Press Inc.

Plucker, J. A., Beghetto, R. A., & Dow, G. T. (2004). Why isn't creativity more important to educational psychologists? Potentials, pitfalls, and future directions in creativity research. *Educational Psychologist, 39*(2), 83–96. https://doi.org/10.1207/s15326985ep3902_1

Poirel, N., Mellet, E., Houdé, O., & Pineau, A. (2008). First came the trees, then the forest: Developmental changes during childhood in the processing of visual local–global patterns according to the meaningfulness of the stimuli. *Developmental Psychology, 44*(1), 245–253. https://doi.org/10.1037/0012-1649.44.1.245

Porche, M. V., Fortuna, L. R., Lin, J., & Alegría, M. (2011). Childhood trauma and psychiatric disorders as correlates of school dropout in a national sample of young adults. *Child Development, 82*(3), 982–998. https://doi.org/10.1111/j.1467-8624.2010.01534.x

Posner, M., & Patoine, B. (2009). How arts training improves attention and cognition. *Cerebrum*, 2–4. http://dana.org/news/cerebrum/detail.aspx?id=23206

Posner, M. I., & Rothbart, M. K. (2007). *Educating the human brain.* American Psychological Association.

Privitera, A. J. (2021). A scoping review of research on neuroscience training for teachers. *Trends in Neuroscience and Education*, 24, 100157. https://doi.org/10.1016/j.tine.2021.100157

Qian, M. & Plucker, J. A. (2017). Creativity assessment. In J.A. Plucker (Ed.), *Creativity & innovation theory, research and practice,* 223-234. Prufrock Press Inc.

Ramsden, S., Richardson, F. M., Josse, G., Thomas, M. S. C., Ellis, C., Shakeshaft, C., Seghier, M. L., & Price, C. J. (2011). Verbal and non-verbal intelligence changes in the teenage brain. *Nature, 479*(7371), 113–116. https://doi.org/10.1038/nature10514

Rao, K., Gravel, J. W., Rose, D. H., & Tucker-Smith, T. N. (2023). Universal Design for Learning in its 3rd decade: A focus on equity, inclusion, and design. *International Encyclopedia of Education, 6*, 712–720. https://doi.org/10.1016/B978-0-12-818630-5.14079-5

Ratey, J. J. (2008). *Spark: The revolutionary new science of exercise and the brain.* Little, Brown and Co.

Rauscher, F. H., Shaw, G. L., & Ky, C. N. (1993). Music and spatial task performance. *Nature, 365*, 611. https://doi.org/10.1038/365611a0

Recht, D. R., & Leslie, L. (1988). Effect of prior knowledge on good and poor readers' memory of text. *Journal of Educational Psychology, 80*(1), 16–20. https://doi.org/10.1037/0022-0663.80.1.16

Rhodes, M. (1961). An analysis of creativity. *The Phi Delta Kappan, 42*(7), 305–310. https://www.jstor.org/stable/20342603

Rice, J., Levine, L., & Pizarro, D. (2007). "Just stop thinking about it": Effects of emotional disengagement on children's memory for educational material. *Emotion, 7*(4), 812–823. https://doi.org/10.1037/1528-3542.7.4.812

Rinne, L., Gregory, E., Yarmolinskaya, J., & Hardiman, M. (2011). Why arts integration improves long-term retention of content. *Mind, Brain, and Education, 5*(2), 89–96. https://doi.org/10.1111/j.1751-228X.2011.01114.x

Ritchhart, R., Church, M., & Morrison, K. (2011). *Making thinking visible: How to promote engagement, understanding, and independence for all learners*. Jossey-Bass.

Roberts, B. R., MacLeod, C. M., & Fernandes, M. A. (2022). The enactment effect: A systematic review and meta-analysis of behavioral, neuroimaging, and patient studies. *Psychological Bulletin, 148*(5–6), 397–434. https://doi.org/10.1037/bul0000360

Robertson, P. (2002). The critical age hypothesis. *The Asian EFL Journal.* http://www.asian-efl-journal.com/marcharticles_pr.html.

Robinson, K. (2010). Changing education paradigms. *YouTube.* https://www.youtube.com/watch?v=zDZFcDGpL4U *The International Journal of Holistic Early Learning and Development, 4*, 35–44. http://ijheld.lakeheadu.ca/

Rogers, J. (2023). Spacing effects in task repetition research. *Language Learning, 73*(2). 445–474. https://doi.org/10.1111/lang.12526

Rogowsky, B. A., Calhoun, B. M., & Tallal, P. (2020). Providing instruction based on students' learning style preferences does not improve learning. *Frontiers in Psychology, 11*, 511773. https://doi.org/10.3389/fpsyg.2020.00164

Rohrer, D., & Pashler, H. (2010). Recent research on human learning challenges conventional instructional strategies. *Educational Researcher, 39*(5), 406–412. https://doi.org/10.3102/0013189X10374770

Rosas, S. R. (2023). Group concept mapping for measure development and validation. *The Sage handbook of survey development and application*, 23. SAGE.

Rose, D. H., & Meyer, A. (2002). *Teaching every student in the digital age: Universal design for learning.* Association for Supervision and Curriculum Development.

Rotherham, A. J., & Willingham, D. (2009). 21st century skills: The challenges ahead. *Educational Leadership, 67*(1), 16–21.

Rousseau, L. (2021). Interventions to dispel neuromyths in educational settings – A review. *Frontiers in Psychology, 12*, 719692. https://doi.org/10.3389/fpsyg.2021.719692

Różańska, A., & Gruszka, A. (2020). Current research trends in multitasking: A bibliometric mapping approach. *Journal of Cognitive Psychology, 32*(3), 278–286. https://doi.org/10.1080/20445911.2020.1742130

Rukminingsih, R., Mujiyanto, J., Nurkamto, J., & Hartono, R. (2021). Comparison of Brain Targeted Teaching Model V/S students' content schemata with online instruction in reading to students different motivation level. In *International Conference on Science, Education, and Technology* (Vol. 7, pp. 511–517). https://proceeding.unnes.ac.id/index.php/iset

Runco, M. A. (2004). Creativity. *Annual Review of Psychology, 55*, 657–687. https://doi.org/10.1146/annurev.psych.55.090902.141502

Runco, M. A., & Jaeger, G. J. (2012). The standard definition of creativity. *Creativity Research Journal, 24*(1), 92–96. doi: 10.1080/ 10400419.2012.650092

Rundus, D. (1971). Analysis of rehearsal processes in free recall. *Journal of Experimental Psychology, 89*(1), 63–77. https://doi.org/10.1037/h0031185

Ruttle, P. L., Shirtcliff, E. A., Serbin, L. A., Ben-Dat Fisher, D., Stack, D. M., & Schwartzman, A. E. (2011). Disentangling psychobiological mechanisms underlying internalizing and externalizing behaviors in youth: Longitudinal and concurrent associations with cortisol. *Hormones and Behavior, 59*(1), 123–132. https://doi.org/10.1016/j.yheb.2010.10.015

Ryan, R. M., & Deci, E. L. (2000). Self-determination theory and the facilitation of intrinsic motivation, social development, and well-being. *American Psychologist, 55*(1), 68–78. https://doi.org/10.1037/0003-066X.55.1.68

Saeed, B. A., & Ramdane, T. (2022). The effect of implementation of a creative thinking model on the development of creative thinking skills in high school students: A systematic review. *Review of Education, 10*(3), e3379. https://doi.org/10.1002/rev3.3379

Sapolsky, R. M. (2004). *Why zebras don't get ulcers*. Henry Holt and Co.

Saraji, M., Mirjalili, S., Duarte, A., & Calhoun, V. D. (2024). Investigating the impact of habitual sleep quality on episodic memory performance: An EEG-based representational similarity analysis. *bioRxiv*, 2024-11. https://doi.org/10.1101/2024.11.08.622661

Satpathy, A. (2015, March 1). The futurist: Virtual reality, empathy, and solipsism. *The Daily*. https://www.dailyuw.com/opinion/the-futurist-virtual-reality-empathy-and-solipsism/article_af2863f6-c234-11e4-9977-936582bc832e.html

Sauvé, L., Renaud, L., Kaufman, D., & Marquis, J-S. (2007). Distinguishing between games and simulations: A systematic review. *Journal of Educational Technology & Society, 10*(3), 247–256. https://www.jstor.org/stable/jeductechsoci.10.3.247

Sawyer, R. K. (2006). Educating for innovation. *Thinking Skills and Creativity, 1*(1), 41–48. https://doi:10.1016/j.tsc.2005.08.001

Sawyer, R. K. (2011). What makes good teaching great? The artful balance of structure and improvisation. *Structure and Improvisation in Creative Teaching*, 1–24. Cambridge University Press.

Schneider, S., Nebel, S., Beege, M., Rey, G. D. (2018). The autonomy-enhancing effects of choice on cognitive load, motivation and learning with digital media. *Learning and Instruction, 58*, 161–172. https://doi.org/10.1016/j.learninstruc.2018.06.006

Schomaker, J., & Meeter, M. (2015). Short- and long-lasting consequences of novelty, deviance and surprise on brain and cognition. *Neuroscience and Biobehavioral Reviews, 55*, 268–279. https://doi.org/10.1016/j.neubiorev.2015.05.002

Schwabe, L., & Wolf, O. T. (2010). Learning under stress impairs memory formation. *Neurobiology of Learning and Memory, 93*(2), 183–188. https://doi.org/10.1016/j.nlm.2009.09.009

Seegers, A. (2020). Brain-targeted teaching as a tool to facilitate implementing mind brain and education science into community college pedagogy. University of New England. https://dune.une.edu/theses/289

Serice, L. (2023). Prisms of neuroscience: Frameworks for thinking about educational gamification. *AI, Computer Science and Robotics Technology*, (13). https://doi.org/10.5772/acrt.13

Shapiro, L., & Stolz, S. A. (2019). Embodied cognition and its significance for education. *Theory and Research in Education, 17*(1), 19–39. https://doi.org/10.1177/1477878518822149

Shen, S., Wang, S., Qi, Y., Wang, Y., & Yan, X. (2021). Teacher suggestion feedback facilitates creativity of students in STEAM education. *Frontiers in Psychology, 12*. 723171.https://doi.org/10.3389/fpsyg.2021.723171

Shepard, R. N. (1967). Recognition memory for words, sentences, and pictures. *Journal of Verbal Learning and Verbal Behavior, 6*(1), 156–163. https://doi.org/10.1016/S0022-5371(67)80067-7

Shiffrin, R. M., & Nosofsky, R. M. (1994). Seven plus or minus two: A commentary on capacity limitations. *Psychological Review, 101*(2), 357–361. https://doi.org/10.1037/0033-295X.101.2.357

Shonkoff, J. P., Garner, A. S., Siegel, B. S., Dobbins, M. I., Earls, M. F., Garner, A. S., McGuinn, L., Pascoe, J., & Wood, D. L. (2012). The lifelong effects of early childhood adversity and toxic stress. *Pediatrics, 129*(1), 232–246. https://doi.org/10.1542/peds.2011-2663

Shonkoff, J. P., & Phillips, D. (2000). *From neurons to neighborhoods: The science of early childhood development*. National Academy Press.

Shrestha, P. (2017, November 17). Convergent vs divergent thinking. *Psychestudy*. https://www.psychestudy.com/cognitive/thinking/convergent-vs-divergent

Skinner, E. A., Chi, U., & The Learning-Gardens Educational Assessment Group. (2012). Intrinsic motivation and engagement as "active ingredients" in garden-based education: Examining models and measures derived from self-determination theory. *The Journal of Environmental Education, 43*(1), 16–36. https://doi.org/10.1080/00958964.2011.596856

Smith, S. M., Glenberg, A., & Bjork, R. A. (1978). Environmental context and human memory. *Memory & Cognition, 6*(4), 342–353. https://doi.org/10.3758/BF03197465

Sparacio, A., IJzerman, H., Ropovik, I., Giorgini, F., Spiessens, C., Uchino, B. N., Landvatter, J., Tacana, T., Diller, S. J., Derrick, J. L., Segundo, J., Pierce, J. D., Ross, R. M., Francis, Z., LaBoucane, A., Ma-Kellams, C., Ford, M. B., Schmidt, K., Wong, C. C., Higgins, W. C., ... & Jiga-Boy, G. M. (2024). Self-administered mindfulness interventions reduce stress in a large, randomized controlled multi-site study. *Nature Human Behavior, 8*, 1716–1725. https://doi.org/10.1038/s41562-024-01907-7

Sperling, G. (1960). The information available in brief visual presentations. *Psychological Monographs, 74*, 1–29. https://doi.org/10.1037/h0093759

Squire, L. R., & Kandel, E. R. (1999). *Memory: From mind to molecules*. W.H. Freeman & Co.

St-Amand, J., Smith, J., & Goulet, M. (2024). Is teacher humor an asset in classroom management? Examining its association with students' well-being, sense of school belonging, and engagement. *Curr Psychology, 43*, 2499–2514. https://doi.org/10.1007/s12144-023-04481-9

Starko, A. J. (2018). *Creativity in the classroom schools of curious delight* (6th ed.). Routledge.

Stassinopoulos, R. L. (2023). *Cultivating student engagement and enhancing teaching self-efficacy in higher education stem: A neuroeducation framework* [Doctoral dissertation, Johns Hopkins University]. https://jscholarship.library.jhu.edu/items/9af66281-3593-4042-9fc3-b0b2ec5a7add

Steinberg, L. (2008). A social neuroscience perspective on adolescent risk-taking. *Developmental Review, 28*(1), 78–106. https://doi.org/10.1016/j.dr.2007.008.002

Stumm, S. V., Hell, B., & Chamorro-Premuzic, T. (2011). The hungry mind: Intellectual curiosity is the third pillar of academic performance. *Perspectives on Psychological Science, 6*(6): 574–588. https://doi.org/10.1177/1745691611421204

Sun, Q., Chen, F., & Yin, S. (2023). The role and features of peer assessment feedback in college English writing. *Frontiers in Psychology, 13*, 1070618. https://doi.org/10.3389/fpsyg.2022.1070618

Sweller, J. (1988). Cognitive load during problem solving: Effects on learning. *Cognitive Science, 12*(2), 257–285. https://doi.org/10.1207/s15516709cog1202_4

Sylvan, L. J., & Christodoulou, J. A. (2010). Understanding the role of neuroscience in brain based products: A guide for educators and consumers. *Mind, Brain, and Education*, *4*(1), 1–7. https://doi.org/10.1111/j.1751-228X.2009.01077.x

Tabor, J. (2024). Why creativity is necessary: The passion of Sir Ken Robinson. In *The Palgrave Handbook of Educational Thinkers* (pp. 1803–1815). Cham: Springer International Publishing.

Tan, J., Mao, J., Jiang, Y., & Gao, M. (2021). The influence of academic emotions on learning effects: A systematic review. *International Journal of Environmental Research and Public Health*, *18*(18), 9678. https://doi.org/10.3390/ijerph18189678

Tanner, C. K. (2008). Explaining relationships among student outcomes and the school's physical environment. *Journal of Advanced Academics*, *19*(3), 444–471. https://doi.org/10.4219/jaa-2008-812

Taylor, J. B. (2008). *My stroke of insight: A brain scientist's personal journey*. Viking Penguin.

TeVault, D. L. (2022). *The interrelatedness of self-efficacy, collective teacher efficacy, and pedagogical knowledge in an independent school: A multiple methods case study* [Doctoral dissertation, Johns Hopkins University]. https://j1op-stage.library.jhu.edu/items/bf93aad3-d19c-4833-b502-e907a332f44c

Thalmann, M., Souza, A. S., & Oberauer, K. (2019). How does chunking help working memory? *Journal of Experimental Psychology: Learning, Memory, and Cognition*, *45*(1), 37–55. https://doi.org/10.1037/xlm0000578

The World Bank. (2003). *Lifelong Learning in the Global Knowledge Economy*. World Bank Group. https://doi.org/10.1596/978-0-8213-5475-9

Thompson, W. F., Schellenberg, E. G., & Husain, G. (2001). Arousal, mood, and the mozart effect. *Psychological Science*, *12*(3), 248–251. https://doi.org/10.1111/1467-9280.00345

Timotheou, S., Miliou, O., Dimitriadis, Y., Sobrino, S. V., Giannoutsou, N., Cachia, R., Monés, A. M., & Ioannou, A. (2023). Impacts of digital technologies on education and factors influencing schools' digital capacity and transformation: A literature review. *Education and Information Technologies*, *28*(6), 6695–6726. https://doi.org/10.1007/s10639-022-11431-8

Tobias, S., & Fletcher, J. D. (2011). *Computer games and instruction*. Information Age Pub.

Tokuhama-Espinosa, T. (2017). International Delphi panel on Mind Brain, and Education science. *Quito, Ecuador: Author*. Downloaded 4 April 2017 from https://drive.google.com/file/d/0B8Ra-PiQPEZ9ZVTZQbmxaNENJNHc/view?usp=shari

Tokuhama-Espinosa, T. (2018). *Neuromyths: Debunking false ideas about the brain*. W.W. Norton & Co.

Tokuhama-Espinosa, T. (2024). *Questions kids ask about their brains*. Teachers College Press.

Tomlinson, C., & McTighe, J. (2006). *Integrating differentiated instruction & understanding by design: Connecting content and kids*. Association for Supervision and Curriculum Development.

Torrance Jenkins, R. (2018). Using educational neuroscience and psychology to teach science. Part 2: A case study review of 'The Brain-Targeted Teaching Model' and 'Research-Based Strategies to Ignite Student Learning.' *School Science Review*, *100*(371), 66–75. https://www.ase.org.uk/resources/school-science-review/issue-371/using-educational-neuroscience-and-psychology-teach

Torre, J. B., & Lieberman, M. D. (2018). Putting feelings into words: Affect labeling as implicit emotion regulation. *Emotion Review*, *10*(2), 116–124. https://doi.org/10.1177/1754073917742706

Trochim, W. M., & McLinden, D. (2017). Introduction to a special issue on concept mapping. *Evaluation and Program Planning*, *60*, 166–175. https://doi.org/10.1016/j.evalprogplan.2016.10.006

Tyng, C. M., Amin, H. U., Saad, M. N. M., & Malik, A. S. (2017). The influences of emotion on learning and memory. *Frontiers in Psychology*, *8*, 235933. https://doi.org/10.3389/fpsyg.2017.01454

Vogel, S., & Schwabe, L. (2016). Learning and memory under stress: Implications for the classroom. *Npj Science of Learning, 1*(1), 1–10. https://doi.org/10.1038/npjscilearn.2016.11

Walker, J. (2016). *Brain-targeted early childhood beginnings: A case study in India* [Doctoral dissertation, The Johns Hopkins University]. https://jscholarship.library.jhu.edu/items/b6a3af75-9049-4073-99b9-8f4a7fc105e4).

Wastila, J. (2015). *The student-centered classroom in EFL classes in Japan: A team-based approach. (Encyclopedia of the Sciences of Learning).* Springer. https://link.springer.com/referenceworkentry/10.1007/978-1-4419-1428-6_1666

Whitescarver, E. L. (2018). Effect of mnemonics on the vocabulary acquisition and retention of high school students with learning disabilities. *Theses and Dissertations, 2567.* https://rdw.rowan.edu/etd/2567

Willingham, D. T. (2009). *Why don't students like school? A cognitive scientist answers questions about how the mind works and what it means for your classroom.* John Wiley & Sons.

Woloshyn, V. W., Bajovic, M., & Worden, M. M. (2017). Promoting student-centred learning using iPads in a grade 1 classroom: using the digital didactic framework to deconstruct instruction. *Computers in the Schools, 34*(3), 152–167. doi: 10.1080/07380569.2017.1346456

Wondim, B. M., Bishaw, K. S., & Zeleke, Y. T. (2024). Effectiveness of teachers' direct and indirect written corrective feedback provision strategies on enhancing students' writing achievement: Ethiopian university entrants in focus. *Heliyon, 10*(2), e24279. https://doi.org/10.1016/j.heliyon.2024.e24279

World Economic Forum. (2022). COVID's impact on education: Worst for the most vulnerable. weforum.org.

World Economic Forum. (2023). The future of jobs report. April 30, 2023. https://www.weforum.org/publications/the-future-of-jobs-report-2023/in-full/4-skills-outlook/

Wullschleger, A., Garrote, A., Schnepel, S., Jaquiéry, L., & Opitz, E. M. (2020). Effects of teacher feedback behavior on social acceptance in inclusive elementary classrooms: Exploring social referencing processes in a natural setting. *Contemporary Educational Psychology, 60*, 101841. https://doi.org/10.1016/j.cedpsych.2020.101841

Xiao, P. L., Li, B. B., Yao, A. N., Yang, A., & Zhang, M. (2024). The impact of virtual reality on student engagement in the classroom–a critical review of the literature. *Frontiers in Psychology.* https://doi.org/10.3389/fpsyg.2024.1360574

Yan, V., Schuetze, B. A., & Eglington, L. G. (2020). *A review of the interleaving effect: Theories and lessons for future research.* https://doi.org/10.31234/osf.io/ur6g7

Yates, E., & Twigg, E. (2017). Developing creativity in early childhood studies students. *Thinking Skills and Creativity, 23*, 42–57. https://doi.org/10.1016/j.tsc.2016.11.001

Yazar, İ. U. (2024). The effects of music on brain development. *Journal of Human Sciences, 21*(3), 234–246. https://doi.org/10.14687/jhs.v21i3.6483

Yuan, X., Kaewsaeng-On, R., Jin, S., Anuar, M. M., Shaikh, J. M., & Mehmood, S. (2022). Time lagged investigation of entrepreneurship school innovation climate and students motivational outcomes: Moderating role of students' attitude toward technology. *Frontiers in Psychology, 13*, 979562. https://doi.org/10.3389/fpsyg.2022.979562

Zadina, J. N. (2023). The synergy zone: Connecting the mind, brain, and heart for the ideal classroom learning environment. *Brain Sciences, 13*(9), 1314. https://doi.org/10.3390/brainsci13091314

Zahran, S., Cliff, D. P., Antczak, D., Aadland, E., Aadland, K. N., Burley, J., ... & Janssen, I. (2024). Optimal levels of sleep, sedentary behaviour, and physical activity needed to support cognitive function in children of the early years. *BMC pediatrics, 24*(1), 1–11.

Zareyan, S., Zhang, H., Wang, J., Song, W., Hampson, E., Abbott, D., & Diamond,

A. (2021). First demonstration of double dissociation between COMT-Met[158] and COMT-Val[158] cognitive performance when stressed and when calmer. *Cerebral Cortex*, *31*(3), 1411–1426.

Zaromb, F. M., & Roediger, H. L. (2009). The effects of effort after meaning on recall: Differences in within- and between-subjects designs. *Memory & Cognition*, *37*(4), 447–463. https://doi.org/10.3758/MC.37.4.447

Zentall, S. (1983). Learning environments: A review of physical and temporal factors. *Exception Education Quarterly*, *4*(2), 10–15. https://doi.org/10.1177/074193258300400211

Zentall, S. S., & Zentall, T. R. (1983). Optimal stimulation: A model of disordered activity and performance in normal and deviant children. *Psychological Bulletin*, *94*(3), 446–471. https://doi.org/10.1037/0033-2909.94.3.446

Zhou, J. (2019). Creativity and brain networks: A review. *Frontiers in Psychology*, *10*, 104. https://doi.org/10.3389/fpsyg.2019.00104

Zormpa, E., Brehm, L. E., Hoedemaker, R. S., & Meyer, A. S. (2019). The production effect and the generation effect improve memory in picture naming. *Memory*, *27*(3), 340–352. https://doi.org/10.1080/09658211.2018.1510966

Index

Helping educators make the greatest impact

CORWIN HAS ONE MISSION: to enhance education through intentional professional learning.

We build long-term relationships with our authors, educators, clients, and associations who partner with us to develop and continuously improve the best evidence-based practices that establish and support lifelong learning.

Zeitfracht Medien GmbH
Ferdinand-Jühlke-Straße 7
99095 Erfurt, Deutschland
produktsicherheit@kolibri360.de